Implementing Personalized Learning Techniques with AI

Kristina Posavec
University of Zagreb, Croatia

IGI Global
Scientific Publishing
Publishing Tomorrow's Research Today

Vice President of Editorial	Melissa Wagner
Managing Editor of Acquisitions	Mikaela Felty
Managing Editor of Book Development	Jocelynn Hessler
Production Manager	Mike Brehm
Cover Design	Phillip Shickler

Published in the United States of America by
IGI Global Scientific Publishing
701 East Chocolate Avenue
Hershey, PA, 17033, USA
Tel: 717-533-8845
Fax: 717-533-8661
Website: https://www.igi-global.com E-mail: cust@igi-global.com

Library of Congress Cataloging-in-Publication Data

Names: Posavec, Kristina, 1984- author.
Title: Implementing personalized learning techniques with AI / Edited by Kristina Posavec.
Other titles: Implementing personalized learning techniques with artificial intelligence
Description: Hershey, PA : IGI Global Scientific Publishing, [2025] | Includes bibliographical references and index. | Summary: "This book explores how AI is not just a tool but a new way of developing personalized education, that offers diverse possibilities for both enhancing and challenging the way we think about learning and teaching"-- Provided by publisher.
Identifiers: LCCN 2024054366 (print) | LCCN 2024054367 (ebook) | ISBN 9798369334744 (hardcover) | ISBN 9798369351505 (paperback) | ISBN 9798369334751 (ebook)
Subjects: LCSH: Individualized instruction. | Artificial intelligence--Educational applications. | Student-centered learning.
Classification: LCC LB1031 .P67 2025 (print) | LCC LB1031 (ebook) | DDC 371.39/4--dc23/eng/20250214
LC record available at https://lccn.loc.gov/2024054366
LC ebook record available at https://lccn.loc.gov/2024054367

British Cataloguing in Publication Data
A Cataloguing in Publication record for this book is available from the British Library.

Table of Contents

Preface

The rapid advancement of artificial intelligence (AI) is transforming various sectors, and education is no exception. This book was created out of an academic curiosity to explore how AI can redefine educational practices and enhance the learning experience for both teachers and students. As educators across the globe continue to tackle challenges such as large class sizes, diverse student needs, and limited resources, AI can be seen and used as an additional educational tool that can help bridge the gap between traditional teaching methods and the demands of modern learning environments. This book seeks to explore the multidimensional role of AI in education, from automating routine tasks to providing personalized learning experiences according to the student's abilities, skills, and needs. This book is an attempt to understand how AI technologies can be used to provide a more inclusive and personalized educational system. Throughout the chapters, readers will find theoretical insights, practical case studies, and trends whose purpose is to provide a comprehensive view of potential AI tools in education. The research questions guiding this work explore broader implications of AI tools on pedagogy, student engagement, and the future of education itself. These chapters offer educators, policymakers, and stakeholders insight into the different ways AI is reshaping the educational landscape and provide considerations for its responsible and effective use with students.

The Introduction discusses the transformative role of AI in education, emphasizing its applications across primary, secondary, and higher education. The chapter outlines how AI is reshaping traditional teaching methods by enabling personalized learning.

"The Role of AI in Education" explores how AI fosters inclusivity, providing support for students with diverse learning needs and removing barriers to accessibility. Tools like generative AI and intelligent tutoring systems are shown to adapt educational content to individual learners' abilities, styles, and progress. The chapter addresses the ethical challenges associated with AI in education, such as data privacy, transparency, and bias. It underscores the importance of implementing ethical frameworks and policies to ensure the responsible and equitable use of AI tools in classrooms.

"AI Tools and Platforms for Personalized Learning" explores various AI-driven tools and platforms designed to enhance personalized learning experiences in educational settings. These tools enable teachers to create tailored educational resources and facilitate individualized learning for students. The chapter discusses several notable tools, including ChatGPT, Gemini, Padlet, DIFFIT, Quizizz, Scholia, Microsoft Copilot, Adobe Firefly, MagicSchool, Perplexity, and Briskteaching. The chapter demonstrates how AI tools and platforms can improve education by making learning more personalized, accessible, and efficient.

"Personalized Learning With Generative AI" explores the concept of personalized learning while focusing on its significance in contemporary education. It discusses the role of AI tools, like ChatGPT and Gemini, in enhancing personalized learning. The chapter details how generative AI can produce activities and exercises that cater to different learning preferences, such as kinesthetic or visual learners, and varying levels of ability. Examples include adaptive grammar exercises, creative storytelling, and role-playing scenarios.

"Case Study of Using AI Tools in Higher Education" investigates the implementation of generative AI tools in higher education through a detailed case study. The study focuses on students in a Computer Science course using AI tools independently for learning and completing tasks during the 2023/2024 academic year. It evaluates their experiences, perceptions, and challenges.

"Case Study of Using AI Tools in Vocational School" examines the application of generative AI in secondary education, focusing on personalized learning strategies implemented by a computer science teacher in a vocational school. Conducted during the 2023/2024 academic year, the study explores how the teacher used AI tools, including ChatGPT and Eduaide.ai, to create customized teaching materials for students.

"Case Study of Using AI Tools in Primary School Education" explores the integration of AI tools, particularly ChatGPT, in a primary school. The research focuses on how AI tools supported a non-native Croatian-speaking student by adapting lesson materials to overcome language barriers.

"Framework for Implementing AI Tools With Personalized Learning" presents a comprehensive approach to integrating generative AI into educational practices. It provides an overview of existing international frameworks for the use of AI in education. In addition, this chapter provides an AI framework for personalized learning which is divided into five main categories: AI Literacy and Training, Pedagogy, Language and Accessibility, Evaluation, and Engagement Strategies.

The Conclusion addresses the transformative role of AI in conducting personalized learning, underscoring its potential to create personalized, inclusive, and effective learning environments. Also, this chapter summarizes the main research questions and highlights the research findings.

I hope that this book will serve as a valuable resource for anyone interested in understanding the intersection of AI and education. It is written not only for academics and educators but also for those outside the field who are curious about the future of learning with AI tools integrated into the educational environment.

I would like to express my gratitude to the teachers, whose work and insights contributed to the creation of this book. Their dedication to advancing educational processes using technology.

With this book, I invite readers to explore how AI is not just a tool but a new way of developing personalized education, which offers diverse possibilities for both enhancing and challenging the way we think about learning and teaching.

Kristina Posavec

Institute for Migration Research, University of Zagreb, Croatia

Acknowledgment

The writing of the book was a collaborative effort, and I am grateful to everyone who contributed to its completion. First of all, I am sincerely thankful to teachers who have been involved in the exploration of innovative solutions and improving educational practices as a constant source of motivation throughout this project.

For my family and friends, your indelible support and patience have meant the world to me. Your belief in the importance of this work has been a constant source of strength and inspiration.

Finally, I want to thank teachers around the world who strive every day to provide the best learning experience for their students. I hope that this book will serve as a useful resource in your ongoing efforts to use artificial intelligence to create an inclusive, effective and innovative educational environment.

Thank you all for being a part of this journey.

Chapter 1
Introduction

ABSTRACT

The chapter introduces the impact of AI on education, focusing on its applications across primary, secondary, and higher education. It explores how AI tools, such as intelligent tutoring systems and adaptive learning environments, enhance personalized learning and automate routine administrative tasks, freeing educators to engage more deeply with students. Key topics include the integration of AI in classroom instruction, the role of AI in supporting personalized learning, and the ethical considerations surrounding AI in education, such as privacy, bias, and fairness. Through case studies and practical frameworks, the chapter provides educators with insights into implementing AI to create more individualized and inclusive learning experiences.

INTRODUCTION

Artificial Intelligence (AI) is reshaping numerous industries and education is no exception. This book investigates the transformative potential of AI in education, focusing on its applications in primary, secondary, and higher education. With AI technologies rapidly advancing, they are increasingly being integrated into both the preparation of teaching materials and direct classroom instruction, affecting how teachers and students interact with educational content. The central aim of this book is to explore how AI tools

DOI: 10.4018/979-8-3693-3474-4.ch001

are changing traditional teaching methods, improving personalized learning experiences, and addressing educational challenges.

According to Holmes and Bialik (2020), AI-driven systems such as intelligent tutoring platforms and adaptive learning environments are able to tailor instruction based on individual student needs, providing real-time feedback and adjusting learning materials according to student performance. These systems use data-driven algorithms to track student progress and identify areas where additional support is needed, which can lead to improved learning outcomes, especially for students who struggle with traditional, one-size-fits-all approaches to teaching. A systematic review by Zawacki-Richter et al. (2019) examined the role of AI in higher education and found that AI applications significantly enhance personalized learning experiences, particularly through intelligent tutoring systems and automated assessments. These tools not only provide immediate feedback to students but also allow educators to focus on more complex teaching tasks, such as fostering critical thinking and creativity. The authors emphasize that AI in education enables more individualized learning pathways, which can address the diverse needs of students in large, heterogeneous classrooms. Additionally, AI has been instrumental in automating routine administrative tasks, freeing up teachers' time to focus on pedagogical activities. Schmidt and Niekler (2020) highlighted how AI can streamline processes like grading, attendance tracking, and lesson planning, reducing the administrative burden on educators. This automation allows teachers to spend more time engaging with students, crafting personalized content, and fostering deeper learning experiences. However, as Gašević, Siemens, and Sadiq (2023) point out, while AI can handle administrative tasks effectively, it is essential to ensure that human oversight remains in place to maintain the integrity and quality of educational practices. Saylam et al. (2023) stress that AI systems must be designed with ethical considerations in mind, as the data used to train these systems can reflect societal biases, which can inadvertently be encoded into educational technologies. AI-driven decision-making processes, such as automated grading or student progress predictions, may risk perpetuating inequalities if these systems are not carefully monitored for fairness. Moreover, Adams et al. (2023) argue that transparency and accountability are crucial in developing AI tools, especially when these tools are used in sensitive environments like K-12 classrooms, where student data privacy is a major concern. Another aspect of AI in education is its potential to enhance inclusion and accessibility. Hwang and Tu (2021) highlight the role of AI in supporting students with special needs, through personalized learning environments that adapt to different abilities. However, there are limitations to the current research on AI in education. Much of the existing literature, as noted by Zawacki-Richter et al. (2019), is focused on technologically advanced regions and does not sufficiently address how AI can be scaled and adapted to low-resource settings. Furthermore, most studies have short-term focuses, limiting our understanding of the long-term impacts of AI on student outcomes and teacher practices (Gašević, Siemens, & Sadiq, 2023). Also, AI plays an essential role in the personalization and adaptation of learning strategies, offering content and assessments that align with individual learner profiles (Abbes et al., 2024). There is also a need for more interdisciplinary studies that explore the technological, pedagogical, and ethical dimensions of AI in education.

This research focuses on several aspect of using AI tools in educational environment. First, how can AI tools be effectively implemented in classroom instruction and educational planning? This question seeks to understand the best practices for integrating AI in a way that benefits both educators and students. Second, the book explores the implications of AI on the role of educators, asking how these technologies transform not only the teaching process but also the teacher's responsibilities in the classroom. Third, the book examines how AI can be used to support personalized learning, offering students educational experiences that take to consideration their individual needs and learning styles. In addition, the research considers the ethical implications of AI in education, such as issues of privacy, bias, and fairness.

The book consists of 8 chapters which deal with different aspects of using AI in conducting personalized learning and teaching. Chapter 2 titled The Role of AI in Education, examines how AI is applied across primary, secondary, and higher education settings. The chapter highlights how AI supports teachers by automating time-consuming tasks such as grading, while also offering students feedback and identifying gaps in their learning. Through these capabilities, AI is shown to have a profound impact on personalizing the educational experience and facilitating more effective learning outcomes. In Chapter 3, titled AI Tools and Platforms for Personalized Learning, the focus is on practical applications of AI tools. This chapter introduces various AI-driven platforms that personalize learning by analyzing student performance data, identifying areas for improvement, and recommending targeted learning paths. The chapter explores how AI-powered tutoring systems and interactive environments can provide individualized support, fostering deeper student engagement and understanding. Chapter 4, Personalized Learning with Generative AI expands on the concept of personalized learning by exploring use of generative AI tools and writing prompts. It offers a literature review on personalized learning, defining its core characteristics and exploring how generative AI can enhance this approach. The chapter shows how AI adapts to individual learning needs, customizing lessons and materials based on each student's progress and abilities. The book continues with two case studies, offering examples of AI implementation in education. Chapter 5, Case Study of Using AI Tools in Higher Education, analyzins how AI tools assist students in task management, learning, and engagement. This chapter explores both the advantages and the limitations of AI in a higher education context, providing valuable insights into how AI tools influence student motivation and performance. Chapter 6, Case Study of Using AI Tools in Vocational School, follows with a case study focused on vocational education, specifically examining AI tools in a vocational school setting in Croatia. This chapter discusses how AI was used to support students who faced difficulties in data analysis and Excel-related tasks, highlighting both the benefits and challenges experienced by teacher and learners. The case study presents the practical applications of AI in adjusting learning to students' needs, especially in vocational training. In Chapter 7, Case Study of Using AI Tools in Primary School, analyzes how AI tools were used to adapt lessons for a non-native Croatian speaker, simplifying complex topics. It offers insights into how AI can be used for personalized learning in younger students and the impact it has on motivation and learning outcomes. Chapter 8, Framework for Implementing AI Tools in Personalized Teaching and Learning presents European and international frameworks as well as the case studies discussed earlier. This chapter provides teachers with practical guidelines for integrating AI into their teaching practices. It offers strategies for addressing the diverse needs of students, from primary education to higher education, and highlights how AI can be effectively employed for personalized learning. In addition, this chapter offers a framework for teachers that they can use to incorporate personalized learning and teaching in their everyday work regarding the adaptation of learning material and conducting in-class use of AI tools directly with students. Through these eight chapters, the book provides an exploration of how AI is changing education. It combines theoretical analysis with practical case studies, making it a valuable resource for educators, policymakers, and researchers seeking to understand and implement AI in educational settings. The book emphasizes the importance of ethical considerations, inclusivity, and ongoing training to ensure that AI improves rather than replaces human-driven educational experiences.

The book investigates several research questions related to the use of AI tools in education, specifically focusing on how these tools impact learning processes, student engagement, and teaching methods. These questions aim to understand both the benefits and limitations of AI integration in various educational settings. One of the research questions examines how AI tools can improve the understanding of new concepts compared to traditional learning methods. Another research question focuses on the benefits, challenges, and limitations students experience when using AI tools independently. The book also addresses the question of how AI tools impact students' confidence and self-efficacy in learning. In addition, the research explored whether AI tools can effectively supplement traditional learning models. In case studies focused on vocational and primary school education, the research explored additional questions. These include how AI tools can support the personalization of learning materials for students with learning difficulties, how AI tools influence student engagement and motivation, and how AI can assist teachers in adapting lessons to suit diverse abilities.

REFERENCES

Abbes, F., Bennani, S., & Maalel, A. (2024). Generative AI and Gamification for Personalized Learning: Literature Review and Future Challenges. *SN Computer Science*, 5(8), 1154. DOI: 10.1007/s42979-024-03491-z

Adams, C., Pente, P., Lemermeyer, G., & Rockwell, G. (2023). Ethical principles for artificial intelligence in K-12 education. *Computers and Education: Artificial Intelligence*, 4, 100131. DOI: 10.1016/j.caeai.2023.100131

Gašević, D., Siemens, G., & Sadiq, S. (2023). Empowering learners for the age of artificial intelligence. *Computers & Education: Artificial Intelligence*, 4, 100130.

Holmes, W., & Bialik, M. (2020). *Artificial intelligence in education: Learning systems and intelligent learning environments for personalized education.* Springer.

Hwang, G. J., & Tu, Y. F. (2021). Roles and research trends of artificial intelligence in education. *Computers & Education: Artificial Intelligence*, 2, 100011.

Saylam, S., Duman, N., Yildirim, Y., & Satsevich, K. (2023). Empowering education with AI: Addressing ethical concerns. *London Journal of Social Sciences*, 6(6), 39–48. DOI: 10.31039/ljss.2023.6.103

Schmidt, P., & Niekler, A. (2020). Challenges and opportunities: Artificial intelligence in education. *Proceedings of the 13th International Conference on Educational Data Mining*, 1-9.

Zawacki-Richter, O., Marín, V. I., Bond, M., & Gouverneur, F. (2019). Systematic review of research on artificial intelligence applications in higher education – Where are the educators? *International Journal of Educational Technology in Higher Education*, 16(39), 1–27. DOI: 10.1186/s41239-019-0171-0

Chapter 2
The Role of AI in Education

ABSTRACT

This chapter explores the role of AI tools within educational systems, in primary and secondary schools as well as in higher education. It examines the application of AI in both the preparation of teaching materials and its direct integration into classroom instruction with students. Through examining the functionalities and applications of the AI tools, the chapter will give insight on the implications and potential impact of AI on teaching and learning practices across various educational levels. The chapter offers insight into the evolving educational landscape shaped by AI technologies, fostering a deeper understanding of its implications for educators and learners.

INTRODUCTION: AI IN EDUCATION

The term Artificial Intelligence (AI) was defined by John McCarthy where he states that AI is "the science and engineering of making intelligent machines" (McCarthy, 1956). There is a growing need for a responsive education system that ensures the access and continuity of educational curricula for every child, irrespective of their socioeconomic status, language, or cultural background (Jauhiainen & Guerra, 2023, p. 4). Artificial Intelligence (AI) has a transformative role in education, revolutionizing traditional teaching methods and empowering both students and educators. Artificial Intelligence is the process of modeling human thinking and designing a machine so that it can behave like humans or other terms called cognitive tasks, namely how

DOI: 10.4018/979-8-3693-3474-4.ch002

machines can learn automatically from programmed data and information (Fitria, 2021, p. 135). AI-driven educational tools foster inclusivity by addressing diverse learning needs while overcoming accessibility barriers remains crucial for equitable education (Ayeni et al., 2024). Research *Generative AI in Education: A Study of Educators' Awareness, Sentiments, and Influencing Factors* shows that educators are increasingly aware of generative AI tools, with more than 40% using them at least periodically or regularly and they see these tools as valuable for boosting efficiency and personalizing teaching (Ghimire, Prather, & Edwards, 2024).

It can facilitate teaching and learning tasks, making them more efficient and faster, but it is crucial to maintain an understanding of the processes and ensure the accuracy of the information being generated (Jauhiainen & Guerra, 2023, p. 3). Artificial intelligence simplifies time-consuming tasks such as rating and enables teachers to focus on personalized interactions with students. In addition, AI-driven tutoring programs offer invaluable support to students, especially in understanding fundamental concepts. Although current AI tutoring is limited to basic subjects, there are potential for future progress in teaching complex subjects. AI also facilitates feedback mechanisms, allowing students to get a first-hand view of their performance and supporting educators to refine their teaching strategies. In addition, AI-driven programs help to identify learning gaps and provide personalized solutions that improve overall understanding. As AI develops, it could redefine the role of educators and move to facilitators rather than merely knowledge providers. In addition, AI enables personal learning experiences that meet the needs and learning styles of each student. Generative AI can play a significant role by serving as a mediator between educational institutions, teachers and pupils, providing educational support anytime and anywhere. Properly implemented generative AI allows teachers to better focus on education opportunities and challenges, while pupils can receive guidance and support suitable to their knowledge backgrounds and levels (Jauhiainen & Guerra, 2023, p. 4) . By generating smart content, AI enhances the accessibility and effectiveness of educational materials, making learning more engaging and interactive. AI ensures universal access to education, empowering students with diverse learning needs to thrive in their academic journey. In education, AI automates tasks, provides additional student support, offers feedback, identifies learning gaps, and generates smart content. It transforms the role of educators, fosters personalized learning experiences, and ensures universal access to education, benefiting students with diverse learning needs.

The OECD (2022), "OECD Framework for the Classification of AI systems" provides several examples for use of AI systems in education:

- Personalizing learning with AI (e.g. adaptive tests and learning systems)
- Supporting students with special needs with AI (e.g. wearables using AI)
- Reducing dropout rates (e.g. predictive and diagnosis models)
- Construction of scoring of tests or exams
- Fraud detection during exams
- Chatbots

Miao et al. (2021) in *AI and education: Guidance for policy-makers* states that AI can be used to improve educational systems in various ways which include personalized learning where AI can help gather data about students' strengths and weaknesses to tailor learning experiences that suit their needs, intelligent tutoring systems where AI can create intelligent tutoring systems that can interact with students and provide customized solutions and feedback, smart assessment where AI can evaluate students' responses and provide immediate feedback, which can help improve learning outcomes, automated grading where AI can assist in grading, saving valuable time and energy for teachers, language learning where AI can also be used in language learning to track and assess a student's pronunciation, grammar, and vocabulary, smart content where AI can assist with the creation of adaptive and interactive content, providing engaging learning experiences for students and predictive analytics where AI can analyze student data to predict future outcomes and enable early intervention to prevent students from falling behind. The document further explores how AI can empower teachers and enhance instruction, as well as the execution of automatic administrative tasks, such as grading, student performance tracking, and lesson planning, which frees teachers time to focus on teaching, and provides personalized feedback, as well as providing teachers with data-based insights into how their students are progressing and enabling them to adapt their teaching style to the needs of individual students. Using intelligent tutoring systems to provide teachers with an adaptive and personalized learning experience for students. AI can generate resources for the teachers and create personalized resources to supplement teacher-led instruction. It could be used for the professional development of the teachers where AI can analyze data about teacher-student interactions to provide targeted feedback and support for professional development and for the social and cognitive analysis in which AI-powered tools can assess social and cognitive factors that affect learning, such as student engagement and emotional states, and provide insights to teachers to support student learning outcomes.

According to the Beijing Consensus on Artificial Intelligence and Education, the development and use of AI in education provides opportunities to advance inclusion and equity in education. These activities include improving access to education, and AI can help remote or underprivileged students receive quality education through intelligent content, intelligent tutoring, and personalized learning experiences. Using artificial intelligence, personalization can improve personalization and provide personalized learning plans to bridge knowledge gaps between underprivileged students and their more privileged colleagues. The AI-powered tools help students with disabilities and learning disabilities in classrooms by providing targeted assistance and feedback. Artificial intelligence can help to help people learn languages by providing language recognition and translation services to non-native speakers or facilitating communication in multilingual classrooms. AI algorithms can be used to avoid cognitive biases, contribute to more equitable results, eliminate human biases, and create more objective classification systems by avoiding cognitive biases that exist in traditional teaching and classification methods, thereby ensuring fair assessment. Artificial Intelligence can also generate multiple representations of training information, making it easy to access training from whatever platform is optimal for the user (Makhambetova et al., 2021, p. 3). On the other hand, AI tools such as intelligent agents and block-based programming software support personalized learning by tailoring activities to individual cognitive levels and enabling students to create and explore AI-driven solutions (Yim & Su, 2023).

The research *Artificial Intelligence (AI) in Education: Unlocking the Perfect Synergy for Learning* highlights the transformative impact of AI in education, emphasizing personalized learning through intelligent agents that adapt to individual needs, enhance engagement, and improve learning outcomes while promoting inclusivity and accessibility. However, it also underscores the need to address ethical concerns like data privacy and transparency to ensure responsible and effective implementation (Ramirez & Fuentes Esparrell, 2024). For implementation of AI in education to be successful it requires well-informed policies, stakeholder engagement, and ethical frameworks to address potential risks and maximize benefits for diverse educational contexts (Jimerson & Childs, 2017; Ifenthaler et al., 2024). While research shows that AI tools can support education, they also raise concerns about academic dishonesty, such as cheating and plagiarism and this necessitates policy updates and innovative assessment strategies to maintain integrity (Katsamakas, Pavlov, & Saklad, 2024).The integration of AI in education can help students develop AI-complementary skills such as critical thinking, creativity, and management, which are crucial for future job markets (Katsamakas, Pavlov, & Saklad, 2024). The AI in education has moved beyond traditional drill-and-practice approaches by integrating diverse pedagogical methods, such as exploratory learning, collaborative learning, and self-regulated learning (Porayska-Pomsta, 2023) and generative AI tools can enhance engagement by serving as thought starters and generating ideas, they can boost efficiency by generating test questions (Ghimire, Prather, & Edwards, 2024). It can be stated that AI enables tailored educational experiences by analyzing individual learning patterns and providing adaptive content, feedback, and learning pathways, improving student engagement and outcomes (Almasri et al., 2024).

TYPES OF AI

The IBM (2023) in their blog post explores the concept of Artificial Intelligence (AI) and categorizes it based on capabilities and functionalities. They divided AI into two categories, AI by capability and functionality. Under capabilities, they outline three types of AI, Narrow AI, General AI, and Super AI. Narrow AI, exemplified by Siri and Alexa, focuses on specific tasks, while General AI and Super AI remain theoretical, with the latter surpassing human cognitive abilities, including emotions and beliefs. Narrow or weak AI are limited to systems trained for one specific task (Marrone, Cropley & Medeiros, 2024). According to ISO (International Organization for Standardization) narrow AI applications, characterized by their specialized algorithms designed for specific tasks, are prevalent in various aspects of daily life. Smart assistants, often cited as prime examples of weak AI, utilize natural language processing for tasks like setting alarms, answering questions, and controlling smart home devices. Chatbots, frequently encountered on customer service platforms of e-stores, employ ANI algorithms to handle common inquiries, freeing humans to tackle more complex tasks. Recommendation engines on platforms like Netflix and Amazon analyze viewing or purchasing habits to deliver personalized suggestions, demonstrating the capabilities of ANI in tailoring user experiences. Navigation apps, such as Google Maps, use ANI to provide real-time directions, ensuring users reach their destinations efficiently. Email spam filters leverage ANI to identify and redirect spam messages away from the inbox. Additionally, autocorrect features on smartphones, like the iPhone, harness the power of weak AI to rectify typos and enhance text composition. Each of these applications underscores the ability of ANI to perform well-defined tasks by analyzing large datasets and following specialized algorithms. As you marvel at these technological advancements, remember that it is weak AI driving these remarkable innovations, shaping our world in ways once deemed unimaginable.

On the other hand, there is General AI, also known as strong AI, which remains as a theoretical concept, and it does not have any practical example yet. It possesses the ability to use previous learnings and skills to accomplish new tasks in different contexts without requiring human intervention to train the underlying models. This capability enables General AI to learn and perform any intellectual task that a human can. ISO states that General AI aspires to create systems capable of performing a wide array of tasks with human-like proficiency. Unlike narrow AI, which is designed for specific functions, strong AI aims to develop a form of general intelligence that can adapt, learn, and apply knowledge across various domains. The goal is to create artificial entities with cognitive abilities similar to humans, enabling them to engage in diverse intellectual activities. Although strong AI remains theoretical with no practical examples currently in use, researchers are actively exploring its potential. The concept of AGI, which could theoretically perform any human job, holds promise for transformative impacts in numerous fields such as language, healthcare, transportation, arts and entertainment, domestic tasks, manufacturing, engineering, and security. Despite the significant challenges in achieving true general intelligence, advancements in AI technology and machine learning suggest that the realization of General AI is a matter of when, not if.

The third type of AI that IBM is writing about is Super AI that is also just theoretical and it is referred to as artificial superintelligence. If ever realized, Super AI would surpass human cognitive abilities, capable of thinking, reasoning, learning, and making judgments. Applications with Super AI capabilities would evolve beyond understanding human sentiments and experiences to the point of feeling emotions, having needs, and possessing their own beliefs and desires.

Furthermore, the IBM introduces four categories of AI based on its functionalities, primarily focusing on Narrow AI including Reactive Machine AI, Limited Memory AI, Theory of Mind AI, and Self-Aware AI.

Reactive Machine AI, which operates without memory and performs specific tasks based on present data, such as IBM Deep Blue's chess-playing abilities or Netflix's recommendation engine. Reactive Machines are highly reliable within their designated functions but lack the capacity for interactive engagement or understanding of the wider world. They consistently respond the same way to identical situations and lack emotional states or curiosity. While this reliability is beneficial for tasks like autonomous driving, it impedes the development of AI systems capable of true engagement and responsiveness to diverse real-world scenarios.

Limited Memory AI, capable of recalling past events and outcomes, exemplified by virtual assistants, chatbots, and self-driving cars. An example of this is self-driving cars, which observe and monitor other vehicles' speed and direction over time to make decisions. These observations, along with preprogrammed representations of the world such as lane markings and traffic lights, influence the car's decision-making process, like when to change lanes safely. The challenge lies in developing AI systems that can build comprehensive representations, remember past experiences, and adapt to new situations.

Theory of Mind AI, a theoretical form of AI that understands the thoughts and emotions of others, aiming to simulate human-like relationships. In this category of AI, machines not only form representations of the world but also of other agents or entities within it. This concept is similar to the psychological concept of "the theory of the mind", in which one understands that people, animals and objects have thoughts and emotions that affect their behavior. Mental theory is essential to human social interaction and social formation, as it helps to understand the motives, intentions and perspectives of others. Without this understanding, collaboration becomes challenging or even impossible. For AI systems to integrate into human society, they must acknowledge that individuals possess thoughts, feelings, and expectations about their treatment, adjusting their behavior accordingly. This level of understanding and adaptability is crucial for effective interaction and cooperation between humans and AI.

Self-Aware AI, another theoretical category, which, if realized, would understand its internal conditions and human emotions and thoughts. Conscious beings have self-awareness, which allows them to distinguish between desires and their consciences. Understanding your own intentions and emotions allows you to make conclusions about other people's emotions and behaviors. This ability is crucial for social interactions and empathy. While the creation of truly self-aware machines remains a distant goal, current efforts should focus on understanding memory, learning, and decision-making based on past experiences. This not only advances AI capabilities but also aids in understanding human intelligence. Moreover, it lays the groundwork for designing or evolving machines capable of more than just classifying sensory inputs, ultimately bridging the gap between human and artificial intelligence.

Large Language Models (LLMs)

Large language models (LLMs) are artificial intelligence models with complex architecture and a large number of parameters that have been trained on very large amounts of text (billions of words) (Rillig et al., 2023, p. 3464). LLM can be used to create educational content, improve pupils' engagement and interaction, and personalize their learning experiences (Jauhiainen & Guerra, 2023, p. 5). IBM defines LLMs as a class of foundation models, which are trained on enormous amounts of data to provide the foundational capabilities needed to drive multiple use cases and applications, as well as resolve a multitude of tasks. In addition, IBM explains how LLMs work, they utilize advanced deep learning techniques and vast amounts of textual data. Typically structured on transformer architectures, such as the Generative Pre-trained Transformer (GPT), these models excel in processing sequential data like text inputs. Comprising multiple layers of neural networks, each layer's parameters are fine-tuned during training, further enhanced by an attention mechanism layer, which focuses on specific segments of datasets. During training, LLMs predict the next word in a sentence by analyzing the context provided by preceding words. This prediction is based on assigning probability scores to tokenized words—broken into smaller character sequences—and transforming them into numerical embeddings representing context. To ensure accuracy, LLMs undergo extensive training on massive corpora of text, often billions of pages. This training allows them to grasp grammar, semantics, and conceptual relationships through zero-shot and self-supervised learning. Once trained, LLMs autonomously generate text by predicting the next word based on input and leveraging acquired patterns and knowledge. The outcome is coherent and contextually relevant language generation suitable for various natural language understanding (NLU) and content generation tasks. Improving model performance involves prompt engineering, prompt-tuning, fine-tuning, and tactics like reinforcement learning with human feedback (RLHF). These methods aim to mitigate biases, hateful speech, and factually incorrect answers, known as "hallucinations," which may arise from training on unstructured data. Addressing these issues is crucial for deploying enterprise-grade LLMs, ensuring they do not pose liabilities or harm organizational reputations.

Google provides use cases for LLMs where they state that the primary function is generating highly plausible text in response to input. They're also showcasing impressive performance in additional tasks such as summarization, question answering, and text classification, known as emergent abilities. Moreover, LLMs demonstrate capability in solving certain math problems and even writing code, although it's recommended to verify their outputs. Their adeptness extends to mimicking human speech patterns and seamlessly blending information with various styles and tones. Furthermore, LLMs serve as integral components in models beyond text generation. Recent advancements have seen LLMs utilized in constructing sentiment detectors, toxicity classifiers, and generating image captions.

The European Data Protection Supervisor (2024) states that the use of LLMs poses several concerns regarding data protection. Training LLMs is a resource-intensive process that often involves personal data. A significant portion of the data used for training LLMs is obtained from publicly available Internet sources, potentially containing personal information of individuals, including public figures. However, this data might be inaccurate or even contain misinformation. Managing the data protection risks associated with such datasets is challenging, and if not properly secured, LLM outputs could inadvertently reveal sensitive information, leading to data breaches. One notable issue is the occurrence of "hallucinations" within LLMs, where they generate incorrect information that appears plausible. These inaccuracies, if disseminated, can harm individuals' reputations and influence decisions affecting them. Moreover, if LLMs are trained on biased data, they may perpetuate or exacerbate existing biases, resulting in unfair or discriminatory outcomes, contravening principles of fair data processing. Another challenge lies in implementing data subjects' rights concerning information learned by LLMs. Unlike traditional databases, LLMs store data in the form of parameters, making rectification, deletion, or access requests difficult or even unfeasible. This includes both accurate data and data resulting from "hallucinations," further complicating compliance with data protection regulations. LLMs could act as pedagogical agents and prompt learners to engage in specific cognitive and metacognitive self-regulation strategies that increase learning effectiveness beyond simple knowledge acquisition (Laak, Aru, p. 7, 2024).

Jackley (2024) in Oracle article is pointing out to the key concepts about LLMs which include:

- Natural language refers to any language that humans use in everyday situations, such as in conversations or written reports, as opposed to languages specifically developed for technical purposes, like computer code.
- Natural-language processing is a type of data processing that analyzes the structure and meaning of written or spoken text.
- A language model is a representation of a natural language that predicts the most suitable next word in a phrase or sentence based on the given context.

According to Jackley (2024) difference between AI and generative AI which refers to LLMs that AI is a broad term that includes various technologies designed to mimic human-like behavior or capabilities and LLMs are a specific type of generative AI, which refers to AI models that create content such as text, images, video, spoken language, and music.

Large Language Models hold promise for overcoming some of the limitations of traditional AI systems where LLMs could act as pedagogical agents, encouraging students to reflect, engage deeply with content, and develop self-regulated learning skills, however, careful implementation is required to ensure these tools are used effectively (Laak, Aru, 2024).

ETHICAL ISSUES OF USE OF AI IN EDUCATION

European Commission (2022) in document *Directorate-General for Education, Youth, Sport and Culture, Ethical guidelines on the use of artificial intelligence (AI) and data in teaching and learning for educators* states that the ethical use of AI in education is guided by four key considerations, human agency, fairness, humanity, and justified choice. Human agency involves enabling individuals to make and be responsible for their life choices. Fairness ensures equitable treatment and access to opportunities. Humanity focuses on respecting individuals' dignity and fostering meaningful connections. Justified choice requires transparent, collaborative decision-making based on facts and data.

The AI Act proposed by the Commission has the aim to establish legally binding requirements for high-risk AI systems, including those in education and vocational training. Educational institutions will rely on the certification of the reliability of these AI systems while complying with certain obligations. Companies developing artificial intelligence are encouraged to incorporate ethical guidelines focused on human action, transparency, fairness, social welfare, privacy, technical flexibility and responsibility. These guidelines help educators and technology providers assess impacts and manage risks to ensure responsible use of artificial intelligence in education. Gašević et al. (2023) emphasis that with the impact of AI expands, concerns about ethics, bias, and fairness take center stage. The data used to train these systems often contains hidden biases, either within itself or introduced during algorithm creation and this can lead to problematic, and even harmful, outcomes for certain groups of people. du Boulay (2023) emphasis that the growing use of AI in various systems, from apps to complex financial tools, has brought ethical concerns to the forefront.

The EU is even proposing legislation to address these issues during design, implementation, and deployment. Frameworks are being developed to guide ethical AI development, which is particularly important in education, where student data privacy is a growing concern due to the vast amount collected and potential for commercial misuse. Researchers are becoming more aware of these issues, and dedicated organizations like the Institute of Ethical AI in Education are providing guidelines for responsible AI use in classrooms. Foltynek et al. (2023) proposes for all types of unauthorized content generation including contract cheating and inappropriate use of AI.

The definition introduces the term unauthorized content generation (UCG) that is the production of academic work, in whole or part, for academic credit, progression or award, whether or not a payment or other favor is involved, using unapproved or undeclared human or technological assistance (Foltynek et al., 2023, p. 2). Incorporating AI education for students and teacher training is essential because without learning about the ethical use of AI, students may misuse it which could lead to academic misconduct.

Foltynek et al. (2023) emphasize that students should be included and educated about the purpose of all activities related to learning and assessment and why they should develop (e.g. write) their individual/group work assignments, and how they can develop their ethical writing and content production skills (Foltynek et al., 2023, p. 3). On the other hand, Foltynek et al. (2023) advocate the development of the national and institutional polices about using AI in education that can be used by teachers and students. According to them the policies should define "default rules on when and how the students, teachers, researchers and other educational stakeholders are allowed to use different kinds of AI tools. There should be space for specific rules at course level. The policy and the rules should be clearly communicated to all stakeholders. It is important to "guide the users on how to correctly and transparently acknowledge the use of AI tools in an assignment, dissertation, thesis, paper, article, book chapter, computer program, graphic, artwork and other types of artefact" (Foltynek et al., 2023, p. 4).

Given the various forms of ethical challenges in AI applications within educational environment, Akgun & Greenhow (2022) concentrate on issues related to privacy, surveillance, autonomy, bias, and discrimination (Wu, et al., 2024). According to Akgun & Greenhow (2022, pp. 434 - 436), privacy is a significant concern in the realm of AI, particularly regarding user consent for accessing personal data, which users may not fully comprehend. The second issue is called surveillance and it is related with the surveillance mechanisms that can be integrated into AI predictive systems to update students' academic progress, strengths, weaknesses, and learning styles. Continuous monitoring and tracking of students' online interactions may hinder their active participation in learning activities and undermine their sense of ownership over their ideas. This dual nature of surveillance in education poses challenges in balancing safety with privacy and autonomy. The third issue is related to autonomy which is related to the use of algorithms by AI systems, for tasks like predicting students' test performance, which can undermine the sense of independence for both students and teachers. The fourth issue concerns bias and discrimination issues because in AI platforms, existing power dynamics and biases are ingrained within machine-learning models. Gender bias is evident, especially in language translation tasks, where AI systems may reinforce gender stereotypes. When people create algorithms, they rely on data that reflects the historical and systemic biases present in society. This data can encode these biases into the algorithm itself, leading to algorithmic bias that reinforces existing inequalities.

The ethical use of AI in education according to Saylam et al. (2023) requires establishing guidelines based on core ethical principles, such as justice, transparency, privacy, and less common concepts such as not causing harm, promoting welfare, and autonomy (freedom of choice). Saylam et al. (2023) states that to adapt these principles to education, it is necessary to take into account the well-being and development of children. Additional principles such as pedagogical appropriateness and AI literacy become crucial. Pedagogical appropriateness ensures teachers retain control over how AI is used in the classroom, focusing on what benefits students. AI literacy means students and teachers should have the knowledge to critically evaluate AI tools. By establishing and promoting awareness of these principles, educators can leverage AI responsibly while preventing misuse in educational environment.

Reiß (2021) considers that the increasing role of AI in education necessitates a critical examination of teaching aims, as AI-driven education lacks the self-awareness and reflexivity inherent in human teachers. In Reiß (2021) research, current AI education systems emphasize subjects like mathematics, potentially narrowing education to mere knowledge acquisition and skill development. This focus may overshadow the importance of teaching subjects like literature, which are more challenging for AI to handle effectively. To foster informed and active citizenship, education should encourage students to engage with political affairs and uphold values such as freedom, autonomy, equality, and cooperation, which may be difficult to achieve with AI-centric education models. Adams et al. (2023) conducted research about existing ethical guidelines and policies for AI in K-12 education and their analysis highlights the need for pedagogically responsive, developmentally, and context-sensitive ethical approaches to integrating AI in K-12 education. While the suitability of specific AI technologies for different educational situations is outside this paper's scope, we stress the importance of strong policy guidance for developers, educators, and stakeholders to ensure ethical and prudent AI use. Current AIEd ethics policies lack a robust theoretical understanding of AI-human interactions and their evolution. Policies must address the long-term cognitive, physical, social-emotional, political, and cultural implications of children growing up in AI-integrated environments. Children are vulnerable yet adaptive to the transformative effects of AI on their lives. The research AI *and Personalized Learning: Bridging the Gap with Modern Educational Goals* (2024) emphasizes challenges such as privacy risks, misinformation, algorithmic bias, and the digital divide and ethical implementation is essential to avoid excluding disadvantaged learners and to address disparities in technology access. While AI is promising to transform education, its potential can only be fully realized through ethical, inclusive, and collaborative implementation that addresses privacy concerns, algorithmic biases, and the digital divide (Ayeni et al., 2024).

REFERENCES

Adams, C., Pente, P., Lemermeyer, G., & Rockwell, G. (2023). Ethical principles for artificial intelligence in K-12 education. *Computers and Education.Artificial Intelligence*, 4, 100131. DOI: 10.1016/j.caeai.2023.100131

Akgun, S., & Greenhow, C. (2022). Artificial intelligence in education: Addressing ethical challenges in K-12 settings. *AI and Ethics*, 2(3), 431–440. DOI: 10.1007/s43681-021-00096-7 PMID: 34790956

Almasri, F. (2024). Exploring the Impact of Artificial Intelligence in Teaching and Learning of Science: A Systematic Review of Empirical Research. *Research in Science Education*, 54(5), 977–997. DOI: 10.1007/s11165-024-10176-3

Ayeni, O. O., Al Hamad, N. M., Chisom, O. N., Osawaru, B., & Adewusi, O. E. (2024). AI in education: A review of personalized learning and educational technology. *GSC Advanced Research and Reviews*, 18(2), 261–271. DOI: 10.30574/gscarr.2024.18.2.0062

Bayly-Castaneda, K., Ramirez-Montoya, M. S., & Morita-Alexander, A. (2024, August). Crafting personalized learning paths with AI for lifelong learning: a systematic literature review. In *Frontiers in Education* (Vol. 9, p. 1424386). Frontiers Media SA. *ChatGPT*. https://chatgpt.com/?oai-dm=1&model=auto

Data, I. B. M., & Team, A. I. (2023, October 16). *Understanding the different types of artificial intelligence*. IBM Blog. https://www.ibm.com/blog/understanding-the-different-types-of-artificial-intelligence/

du Boulay, B. (2023). Artificial Intelligence in Education and Ethics. In Zawacki-Richter, O., & Jung, I. (Eds.), *Handbook of Open, Distance and Digital Education*. Springer. DOI: 10.1007/978-981-19-2080-6_6

European Commission. (2022). Directorate-General for Education, Youth, Sport and Culture, Ethical guidelines on the use of artificial intelligence (AI) and data in teaching and learning for educators, Publications Office of the European Union. https://data.europa.eu/doi/10.2766/153756

Fitria, T. N. (2021, December). Artificial intelligence (AI) in education: Using AI tools for teaching and learning process. In *Prosiding Seminar Nasional & Call for Paper STIE AAS* (pp. 134-147).

Foltynek, T., Bjelobaba, S., Glendinning, I., Khan, Z. R., Santos, R., Pavletic, P., & Kravjar, J. (2023). ENAI Recommendations on the ethical use of Artificial Intelligence in Education. *International Journal for Educational Integrity*, 19(1), 12. DOI: 10.1007/s40979-023-00133-4

Frąckiewicz, M. (2023). OpenAI and the Risks of AI Bias: Addressing Stereotypes and Discrimination. TS2 SPACE. https://ts2.space/en/openai-and-the-risks-of-ai-bias-addressing-stereotypes-and-discrimination

Gašević, D., Siemens, G., & Sadiq, S. (2023). Empowering learners for the age of artificial intelligence. Computers & Education. *Artificial Intelligence*, 4, 100130. DOI: 10.1016/j.caeai.2023.100130

Gemini. (n.d.). https://gemini.google.com/

Ghimire, A., Prather, J., & Edwards, J. (2024). Generative AI in Education: A Study of Educators' Awareness, Sentiments, and Influencing Factors. *arXiv* preprint *arXiv*:2403.15586.

Ifenthaler, D., Majumdar, R., Gorissen, P., Judge, M., Mishra, S., Raffaghelli, J., & Shimada, A. (2024). Artificial Intelligence in Education: Implications for Policymakers, Researchers, and Practitioners. *Tech Know Learn*, 29(4), 1693–1710. DOI: 10.1007/s10758-024-09747-0

Introduction to large language models. (n.d.). Google for Developers. https://developers.google.com/machine-learning/resources/intro-llms

Jackley, M. (2024, February 16). *What is a Large Language model (LLM)?*https://www.oracle.com/artificial-intelligence/large-language-model/

Jauhiainen, J. S., & Guerra, A. G. (2023). Generative AI and ChatGPT in school Children's education: Evidence from a school lesson. *Sustainability (Basel)*, 15(18), 14025. DOI: 10.3390/su151814025

Katsamakas, E., Pavlov, O. V., & Saklad, R. (2024). Artificial Intelligence and the Transformation of Higher Education Institutions: A Systems Approach. *Sustainability (Basel)*, 16(14), 6118. DOI: 10.3390/su16146118

Laak, K. J., & Aru, J. (2024). AI and personalized learning: bridging the gap with modern educational goals. *arXiv* preprint *arXiv*:2404.02798.

Large language models (LLM). (2024, May 13). European Data Protection Supervisor. https://www.edps.europa.eu/data-protection/technology-monitoring/techsonar/large-language-models-llm_en

Makhambetova, A., Zhiyenbayeva, N., & Ergesheva, E. (2021). Personalized learning strategy as a tool to improve academic performance and motivation of students. *International Journal of Web-Based Learning and Teaching Technologies*, 16(6), 1–17. DOI: 10.4018/IJWLTT.286743

Marrone, R., Cropley, D., & Medeiros, K. (2024). How Does Narrow AI Impact Human Creativity? *Creativity Research Journal*, 1–11. DOI: 10.1080/10400419.2024.2378264

Miao, F., Holmes, W., Huang, R., & Zhang, H. (2021). *AI and education: Guidance for policy-makers*. UNESCO., DOI: 10.54675/PCSP7350

OECD. (2022). *OECD Framework for the Classification of AI systems. OECD Digital Economy Papers, No. 323*. OECD Publishing. DOI: 10.1787/cb6d9eca-

Porayska-Pomsta, K. (2024). A manifesto for a pro-actively responsible AI in education. *International Journal of Artificial Intelligence in Education*, 34(1), 73–83. DOI: 10.1007/s40593-023-00346-1

Ramirez, E. A. B., & Fuentes Esparrell, J. A. (2024). Artificial Intelligence (AI) in Education: Unlocking the Perfect Synergy for Learning. *Educational Process: International Journal*, 13(1), 35–51. DOI: 10.22521/edupij.2024.131.3

Reiß, M. (2021). The use of AI in education: Practicalities and ethical considerations. *London Review of Education*, 19(1). Advance online publication. DOI: 10.14324/LRE.19.1.05

Rillig, M. C., Ågerstrand, M., Bi, M., Gould, K. A., & Sauerland, U. (2023). Risks and benefits of large language models for the environment. *Environmental Science & Technology*, 57(9), 3464–3466. DOI: 10.1021/acs.est.3c01106 PMID: 36821477

Saylam, S., Duman, N., Yildirim, Y., & Satsevich, K. (2023). Empowering education with AI: Addressing ethical concerns. *London Journal of Social Sciences*, 6(6), 39–48. DOI: 10.31039/ljss.2023.6.103

What are Large Language Models (LLMs)? (n.d.). https://www.ibm.com/topics/large-language-models

What is Artificial Intelligence (AI)? (2024, January 31). https://www.iso.org/artificial-intelligence/what-is-ai

Wu, S., Cao, Y., Cui, J., Li, R., Qian, H., Jiang, B., & Zhang, W. (2024). A Comprehensive Exploration of Personalized Learning in Smart Education: From Student Modeling to Personalized Recommendations. *arXiv* preprint *arXiv*:2402.01666.

Yim, I.H.Y., & Su, J. (2024). Artificial intelligence (AI) learning tools in K-12 education: A scoping review. *J. Comput. Educ.* DOI: 10.1007/s40692-023-00304-9

Chapter 3
AI Tools and Platforms for Personalized Learning

ABSTRACT

This chapter explores various AI tools and platforms designed to personalize learning that are available online for teachers to use. The list of selected AI tools will provide information on how AI can analyze student data, notify knowledge gaps, and recommend targeted learning paths. AI-powered tutors and interactive learning environments can provide students with individualized support and foster deeper engagement with the material. Devers functionalities of AI can help educators create a more effective and empowering learning experience for all students. The list of AI tools and platforms is created based on analyzing the features of AI tools and platforms based on criteria that they are free to use, have functionalities for personalized learning, and can be used in educational environments.

CHATGPT

ChatGPT is an advanced AI language model designed to interact with users like you in a natural and informative way. ChatGPT, developed by OpenAI, uses state-of-the-art deep-learning techniques to understand and generate text responses that are human-like in a wide range of fields. ChatGPT has a knowledge base and ability to understand context, providing an understanding and creative solution. ChatGPT has the possibility to adapt to various con-

DOI: 10.4018/979-8-3693-3474-4.ch003

versational styles, update information and provide a variety of companions for exploring ideas, seeking advice, or simply enjoying time in dialogue. ChatGPT aims to provide helpful and useful responses based on user interests and questions, whether it is in discussions about technology trends, exploring philosophical questions or sharing personal anecdotes.

During the research ChatGPT was used to get the answer about a wide range of possibilities and functionalities. The OpenAI ChatGPT provided following information how and for what it can be used:

- **Information Retrieval:** ChatGPT can provide factual information on a vast array of topics, ranging from historical events and scientific concepts to current news and pop culture.
- **Answering Questions:** You can ask ChatGPT questions on virtually any subject, and it will strive to provide accurate and informative responses based on its knowledge base.
- **Language Translation:** ChatGPT can assist with language translation tasks, helping users communicate across different languages by translating text inputs or providing explanations in various languages.
- **Creative Writing:** Whether you need help generating ideas for a story, crafting poetry, or composing song lyrics, ChatGPT can offer creative suggestions and assist with writing tasks.
- **Personal Assistance:** ChatGPT can serve as a virtual assistant, helping with tasks such as setting reminders, scheduling appointments, and organizing your day.
- **Learning and Education:** ChatGPT can support learning and education by explaining complex concepts, providing study tips, and offering guidance on academic subjects.
- **Coding Assistance:** For programmers, ChatGPT can provide coding assistance, offering explanations, code snippets, and troubleshooting tips for various programming languages and frameworks.
- **Entertainment and Fun:** ChatGPT can engage users in entertaining conversations, tell jokes, share interesting facts, and even play text-based games.
- **Therapeutic Conversations:** ChatGPT can provide support and companionship in therapeutic conversations, offering a listening ear and engaging in empathetic dialogue.

- **Customer Support:** ChatGPT can assist with customer support inquiries, answering common questions, troubleshooting issues, and providing assistance with products or services.

Figure 1. ChatGPT interface in Croatian

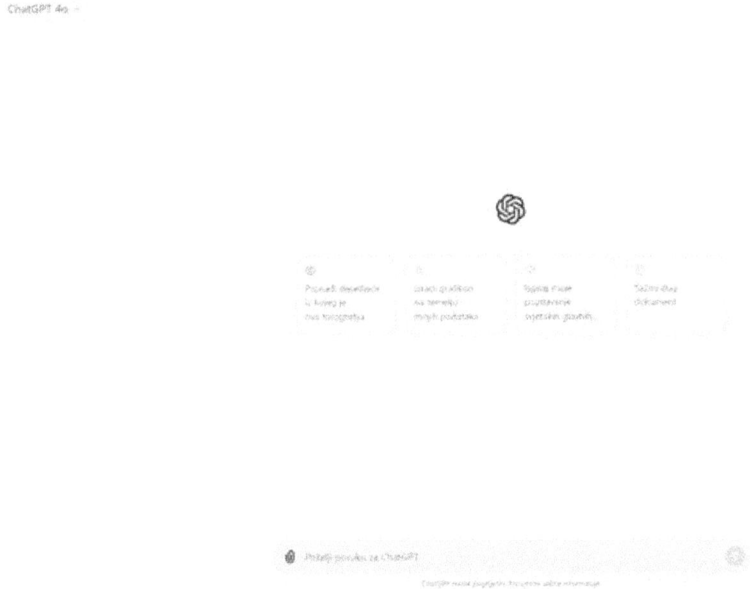

ChatGPT has a wide use in almost any field of human activity from doing everyday tasks like composing emails, providing information, constructing plans and ideas to organizing educational content, creating tests, providing feedback information, etc. The most interesting for this research is its use in learning and education. As it is shown in chapter *Understanding Personalized Learning* the use of OpenAI can help create personalized learning materials for students from different backgrounds and knowledge levels. It is important to mention that all materials which are produced with ChatGPT have to be revised and adapted for further use by the teachers.

ChatGPT offers several valuable applications in education that are related to personalized learning, tutoring and homework help, language learning, research assistance, writing support, virtual lectures and presentations, accessibility and study group facilitation.

ChatGPT enables personalized learning experiences by adjusting explanations and resources to the learning styles and preferences of each student. It provides additional explanations, examples and practice problems to reinforce concepts and improve the overall learning process. ChatGPT can answer complex questions, provide different perspectives, and engage students in interactive learning activities based on the unique needs of each student. This personalized approach helps to address the gaps in understanding and promote deeper understanding. Furthermore, ChatGPT's ability to provide instant feedback and support is an opportunity for continuous learning and development.

It can be used as a virtual tutor to help students with homework assignments, clarify confusing topics and explain difficult concepts. ChatGPT provides step-by-step instructions that help students navigate complex problems and provide hints that facilitate independent problem solving. This virtual assistance not only supports students to complete their tasks, but also promotes a deeper understanding of the subject. ChatGPT is also available 24/7 and ensures that students receive timely assistance when necessary and provides a reliable resource for continuous academic support. This comprehensive method of teaching improves students' learning experience, enabling them to achieve their educational goals more effectively.

The tool can be used also for language learners, offering a range of support to enhance their proficiency in a target language. It provides accurate translations and detailed explanations of grammar rules, facilitating a better understanding of linguistic structures. Additionally, ChatGPT engages learners in practice conversations, helping to improve their speaking and comprehension skills. Beyond language mechanics, ChatGPT offers cultural insights that enrich the learning experience by providing context and understanding of cultural nuances. Furthermore, it recommends resources for further study, enabling learners to explore additional materials tailored to their specific needs and interests. This comprehensive approach ensures that language learners receive a well-rounded education, combining technical language skills with cultural literacy.

In addition, it can be an assistant researcher for students, providing broad support to gather information about academic topics, locate relevant sources, and generate ideas for projects and papers. ChatGPT streamlines the research process and improves the efficiency of information discovery by providing detailed summary of the articles and proposing effective keywords for research.

In addition, he provides expert guidance on the structure of research papers, helping students organize their ideas and present their findings coherently. This multifaceted support not only helps to complete tasks, but also fosters critical thinking and analytical abilities. With ChatGPT's comprehensive support, students are better equipped to conduct thorough research, produce high-quality academic work and achieve their academic objectives.

ChatGPT can help students improve their writing skills through constructive feedback on papers, suggestions for revisions, and valuable tips for effective communication. ChatGPT helps students develop creative and convincing content by helping brainstorming ideas. Furthermore, it guides the development of maps and ensures the logical and consistent structure of their written works. ChatGPT also helps refine arguments, allowing students to present their point of view convincingly and clearly. This comprehensive help not only improves the quality of students' work, but also helps them develop critical and analytical skills. With ChatGPT's support, students are able to produce structured, articulate and impactful texts and strengthen their academic and professional communication skills.

The teachers can use it to create interactive virtual lectures and presentations and improve student learning experiences. By presenting the content of the course in a lively and dynamic manner, ChatGPT helps to maintain the interest and understanding of students. Furthermore, it provides real-time answers to students' questions, ensures quick answers to doubts, and promotes a more interactive learning environment. ChatGPT also facilitates discussions on the topics of the lectures and encourages students to interact critically with the materials and with each other. This interactive approach not only improves the effectiveness of virtual learning, but also promotes student active participation and deeper understanding. With ChatGPT's assistance, educators can create an enriching and interactive educational experience that meets students' needs.

For students with disabilities, ChatGPT offers alternative learning material formats to make education more accessible. For example, it provides simplified audio descriptions and explanations to meet the various needs of learners. ChatGPT also helps students with visual or learning disabilities through reading and understanding to ensure that they receive the same quality of education as their peers. This support is essential for the removal of learning barriers and for the promotion of inclusivity in the educational environment. By using ChatGPT's capabilities, educators can create a more equitable learning experience and empower all students to achieve success regardless of their individual challenges. This commitment to accessibility strengthens the entire educational environment and promotes an inclusive and supportive environment for all learners.

ChatGPT can improve the effectiveness of online research groups by supporting discussion questions, moderate conversations, and summarize key points. ChatGPT stimulates constructive and productive discussions between group members by creating stimulating questions. Its moderation capacity ensures that discussions are focused and respectful and fosters a learning environment for collaboration and support. Furthermore, ChatGPT's ability to summarize key points helps students retain key information and keep their classroom organized. This structured approach not only improves the efficiency of group cooperation, but also ensures that all participants contribute meaningfully and enjoy the same benefits. By integrating ChatGPT into student group activities, students can maximize learning opportunities and achieve academic goals through improved teamwork and communication.

The ChatGPT can enhance the learning experience for students by providing personalized support, facilitating interactive learning activities, and promoting engagement and collaboration in educational settings for teachers and students. Concrete examples of ChatGPT use for personalized learning can be found in Chapter Personalized Learning with Generative AI.

GEMINI

Gemini is a family of large language models developed by Google. In this phase Gemini was asked to describe itself and the response is as follows:

- Capabilities: Gemini boasts an impressive understanding of various inputs, including text, code, images, and even video. It can process and combine this information to generate different creative text formats, translate languages, write different kinds of creative content, and answer your questions in an informative way.
- Flexibility: One of Gemini's strengths is its ability to run efficiently on a wide range of devices. This means you can potentially interact with Gemini on powerful machines in data centers or even on your mobile phone.

- Accessibility: Google offers access to Gemini models through different avenues. You can interact with it directly through the Gemini app or use cloud platforms like Vertex AI to integrate its capabilities into your applications.
- Versions: There are three main versions of Gemini available, each catering to different needs:
- Ultra (1.0): This is the most capable and feature-rich version, ideal for tackling highly complex tasks.
- Pro (1.0 - 1.5): This version strikes a balance between capability and efficiency, making it suitable for a wide range of tasks.
- Nano (1.0): Designed for on-device use, this lightweight version offers the benefits of Gemini on your mobile device.

Based on the information provided by the Gemini it can be stated that Gemini offers a multifaceted approach to enhancing creativity and productivity across various domains. In content creation, it serves as a versatile tool, aiding in the generation of diverse creative text formats such as poems, code, scripts, musical pieces, emails, and letters. Beyond mere assistance, Gemini facilitates the creative process by helping users brainstorm ideas, overcome writer's block, and refine their content to be compelling and engaging. In the realm of research and learning, Gemini functions as an intelligent research companion, capable of sifting through vast amounts of information to provide succinct summaries, informative answers to questions, and even language translations to broaden users' learning horizons. Moreover, Gemini excels in improving communication and understanding through its natural language processing capabilities. Users can interact with Gemini in a conversational manner, receiving clear, concise, and informative responses to their queries. Additionally, its machine translation feature bridges language barriers, facilitating smoother communication and information sharing across different cultures. Gemini also offers next-level applications, particularly in software development, where developers can harness its capabilities to create innovative AI-powered applications. By integrating Gemini models through platforms like Vertex AI, developers can enhance their applications with advanced features such as natural language processing and content generation. Furthermore, the lightweight Nano version of Gemini opens doors to on-device intelligence, enabling smartphones and other mobile devices to utilize Gemini's capabilities for tasks like voice assistants and real-time creative text generation, thereby enhancing user experiences on the go.

Figure 2. Gemini interface in Croatian

Gemini as ChatGPT in their responses always inform users that it is important to remember that tools are still under development, and its functionalities are constantly evolving and that tools can make mistakes.

Gemini also has it use in the education sector, empowering educators and enriching the learning experience for students. According to the Gemini it can be used as teacher's assistant, for personalized learning, as accessibility tool, for interactive learning and material creation, and for busting creativity.

The concept of a teacher's assistant envisions an AI companion designed to assist educators in crafting dynamic and effective lesson plans. Gemini, possesses the capability to analyze a given topic and produce comprehensive lesson frameworks, encompassing diverse instructional activities and thought-provoking discussion prompts customized to accommodate various age demographics and learning modalities. By leveraging Gemini's functionalities, instructors can significantly alleviate the burdens associated with lesson planning, thereby affording them ample opportunities to allocate resources towards individualized pedagogical approaches and fostering meaningful student engagement. Consequently, the integration of such technological support not only streamlines administrative tasks but also enriches the educational experience by nurturing tailored learning environments conducive to academic growth and development.

Personalized learning recognizes the inherent diversity of students' learning styles and abilities. In this context, Gemini offers tailor-made educational experiences by assessing the strengths and areas of improvement of individual students. Through this analysis, Gemini can design educational materials and propose alternative explanations for difficult concepts that meet each student's unique needs and preferences. By adopting this personalized approach, students are empowered to progress their educational journey at the fastest pace that suits them, thus promoting a deeper understanding and mastery of academic content. This individual support not only improves learning outcomes, but also cultivates the feelings of autonomy and self-efficacy of students, and ultimately promotes a more inclusive and effective educational environment.

Gemini can be used as a means of accessibility, as it can provide essential assistance to students with learning disabilities and promote a multicultural education environment. Using its capabilities, Gemini facilitates access through various means. It primarily serves as a text-to-speech converter to enable students with reading disabilities to understand written content more effectively. This feature ensures that people who face challenges in traditional text-based learning can access educational materials more easily. In addition, Gemini's versatility extends to the creation of content in a variety of formats that accommodate student learning preferences and modes. Through visual aids, hearing hints, or tactile materials, Gemini ensures that educational content is presented in a way that allows optimal understanding and participation. It not only improves the learning experience of students with disabilities through such comprehensive support, but also demonstrates commitment to the promotion of equality and inclusion in the educational environment.

Gemini can be used for developing interactive learning experiences because it can complement traditional textbooks with dynamic engagement opportunities. By leveraging Gemini, textbooks can be transformed into interactive platforms wherein students can actively participate in their learning journey. This transformative feature enables students to pose inquiries directly to Gemini, prompting real-time responses and supplementary information tailored to their queries. Moreover, Gemini facilitates deeper exploration of subject matter by offering elucidating explanations in a captivating manner, thereby enhancing students' understanding and retention of complex concepts. Through this interactive framework, educational materials transcend their static confines, fostering a collaborative learning environment wherein students are empowered to actively engage with the content and cultivate critical thinking skills.

Gemini can provide support to students through various creative projects, whether they conceptualize ideas for scientific projects or create imaginative narratives. Through its support, Gemini facilitates the generation of creative text formats, provides insights to the development of storyline, and supports projects with relevant factual information to enrich the creative process. Moreover, Gemini is a catalyst of inspiration that energizes students' imagination and encourages them to push the boundaries of traditional thinking. By nurturing creativity in this way, Gemini not only improves the quality of the students' work, but also develops basic skills such as problem solving, communication and adaptability, preparing them for success in an increasingly dynamic and competitive world.

Except the benefits and possibilities that Gemini can offer to teachers and students in their everyday activities Gemini mention also the challenges and some considerations that users need to bear in mind when using it for teaching and learning. These challenges are related to teacher training, reliability and bias and ethical considerations.

Teachers' training is essential to ensure that Gemini is optimally integrated into the classroom environment and that educators can exploit its capabilities to the maximum. Fully developed training programs are indispensable to equip teachers with the necessary skills and knowledge, recognizing Gemini's potential as a transformative educational tool. These training initiatives cover various aspects, including preparing the features of Gemini, understanding its application across different subjects and grade levels, and mastering strategies to implement effectively within educational frameworks. In addition, continuing support mechanisms are essential to maintain teachers' competence and confidence in using Gemini, including troubleshooting opportunities, professional development opportunities, and access to an educator support community. With investment in robust teacher training and support systems, schools can maximize Gemini's impact, enable teachers to facilitate enriched learning experiences, and equip students with the skills necessary to succeed in the 21st century.

T The reliability and impartiality of Gemini information are the main considerations, reflecting the broader need for ethical and equitable AI use. As an AI-driven tool, the effectiveness of Gemini depends on the accuracy and neutrality of the data processed and distributed. Therefore, careful attention should be paid to the mitigation of potential biases inherent in algorithms or data sets, which inadvertently undermine results or perpetuate inequality. This requires strict quality assurance protocols, including detailed validation of sources, transparent documentation of methods and continuous monitoring to detect and correct errors when they occur. In addition, the promotion of interdisciplinary cooperation between AI experts, educators and sector experts can improve the robustness of Gemini algorithms and ensure compliance with established standards of accuracy and fairness. By maintaining the principles of reliability and prejudice mitigation, Gemini can serve as a trusted ally in education efforts to promote informed decision-making and equitable learning outcomes for all stakeholders.

Integrating AI into education practices requires careful attention to ethical considerations and recognition of the multifaceted impact inherent in its adoption. The main concerns are the risk of overdependence on technology, as the role of artificial intelligence replaces human judgment and pedagogical expertise. This excessive dependence can inadvertently diminish the value of interpersonal interaction and the in-depth understanding of students' needs that educators offer. Furthermore, biases in AI models pose significant ethical dilemmas because they perpetuate inequalities and strengthen existing social prejudices. In order to address these challenges, an informed and principled approach to AI implementation is necessary, based on transparency, accountability and commitment to equitable outcomes. This includes strong monitoring mechanisms, comprehensive training for stakeholders and continuous review of AI algorithms to identify and mitigate prejudices. In addition, to promote ethical AI practices, inter-disciplinary collaboration is needed to inform responsible decision-making based on information from the fields of ethics, education and technology. By ensuring the integrity and fairness of the learning environment, educators and policy makers can use the potential of AI integration to improve educational experiences. A concrete example of the use of Gemini to learn personalized is found in the chapter on personalized learning with generation AI.

PADLET

Padlet is a digital bulletin board tool that offers some AI functionalities. It is a versatile digital platform likened to a virtual corkboard, enabling users to pin ideas, notes, multimedia, and hyperlinks in an organized and visually appealing manner. Beyond mere information storage, Padlet facilitates collaborative efforts by allowing users to share and interact with the posted content. While not inherently an AI system, Padlet incorporates AI-driven features powered by machine learning, expanding its utility and enhancing user experience.

One such feature is the 'Create with AI' tool, which enables users to generate entire Padlets based solely on textual descriptions, offering templates like “Lesson Plan” or “Timeline of Events” for structured guidance or a “Custom Board” option for a more flexible approach. The AI analyzes the input to generate relevant content, streamlining the brainstorming process and saving time. Additionally, Padlet's AI assists in content creation, effortlessly generating elements like drawings, slideshows, and short links based on user-provided keywords, thereby enhancing the visual appeal and richness of the shared materials.

Figure 3. Padlet interface

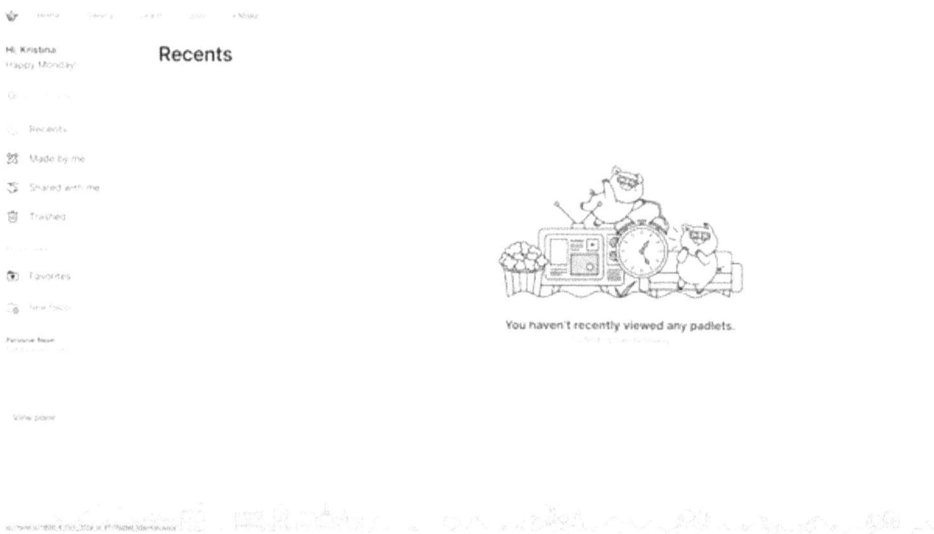

In addition, Padlet incorporated AI-powered moderation tools to facilitate public collaboration and ensure a positive and productive online environment. These features collectively contribute to several benefits, such as time-saving content creation, enhanced collaboration opportunities, and improved accessibility for users with different learning preferences and abilities. However, AI must not replace human creativity and critical thinking, but as a support tool. Users should take care to verify the accuracy of the content generated by AI and reduce the potential prejudices inherent in AI algorithms.

In educational contexts, Padlet is a valuable resource for the promotion of creativity, collaboration and active learning between students and educators. It can facilitate various educational activities such as brainstorming sessions, group projects, interactive presentations and training evaluations, thereby improving participation and knowledge retention. Padlet's AI features further enhance its usefulness in education by supporting lesson planning, personalized learning materials and promoting accessibility and inclusion.

DIFFIT

DIFFIT is an AI-based tool designed specifically for teachers to differentiate classroom instruction. Differentiation refers to tailoring classes to meet the individual needs of students in the classroom. This may include adjusting the difficulty level of the learning materials, providing alternative teaching methods or providing additional support to students who need it. DIFFIT enables teachers to differentiate instruction by making it easy to create different versions of learning materials for students of different levels of reading, previous knowledge, or learning styles. DIFFIT offers a streamlined process for creating customized educational materials and promotes differentiated education to meet the needs of different students. The user starts by providing inputs in the form of text, specific topics, or hyperlinks to existing articles. They then specify the required level for the material to ensure that it is consistent with the level of student competence. Using this information, DIFFIT generates a complete range of resources that are customized for the specific parameters. These include adapted reading passages, carefully rewritten to the appropriate reading level, brief summary explaining key points of the text, curated lists of key vocabulary terms, definitions and examples, and a series of comprehension checks, including multiple choice, short answers, and open-ended questions to evaluate students' comprehensive understanding.

Figure 4. DIFFIT interface

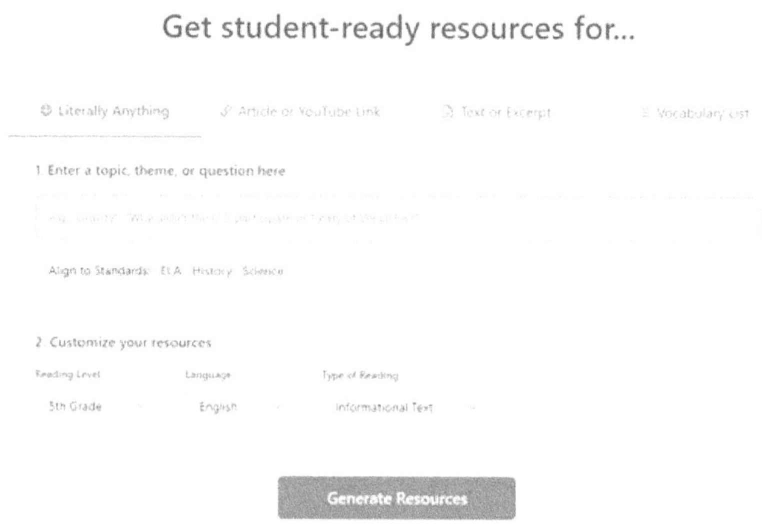

Moreover, DIFFIT offers supplementary features to enhance its utility in educational settings. It supports multiple languages, facilitating accessibility for students in multilingual classrooms by converting the generated content into diverse linguistic formats. Additionally, the platform provides convenient export options, enabling users to seamlessly integrate the generated materials into their instructional materials through formats like Google Docs. This versatility ensures that educators can leverage DIFFIT's capabilities to streamline lesson planning and effectively address the diverse learning needs of their students, ultimately promoting enhanced comprehension and academic success.

The use of DIFFIT in the educational context generates a large number of benefits and improves the teaching and learning experience. First, DIFFIT is a time-saving tool by automating the creation of differentiated learning materials, reducing the burden of developing manual resources and giving educators more time to focus on lesson planning and meaningful student interaction. In addition, DIFFIT promotes the inclusion and adaptation of different student profiles and allows educators to adapt resources to the needs and preferences of individual students and effectively adapt to different learning styles and abilities. In addition, DIFFIT plays a key role in promoting the involvement and motivation of students by providing materials tailored to the students' appropriate reading levels. DIFFIT aims to improve understanding and encourage active participation in learning activities by presenting content in a format compatible with the students' level of competence. In addition, DIFFIT's user-friendly interface increases accessibility and provides a valuable resource for educators of a variety of technical fields. The ease of use ensures that educators can easily incorporate DIFFIT into teaching practices without facing significant obstacles, thus maximizing its usefulness and impact in different educational environments.

DIFFIT, as an AI-powered tool for differentiation, offers a range of benefits in education by allowing teachers to cater to the diverse needs of their students. DIFFIT's versatile functionalities render it a valuable asset across diverse educational settings, offering myriad opportunities to enhance teaching and learning experiences. Firstly, DIFFIT facilitates the creation of accessible learning materials by adeptly adapting texts and articles to various reading levels, ensuring equitable access to core concepts for students with differing reading abilities, including those with learning disabilities like dyslexia. Moreover, its multilingual support capabilities enable the translation of content, accommodating the needs of linguistically diverse classrooms and fostering improved comprehension and engagement among students.

Furthermore, DIFFIT enhances student comprehension through targeted vocabulary building exercises, automatically identifying key terms within texts and furnishing definitions with illustrative examples. Additionally, its provision of comprehension checks, comprising multiple-choice, short answer, and open-ended questions aligned with the adapted reading passages, serves as embedded assessments for teachers to gauge student understanding and identify areas requiring further support.

In terms of promoting student engagement, DIFFIT offers customizable activity templates tailored to different learning styles, fostering active participation and meaningful learning experiences. It supports scaffolded learning by providing summaries or background information alongside adapted reading passages, thereby facilitating comprehension and retention, especially for complex topics.

In addition, DIFFIT streamlines teacher workflow by serving as a time-saving tool, automating the process of differentiating learning materials and enabling educators to allocate more time to essential tasks such as lesson planning and personalized instruction. Additionally, its customizable features afford teachers control over the adaptation process, allowing for tailored resources that align with specific lesson plans and student needs.

QUIZZIZ

Quizizz is a game learning platform that allows students to explore and evaluate more interactively and engage with each other. The tool offers teachers and students several features in educational settings, such as creating interactive quizzes, experiencing live games, producing detailed reports, promoting student engagement, promoting active learning, providing instant feedback, and serving as an evaluation tool.

Quizzz has a wide range of interactive quizzes on various topics. These quizzes include various format of questions, including multiple choices, true/false, open and image-based questions, responding to different learning preferences and facilitating a comprehensive assessment of students' knowledge.

Figure 5. Quizziz interface

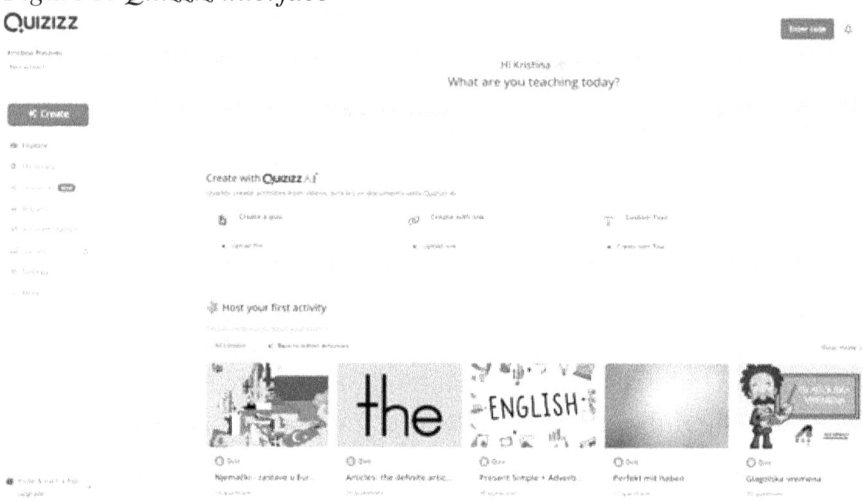

Live Game Show Experience can transform traditional assessments into captivating game shows, Quizizz immerses students in a dynamic learning environment where they engage in real-time competition. Participants answer questions using their devices, with the platform showcasing a leaderboard, thereby infusing an element of excitement and healthy competition into the learning process.

Educators gain invaluable insights into student performance through Quizizz's detailed reports. These reports furnish comprehensive analyses of individual and class-level comprehension across specific topics, empowering teachers to pinpoint areas requiring further emphasis and tailor instructional strategies accordingly.

The gamified format and real-time competition inherent in Quizizz heighten student engagement, transforming learning into an interactive and enjoyable experience. This immersive approach fosters sustained interest and active participation among students, enhancing overall learning outcomes.

By encouraging students to actively recall information and compete with their peers, Quizizz promotes active engagement with course content, thereby reinforcing comprehension and retention. This active learning methodology cultivates deeper understanding and mastery of subject matter.

Quizizz offers students immediate feedback on their responses, enabling them to promptly identify knowledge gaps and refine their learning strategies accordingly. This instantaneous feedback loop facilitates continuous improvement and empowers students to take ownership of their learning journey.

As a assessment tool, Quizizz not only gauges student learning effectively but also serves as a diagnostic tool for educators to identify areas of strength and areas requiring additional support. The platform's gamified approach to assessment ensures that evaluations are conducted in a manner that is engaging and enjoyable for students, fostering a positive attitude towards learning.

In essence, Quizizz is a multi-faceted educational tool that facilitates complete assessment and promotes student engagement, active learning and personalized feedback, thus enriching learning and teaching experiences in various educational contexts. Quizizz is a versatile evaluation and learning platform that serves as the primary tool for educators and students in the K-12 educational environment.

However, its application extends beyond the traditional classroom environment and encompasses higher education, corporate training programs and self-directed learning initiatives. Quizizz offers a number of additional features to improve its functionality, as well as its core functions.

First, teachers can use Quizizz to create customized quizzes adapted to specific education needs or select from a large collection of pre-existing quizzes that cover a wide range of topics. In addition, teachers are able to share quizzes with colleagues, facilitate collaborative resource sharing, and facilitate educational planning. In addition, Quizizz facilitates the assignment of quizzes as homework, enabling educators to monitor students' progress remotely and track individual performance. This feature promotes flexibility in learning and empowers students to participate in the content of the courses at their own pace. Quizizz also provides students with on-the-go learning convenience through mobile applications that enable them to access assigned quizzes and participate in independent training sessions anywhere.

In addition, Quizizz is using Artificial Intelligence (AI) technology to increase its functionality and improve both the creation of quizzes and the participation of students. The platform's AI-powered features include:

- Quizizz AI an integrated AI assistant that accelerates quiz creation processes for educators. By entering text, website URLs, or uploading files, the quizzes AI generates questions autonomously based on the content provided, simplifying the quiz creation process and reducing the time spent by educators.
- Question enhancement. Quizizz AI can improve existing questions by converting multiple choice questions into alternative formats such as filling-the-blank or dragging and dropping. This feature enhances the interactivity and participation of the quiz and provides a platform for adjusting to different learning preferences and promoting deeper understanding among students.

Using AI in Quizizz has many benefits and significantly improves the efficiency and effectiveness of education practices. First, Quizizz AI simplifies the process of creating questions, automates tedious tasks, and frees teachers' valuable time for other educational tasks. Furthermore, AI-driven question generation contributes to the diversification of question formats, enriching questions with a wider variety of interactive options, and increasing their effectiveness in assessing the learning of students. In addition, Quizizz AI promotes accessibility and allows the creation of quizzes adapted to different learning styles. For example, fill-in-the-blank questions generated by AI serve kinesthetic learners, promote inclusion, and ensure equitable assessment experiences for all students. By using Quizizz, educators can use gamification elements and artificial intelligence features effectively to improve classroom learning and assessment practices.

Interactive Review and Assessment sessions benefit from the instantaneous feedback and interactive nature of Quizizz quizzes, enabling formative assessments to gauge student understanding in real-time and inform instructional adjustments accordingly. Additionally, assigning quizzes as homework transforms review and practice sessions into engaging competitions, fostering student participation and motivation. For summative assessments, Quizizz offers an engaging game show format that maintains student interest while providing valuable insights into their learning progress. Moreover, Quizizz serves as a versatile tool for classroom engagement and participation. Introducing new topics with quick, fun quizzes energizes students and sets a dynamic tone for subsequent lessons. Likewise, review sessions become lively and collaborative through Quizizz's team-based competitions, promoting active engagement and knowledge reinforcement among students. Exit tickets provide a seamless conclusion to lessons, allowing teachers to swiftly assess student understanding before transitioning to new topics. This immediate feedback loop empowers educators to address misconceptions promptly, ensuring effective knowledge consolidation. Furthermore, Quizizz AI enhances efficiency through effortless quiz creation, with the AI assistant automating question generation based on provided text or uploaded files. This feature not only saves teachers time but also contributes to personalized learning by diversifying question formats to accommodate different learning styles, thereby fostering inclusive assessment practices for all students.

SCHOOLAI

SchoolAI is a web site that offers a suite of AI tools for teachers. These tools are aimed at saving teachers' time and efforts by automating tasks and creating a variety of educational resources. SchoolAI offers a suite of comprehensive tools equipped with AI to simplify various aspects of teaching and classroom management. Firstly, educators can use SchoolAI's document generation capabilities to create a wide range of learning materials and administrative documents. This includes the creation of comprehensive learning plans adapted to specific topics and learning objectives, as well as the creation of interactive sheets and quizzes with different questions to enhance student understanding. Furthermore, SchoolAI facilitates the development of clear and concise scoring schemes for assignments and assessments and simplifies the process of teacher evaluation. In addition, SchoolAI has expanded support for special education by producing individual educational goals (IEPs) and designing full IEPs tailored to meet the specific needs of students. In addition, SchoolAI empowers educators to maintain effective communication with parents and students by creating Class Newsletters with AI to ensure timely dissemination of important information. In addition, SchoolAI offers additional document generation options, such as behavioral intervention plans (BIPs), syllabuses and even funny jokes, to foster a positive classroom atmosphere.

Figure 6. SchoolAI interface

In addition to document generation, SchoolAI provides innovative tools to enhance instructional content and classroom activities. The Text Leveler feature allows educators to adapt any block of text to different grade levels, making complex topics more accessible for students with varying reading abilities. Moreover, educators can utilize SchoolAI to generate story-based word problems that contextualize math concepts and make learning more engaging for students. Additionally, SchoolAI offers time-based activity ideas to assist educators in designing stimulating and purposeful learning experiences tailored to specific topics and time constraints. Lastly, the Build Your Own feature empowers educators to provide custom instructions and prompts, allowing SchoolAI to generate documents tailored to their specific requirements, thereby enhancing flexibility and adaptability in instructional planning and resource creation. Overall, SchoolAI equips educators with a diverse array of tools and resources to enhance teaching effectiveness, promote student engagement, and streamline administrative tasks in educational settings.

The use of SchoolAI brings many benefits that greatly improve the efficiency and effectiveness of education practices. Firstly, SchoolAI streamlines the production of documents and other administrative tasks, allowing valuable teachers to spend time on basic activities such as lesson planning, personalized instruction, and meaningful interactions with students. This aspect of the SchoolAI saving time contributes to a more productive and fulfilling learning experience for teachers. In addition, SchoolAI facilitates personalized learning experiences with tools such as Text Leveler, which adapt instructional materials to meet students' learning needs. SchoolAI promotes inclusion and fosters a supportive classroom environment that enables all students to thrive by accommodating different reading skills and learning styles. Furthermore, SchoolAI promotes student engagement and learning outcomes by facilitating creative and interactive activities that target diverse interests and learning preferences. These active activities not only make learning more fun, but also promote active participation and deeper understanding among students. In addition, SchoolAI has been designed with the aim of user-friendliness to ensure accessibility for educators of different technical levels. Its intuitive interface and simple functionality allow educators to effectively use its tools and resources, regardless of their technical ability.

COPILOT

Microsoft Copilot is an AI-powered productivity tool, it is designed to enhance productivity, creativity, and data accessibility and it works alongside Microsoft 365 apps such as Word, Excel, PowerPoint, Outlook, Teams, and other Microsoft applications. It assists with tasks like summarizing documents, creating images, and searching the web.

Figure 7. Copilot interface

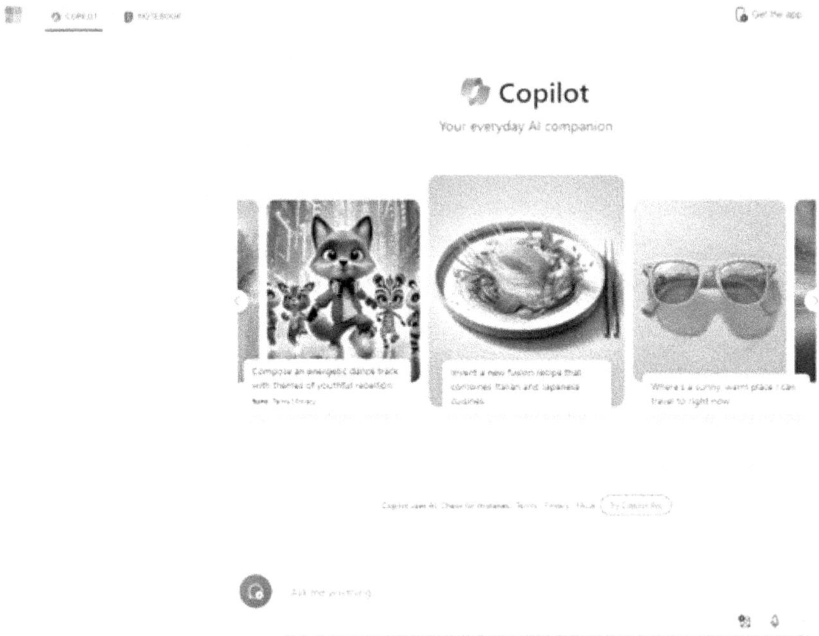

Microsoft Copilot can be used as an AI assistant in educational settings, helping educators and students streamline their work. According to Copilot there are five ways how tool can be used for education:

- **Personalized Learning:** Copilot supports personalized learning by assisting in creating tailored content, feedback, and guidance for students based on their individual needs and learning styles. Whether it is customizing assignments, providing targeted resources, or adapting content, Copilot helps enhance the learning experience.
- **Brainstorming:** Copilot can be used to generate fresh ideas for activities, lesson plans, supporting materials, and assignments. It can spark creativity and help users explore innovative teaching approaches.
- **Lesson Planning:** Copilot aids in lesson planning by suggesting or drafting activities, resources, and assessments aligned with learning objectives. Teachers can also start a rubric for their lessons, making assessment easier.

- **Feedback Generation:** Copilot assists in drafting initial feedback and ideas for student work. Teachers can then personalize and edit this feedback to provide meaningful insights to students.
- **Quick Answers and Content Sources:** Copilot provides quick answers without the need to sift through multiple search results.

It also offers links to content sources, allowing users to assess the credibility of information or explore original content further. These include tools for generating educational content, aligning materials with standards, and creating quizzes. Additional updates focus on AI-driven feedback, interactive learning experiences, and data integration from educational platforms like Teams. The updates are designed to save time, deepen learning, and provide contextual support. Copilot has two interfaces, one for general enquiries and one is called Notebook where users can generate more content based on their prompts. There is a possibility to upload images and export results provided by Copilot. In the results provided by Copilot there are incorporated links to the external results so that users can get information about the original source of the text provided by Copilot. In the user manual *Prompt Lab Working with Minecraft Education and Microsoft Copilot* there are few tips for writing good prompts for educational purposes called GLEAM (Minecraft Education Prompt Lab, 2024):

- **G - Goal:** Define the educational goal or objective of your query.
- **L - Level:** State the educational level or grade level for which the learning is intended.
- **E - Examples:** Request specific examples or analogies to better illustrate the topic.
- **A - Assess:** Critically assess the AI's responses for accuracy and educational value.
- **M - Modify:** Be willing to refine or modify your query based on the responses to get more precise information.

Copilot functions just like other generative AI like ChatGPT and Gemini which are described in previous sections. The base for creating and developing educational materials are prompts and Microsoft has provided users with useful tips on how to integrate Copilot with other Microsoft applications. Based on Redress Compliance there are 10 ways how Copilot can be used in education, for lesson planning, grading and feedback, interactive learning activities, research assistance, student performance analytics, curriculum development, automating administrative tasks, customized learning material creation, language translation and learning and enhancing online teaching (Filipsson, 2024). Microsoft Copilot enhances personalized learning by tailoring educational content to individual student needs. It analyzes student data to identify strengths and weaknesses, then suggests targeted resources and activities to address specific learning gaps, it also offers adaptive learning paths, allowing students to progress at their own pace. Additionally, it can provide personalized feedback and support, helping students understand and master difficult concepts (Filipsson, 2024).

ADOBE FIREFLY

Adobe Firefly is an application designed for exploring AI-assisted creative expression. It allows users to generate images based on text prompts and apply various content styles to achieve their desired artistic vision. Adobe Firefly utilizes AI to generate unique images based on the text descriptions user provide. Users can describe what they have in mind, and Firefly will translate words into a creative visual. Users can apply different content styles to generated images. This allows users to create images with a specific artistic feel, like a painting, a sketch, or a photorealistic style. While AI takes the lead in image generation, Firefly offers control over the final outcome. Users can adjust aspects like aspect ratio, content type (such as photos, illustrations, or patterns), color and tone, lighting, and composition to refine generated image. Adobe Firefly offers several significant benefits for users looking to enhance their design workflow. It sparks creativity by overcoming creative blocks and inspiring new ideas through the generation of unexpected visual interpretations of text prompts. This feature expedites the design process, allowing users to quickly produce draft images or explore various creative directions, thereby saving time in the initial stages of design.

Figure 8. Adobe Firefly interface

Firefly is also accessible to non-artists, enabling those without extensive artistic skills to create unique visuals using simple text descriptions. Through generative AI, Firefly can transform textual descriptions into unique images, aiding in creativity and overcoming creative blocks. Beyond image generation, Firefly provides content style options, allowing users to apply different artistic styles such as paintings, sketches, or photorealistic masterpieces. Users retain creative control with the ability to refine and adjust the final product by selecting aspect ratios, content types, color palettes, lighting effects, and composition. This flexibility ensures that the generated images meet the specific needs and preferences of the user. Adobe Firefly, with its AI-powered image generation and creative exploration functionalities, can be a valuable tool in education by boosting creativity and visual thinking. During brainstorming sessions, Firefly helps students struggling to visualize ideas by generating unexpected visual representations from text prompts, sparking discussions, and igniting creative thinking. In literature, it allows students to generate images depicting scenes, characters, or emotions from stories, deepening their understanding, and encouraging visual interpretation. For art projects, Firefly inspires new ideas by providing starting points from text prompts and allowing exploration of different styles to find their artistic voice. In enhancing learning and communication, Firefly enables students to create unique visuals for presentations, visualize complex scientific concepts, and generate images that capture key moments in their storytelling and narrative writing. It promotes accessibility and differentiation by helping students overcome writer's block through visual representation and catering to visual learners by exploring concepts through images. Firefly can also spark creative project ideas for students with various learning styles and interests. However, there are important considerations. Adobe Firefly likely operates on a subscription model or offers a limited free trial, which could limit its widespread use in educational settings. Additionally, crafting clear and concise text prompts is crucial for successful image generation, requiring some guidance for students in formulating effective prompts. Overall, Adobe Firefly offers a unique and engaging tool for educators to incorporate AI-powered creativity and visual thinking into their classrooms, enhancing the learning experience for students of all ages through brainstorming, concept exploration, and visual communication.

MAGICSCHOOL

MagicSchool.ai, as accessed through the web app app.magicschool.ai, is a platform designed to leverage the power of artificial intelligence (AI) to assist educators and students in the learning process.

Figure 9. MagicSchool interface

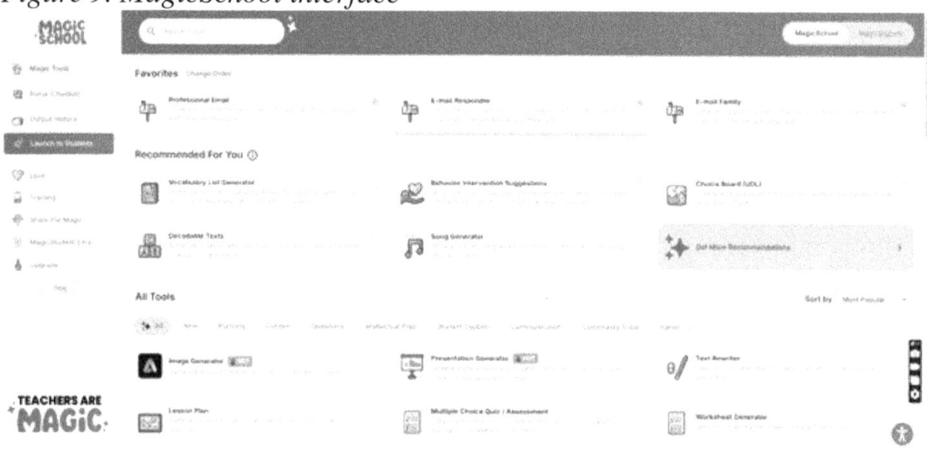

AI-powered tools offer educators the capabilities to streamline various aspects of teaching like lesson planning, differentiation, assessment creation, and it can be used as a communication tool. With tools like educators can streamline lesson planning by generating content that aligns precisely with specific learning objectives. From crafting engaging activities to developing assessments and differentiated materials, tools cater to diverse student needs, enhancing the efficiency and effectiveness of lesson preparation. MagicSchool empowers educators to tailor lessons to meet the unique needs of individual students. By allowing adjustments in the complexity of learning materials based on factors like reading level and learning styles, MagicSchool promotes a more inclusive classroom environment where every student can receive personalized instruction suited to their abilities and preferences. This AI-powered tool facilitate the creation of various forms of assessments, including quizzes and tests, to gauge student understanding. In particular, MagicSchool offers automated scoring for multiple choice questions, significantly reducing the time teachers spend assessing and enabling them to allocate their time more effectively. The tools help educators to create clear and concise reports on student progress and to enhance communication between educators, parents, and students, promote collaboration in education, and facilitate information and participation in the learning process.

It adapts the students' individual learning path and suggests activities and resources based on their strengths and weaknesses. Students have access to interactive exercises and practice activities that strengthen their understanding of concepts. Furthermore, Magic School provides comprehension support tools such as vocabulary building exercises and text summary features to help students improve their comprehension of reading. Interaction with AI tools helps students develop understanding of AI's processes and potential applications in various fields, improving their AI literacy and readiness for the future of technology.

MagicSchool automates tasks such as teaching planning, assessment creation, and differentiation, thus saving valuable time for teachers, enabling them to focus on personalized instruction and interaction with students. MagicSchool improves efficiency by providing educators with tools to efficiently manage their workloads and adapt learning experiences to the needs of individual students. MagicSchool's AI-powered capabilities promote engagement by making learning more interactive and fun for students, creating a positive learning environment that improves student satisfaction and overall motivation. It supports students from different backgrounds by providing differentiation tools to ensure that all students have access to appropriate learning materials adapted to their individual needs and thus foster inclusivity and equality in the classroom.

MagicSchool significantly reduces teacher workload by automating administrative tasks and content generation, thereby affording educators more time to devote to personalized instruction and meaningful student interaction. Moreover, the AI-powered features integrated into MagicSchool enhance student engagement by fostering interactive and dynamic learning experiences, consequently cultivating a more positive and immersive educational environment. Furthermore, MagicSchool promotes equity and inclusion through its differentiation tools, ensuring that all students have access to learning materials and support tailored to their individual needs, thereby addressing diverse learning styles and abilities.

Additionally, MagicSchool facilitates data-driven instruction by enabling educators to analyze student performance data, providing valuable insights that inform instructional decisions and enable further personalization of the learning experience. The free version may offer limited access to basic functionalities such as lesson plan templates or simple quiz creation, and advanced features like AI-powered content generation or personalized learning paths for students (MagicSchool for Students) may not be available. Usage limitations, such as restrictions on the number of resources that can be created or accessed, may also apply to the free plan. Paid versions, such as MagicSchool Plus and Enterprise tiers, likely provide access to the full range of AI-powered tools and features, with differentiated pricing structures and varying functionalities tailored to school size or individual teacher needs.

PERPLEXITY

Perplexity.ai is a search engine and AI-powered chatbot designed to provide users with comprehensive and useful answers to their questions. Unlike traditional search engines that return a list of websites, Perplexity.ai uses a conversational approach. Users can ask questions in natural language, and AI tries to understand intent and provide a clear and concise answer. Perplexity.ai cites the sources it uses to generate its answers, allowing users to verify the information and explore further if needed which can be useful for writing scientific papers. This transparency builds trust and helps users evaluate the credibility of the information presented. Perplexity offers different focus modes that allow users to refine search results. Users can choose to search the entire internet ("All") or limit search to specific categories like news articles ("News"), academic papers ("Scholar"), or code repositories ("Code"). Perplexity'ai is trained on a massive dataset of text and code, allowing it to understand complex queries and provide informative responses. While the primary interface might be in English, Perplexity.ai offers multilingual support to a certain extent. It can potentially understand and respond to queries in various languages. Perplexity.ai allows users to upload and analyze local files, including images. This could be useful for tasks like image recognition or extracting information from documents. Tool might offer an API (Application Programming Interface) that allows developers to integrate its search and chatbot functionalities into their own applications.

Figure 10. Perplexity interface

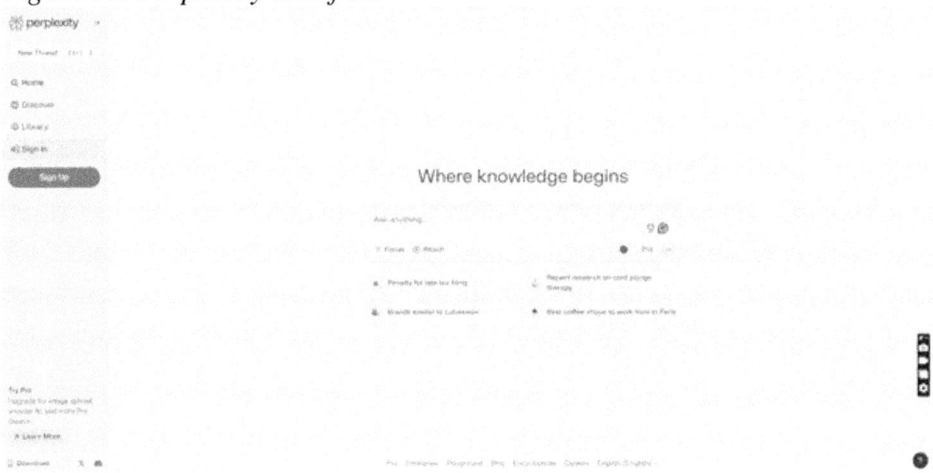

Perplexity.ai offers a free version with basic functionalities. Advanced features like file analysis or the API might be limited or require a paid subscription. As with any AI tool, it is important to critically evaluate the information provided and double-check facts from reputable sources when necessary. By combining conversational search, source citation, and AI-powered understanding of complex queries, Perplexity.ai strives to deliver informative and user-friendly search experiences. Perplexity.ai, with its conversational search engine and AI chatbot functionalities, can be a valuable tool in education and the classroom because it can enhance research and inquiry by formulating research questions where students can use it to explore topics and refine their research questions. Teachers and students can get credible sources which allows students to not only find information but also learn to evaluate the credibility of sources, a crucial skill for academic research. The ability to follow up with related questions within Perplexity.ai allows students to delve deeper into a topic and gain a more comprehensive understanding. Students can use tool to clarify complex concepts encountered in class lectures or textbooks. By asking questions and receiving clear, concise answers, they can solidify their understanding. The tool has multilingual capabilities that can be particularly helpful for students learning English or those who are more comfortable with another language. Functionality of uploading and analyzing images could be beneficial for visual learners to grasp concepts or explore topics visually. The diversity of information from various sources, can help students to practice critical thinking skills by evaluating the credibility and bias of the presented information. Teachers can use it as starting point for researching different perspectives on a topic, which can be useful for preparing for debates or discussions in class and students can develop stronger arguments and counterarguments, fostering deeper exploration of complex issues. While Perplexity.ai empowers independent learning, it is important for teachers to guide students in formulating effective research questions, evaluating information, and integrating their findings into their learning. In addition. It is important that teachers emphasize the importance of understanding where information comes from and how Perplexity.ai cites its sources.

BRISKTEACHING

Briskteaching.com is the website for a free AI-powered Chrome extension called Brisk Teaching. This extension aims to help educators save time and streamline their workload by utilizing AI functionalities directly within the tools they already use.

Figure 11. Briskteaching menu

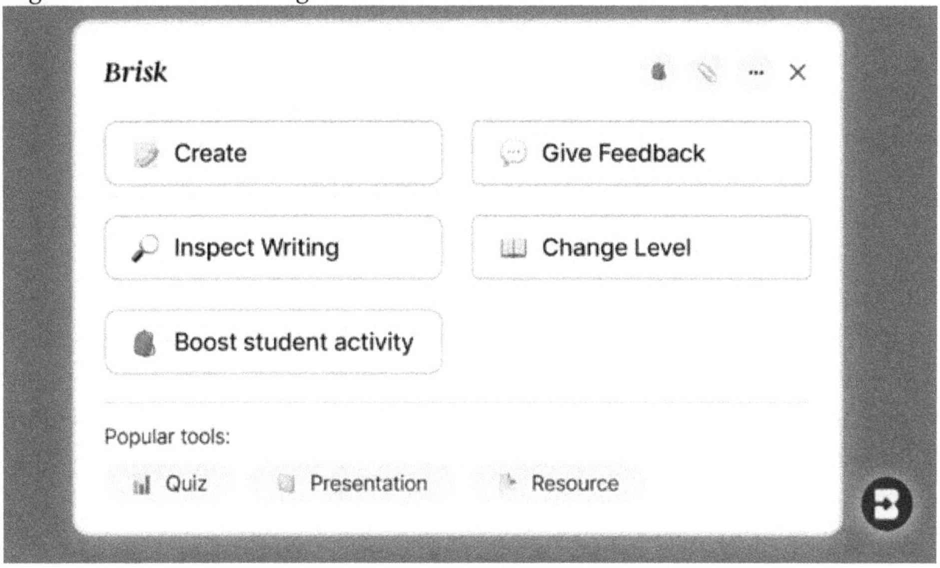

Brisk works within popular tools like Google Docs, Slides, YouTube, and web articles. This eliminates the need to switch between different platforms and allows educators to leverage AI features directly within their workflow. It generates personalized curriculum materials in just a few seconds based on teachers' prompt, potentially saving time on lesson planning. It utilizes AI to provide students with more feedback opportunities on their assignments, allowing teachers to focus on personalized feedback for complex areas. Brisk can be used to improve reading of the students in a way that help students access complex information by adjusting the reading level of news articles or other online content. Students can utilize Brisk features, like reading level adjustment for online articles or feedback generation on short writing exercises, to support their independent learning efforts outside of class. Teachers can follow the progress of their students by analyzing student work and class progress without manually reading through every assignment. This allows teacher to identify areas where students might need additional support. Tool has integrated extension for ChatGPT detection, e.g., it can detect if students are using AI tools like ChatGPT to complete their work. Benefits of using Brisk in teaching is performance of tasks like content creation, feedback generation, and progress analysis that saves teacher time for lesson preparation. Generate lesson plans, presentations, or other instructional materials in seconds using AI prompts. This allows teachers to focus on refining the content and tailoring it to their specific curriculum and teaching style. AI-powered features can help cater to diverse student needs and learning styles. Brisk Teaching is currently a free Chrome extension, and it is designed to empower educators by streamlining workflows, personalizing learning, and providing time-saving functionalities. In addition, it offers various functionalities that can be utilized in education and the classroom to enhance teaching efficiency, personalize learning, and improve student engagement. Utilize AI-powered feedback features to provide students with quick and efficient feedback on their assignments. Brisk can potentially highlight areas for improvement, saving teachers time from manually reading and commenting on every piece of work. AI-powered tools within Brisk can potentially generate interactive elements for presentations or lessons, fostering a more engaging learning experience for students.

FORMATIVE AI

Formative (https://app.formative.com/) is a web application that specializes in creating and delivering high-quality assessments and educational content for educators. Various functions enhance teaching and learning processes and become valuable tools in classrooms around the world. The formative tool allows teachers to create assessments in different question formats, including multiple choice, open-ended, matching, short answers, and drag and drop activities. This adapts to different learning styles and assessment needs. Students can immediately receive feedback on their responses, identify areas for improvement, and adjust their understanding during the assessment process. Teachers can align their assessments with specific learning standards to evaluate students' mastery of important concepts.

Figure 12. Formative AI interface

The platform provides user-friendly tools for educators to create new assessments or upload existing content like PDFs or Docs and it allows access a library of pre-built formative assessments and activities on various topics, saving teachers' time on content creation. There are collaboration features which enables sharing of assessments with colleagues or co-creation of formative activities within the platform.

Teachers can tailor assessments to individual student needs by offering different question sets or difficulty levels. Formative assessments go beyond traditional tests, offering interactive activities that can make learning more engaging and students receive immediate feedback on their performance, promoting self-assessment and a growth mindset. Based on student performance, formative assessments can inform personalized learning paths for students. Formative provides educators with data analysis tools to track student progress and identify areas where the class might need more support. As of summer 2023, Formative offers an optional beta feature that utilizes AI to generate question prompts and hints, potentially streamlining content creation for educators.

Using Formative offers several significant benefits for educators and students alike. It improves assessment practices by promoting a growth mindset and a deeper understanding of concepts compared to traditional tests. The streamlined workflow, facilitated by features like the formative library and easy content creation tools, saves teachers valuable time. Additionally, Formative makes differentiation easy, allowing teachers to cater to diverse learning styles and needs with various question formats and differentiation options. Enhanced student engagement is another benefit, as interactive assessments and immediate feedback make learning more engaging for students.

However, there are some considerations that must be taken into account. Formative offers a limited free version, and upgrading to a paid plan unlocks more features, such as student performance reports and advanced analytics. Although Formative has performed well in assessing, it may not be a comprehensive learning management system, so it can provide a more complete classroom experience by integrating it with other educational tools.

The formative assessment provides students with immediate feedback on their performance and helps them understand their strengths and weaknesses. This promotes a growth mindset and focuses on continuous improvement. Based on feedback, students and teachers can develop personalized learning strategies to meet individual needs, including additional practice exercises, targeted instruction or alternative learning resources.

Formative allows teachers to create tailored assessments with different difficulty levels, question formats, or answer choices, catering to diverse learning styles and ensuring all students have the opportunity to demonstrate their understanding. The data analysis tools within Formative reveal patterns in student performance, allowing teachers to identify groups of students who might require similar support and create differentiated instruction plans accordingly. The platform also offers a library of pre-built assessments with varying difficulty levels, enabling teachers to select activities that best suit the needs of individual students.

The interactive nature of formative assessments encourages students to actively engage with the feedback they receive, helping them develop self-assessment skills and take ownership of their learning journey. Formative assessments can inform personalized learning paths for students, enabling access to targeted learning resources, practice activities, or mini-lessons to address specific knowledge gaps.

Unlike traditional examinations, which measure mastery at the end of a unit, a formative assessment occurs during the learning process. This allows adjustments and interventions before summary assessments, thus promoting deeper understanding and knowledge retention. In addition, the formative assessment can serve as a springboard for discussions and collaborative learning activities in classes, strengthening communication skills and enabling students to learn from the perspectives of others.

REFERENCES

Adobe Firefly. (n.d.). Retrieved May 18, 2024, from https://firefly.adobe.com

Briskteaching. (n.d.). Retrieved March 6, 2024, from https://briskteaching.com

ChatGPT. (n.d.). Retrieved May 25, 2024, from https://chatgpt.com/

Copilot. (n.d.). Retrieved May 10, 2024, from https://copilot.microsoft.com/

DIFFIT. (n.d.). https://web.diffit.me/

Filipsson, F., & Filipsson, F. (2024). Top 10 use cases for Microsoft Copilot in Education. *Redress Compliance - Just another WordPress site*. https://redresscompliance.com/top-10-use-cases-for-microsoft-copilot-in-education/

Formative, A. I. (n.d.). Retrieved June 13, 2024, from https://www.formative.com/

GEMINI. (n.d.). Retrieved June 13, 2024, from https://gemini.google.com

MagicSchool. (n.d.). Retrieved May 30, 2024, from https://app.magicschool.ai

Padlet. (n.d.). Retrieved June 12, 2024, from https://padlet.com/

Perplexity. (n.d.). Retrieved June 2, 2024, from https://perplexity.ai

Prompt Lab working with Minecraft Education and Microsoft Copilot: Vol. 1.3. (2024). Microsoft Corporation. https://aka.ms/promptlab1

QUIZZIZ. (n.d.). Retrieved May 10, 2024, from https://quizizz.com/?lng=en

School, A. I. (n.d.). Retrieved May 10, 2024, from https://schoolai.com/tools

Chapter 4
Personalized Learning With Generative AI

ABSTRACT

This chapter conducts a comprehensive literature review to explain the concept of personalized learning, exploring its various definitions, key characteristics, and fundamental elements. By synthesizing existing definitions, it aims to provide a clear understanding of personalized learning and its implications for educational practice. Through an analysis of the diverse perspectives and approaches within the field, this chapter offers insights into the principles and strategies that underpin effective personalized learning. Researching the theoretical foundations and practical applications of personalized learning, this chapter aims to contribute to a deeper understanding of this evolving educational paradigm.

WHAT IS PERSONALIZED LEARNING?

There are many definitions of personalized learning. The National Education Technology Plan (NETP) developed by the U.S. Department of Education (2016) defines personalized learning as "instruction in which the pace of learning and the instructional approach are optimized for the needs of each learner" (p. 7). Personalized learning is an educational approach which is aimed at students and their needs that aims to personalize the learning experience according to the unique needs, goals, and skills of individuals which can be achieved by using current instructional technology that provides unique learning experiences in different learning environments" (Shemshack et al., 2021, p. 485). In *Personalized learning: The simple, the complicated, the complex and the chaotic* (Gunawardena, Bishop & Aviruppola, 2024) authors are elaborating about personalized learning and are mentioning research from Pane et al. (2015) with conclusion that "students who learned in personalized learning environments made considerable progress in comparison to

DOI: 10.4018/979-8-3693-3474-4.ch004

their counterparts" (Gunawardena, Bishop & Aviruppola, p. 2, 2024). In another study conducted by Alamri et al.'s (2020) is mentioned by Gunawardena, Bishop & Aviruppola (2024) where "students who participated in the latter had positive perceptions overall and felt that the personalized learning design enhanced their sense of autonomy, competence, intrinsic motivation, and learning" (Gunawardena, Bishop & Aviruppola, p. 2, 2024). Personalized learning is touted to provide opportunities for learners to achieve their full potential while developing a love of learning (Gunawardena et al., 2024, p. 1).

Personalized learning empowers students to pursue their unique learning objectives at their preferred speed and this advantage is realized through comprehension of each student's specific needs, therefore, implementing personalized learning becomes crucial to cater to the diverse individualities of students (Chen & Wang, 2021). In addition, personalized learning, driven by AI algorithms, tailors instructional content, pacing, and assessment to the unique needs of learners, fostering a more inclusive and effective education (Ayeni et al., 2024) thus the integration of technology has spawned a new development path: personalized learning empowered by technology (Peng & Spector, 2019, p. 3).

Popular critiques of personalized learning have emphasized how it ironically "de-personalizes" learning with technology and serves the interests of corporate education reform (Brass & Lynch, 2020, p. 3). Personalized learning is teaching and learning that is focused on the background, needs, potential and perception of the learner. It is learner-centered education (UNESCO, 2017, p. 5).

In (UNESCO, 2017, p. 6). Bloom's 1968 paper "Learning for Mastery" outlined some of the essential principles for personalized learning:

- a good tutor for each student
- permitting students to go at their own pace
- guiding students with respect to courses they should or should not take
- providing different tracks or streams for different learners (Bloom 1968).

(UNESCO, 2017). For personalized learning to be successful, the following context and system alignment is required:

- One where there is an agreed understanding of what personalized learning means. This should be understood by the whole learning community: teachers, administrators, leaders, parents and teachers. It has to be a critical part of the school's mission to recognize that student learning is improved dramatically when it is personalized.
- A culture of continual dialogue about learning and about students' needs.

- A context that is willing to listen to the learner's voice – and in many cases this will be a child's voice – to take his or her concerns seriously and to be prepared to act on them.
- A context where continual re-evaluation and re-visiting of goals and strategies is valued and promoted.
- A classroom and entire school environment where making mistakes is not seen as something bad or wrong but as a vital step towards learning. Students should be happy to say that they do not understand because they know that this means that they will be given a further opportunity to do so. This enabling context is vital for without that element of trust and confidence to share understanding and misunderstanding, students will be afraid to express where they are in the learning continuum.
- Although personalized learning does not rely solely on new technologies, access to the internet and some computing devices can allow individual learners to take their learning further.
- Access for teachers and students to a library or some learning materials that allow for the independent exploration of domain knowledge (textbooks, collated notes, past examples of good work).
- A coherent approach that triangulates curriculum, assessment, teaching and learning with the principles of personalized learning.
- A school culture that not only tolerates, but encourages outdoor education, fieldtrips, community and service activities.

Martinez (2002) describes personalization in learning through five levels of sophistication: name-recognized, self-described, segmented, cognitive-based, and whole-person-based. Each level offers a specific strategy for tailoring the learning experience. Name-recognized personalization, the simplest form, involves acknowledging individuals by incorporating their names or previous achievements into instruction. Self-described personalization allows learners to express preferences and attributes through surveys or quizzes, shaping subsequent learning experiences accordingly. Segmented personalization categorizes learners based on demographics or common traits, delivering content tailored to specific groups. Cognitive-based personalization targets learners' cognitive processes and preferences, offering content in preferred formats or sequences. This level employs complex algorithms to predict user preferences based on data and activity monitoring. While these strategies can function independently, their combined application can create a more comprehensive and effective personalized learning experience (Martinez, 2002, pp. 154 - 155).

The process of personalizing learning requires that a learning environment—whether it be face-to-face vs. digital or human-driven vs. automated—take into account the learner and some combination of their prior knowledge, motivations, goals, beliefs, interests, skills, experience, and culture (and likely other factors) and provide an instructional experience that is responsive to these features in ways that should promote superior engagement in a learning task and performance on it (Bernacki et al., 2021, p. 2). The use of digital course content and assessment and technological devices to deliver content is meant to increase teachers' capacities to personalize students' pacing and learning paths and make the process of designing and delivering PL more manageable for teachers (pp. 459 - 460).

In *Innovate to Educate: System [Re]Design for Personalized Learning - A Report* from the 2010 Symposium the conclusion was that personalization is frequently conflated with individualization and differentiation, terms commonly used in education circles, but often indicating minor adjustments within the traditional mass-production paradigm. Authentic personalization demands a significant pivot, shifting away from institution or teacher-centric methodologies towards a genuine, student-centered ethos. True personalization involves crafting a learning program and methodology that are precisely attuned to the unique abilities, interests, preferences, and requirements of each individual student (Wolf, 2010).

The standard definition of "personalized learning" stresses instruction that is varied in pace, method, objectives, and content for each student and tailored to the student's interests and preferences. Technology is seen as a means to efficiently manage this level of differentiation, access a cornucopia of learning opportunities and resources, and give the student greater control over his or her learning (Redding, 2013, p. 3).

Redding (2013) states that the teacher's role transcends merely guiding students towards discovery, whether through technology or other means. They are not simply facilitators, but architects of a structured curriculum from an abundance of potential content. The teacher actively imparts new concepts and skills, expands students' interests, and cultivates logical thinking through inquiry and dialogue. Their influence extends beyond what technology can achieve, as they wield the power of relational persuasion. By setting examples and providing guidance, teachers instill values of mastery, elevate expectations, and empower students to manage their own learning journeys. Moreover, teachers excel in teaching social and emotional competencies and involving families in their children's academic and personal growth.

Lexically, personalization is the action or process that aims to design and produce something that meets the individual requirements. When borrowing this idea to the educational context, it refers to how the individual students' learning needs can be addressed in the teaching and learning process (Cheung et al., 2021, p. 179).

Lee (2018) explains a Personalized Learning Plan (PLP) as a tailored instructional roadmap that considers individual variations in career aspirations, traits, interests, and academic proficiency. It encompasses the concepts of individualization, differentiation, and personalization. Crafting and executing PLPs enable the adaptation of learning pace to suit individual learners, customization of teaching approaches to match individual traits, and establishment of diverse learning objectives aligned with individual interests.

Characteristics of Personalized Learning

The main characteristic of personalized learning is that is "student-centered system that supports their diverse needs and the development of abilities" (Lee et al., 2018, Makhambetova et al., 2021) and it is focused on the background, needs, potential and perception of the learner and it is learner-centered education (UNESCO, 2017, p. 5). AI tools like ChatGPT provide opportunities for personalized learning experiences by acting as 24/7 teaching assistants, automating repetitive tasks, and adjusted feedback to individual needs of users (Ghimire, Prather, & Edwards, 2024). In addition, AI can assist in course design, improve faculty research productivity, and optimize administrative processes, allowing more focus on teaching and innovation (Katsamakas, Pavlov, & Saklad, 2024). Furthermore, AI enables tailored learning experiences by adapting to individual student needs through intelligent tutoring systems, personalized feedback, and adaptive curricula, significantly improving student engagement and learning outcomes (Ifenthaler et al., 2024).

UNESCO (2017) explains the three core principles that underline the essence of personalized learning: creativity, research, and challenge. Creativeness is a cornerstone, and teachers are responsible for nurturing the environment where students can explore ideas autonomously from different perspectives and nurture their creativity in the process. This method encourages students to take ownership of their learning journey and to allow creative thinking to permeate all aspects of the educational experience. Research, similar to the pursuit of lifelong knowledge, transcends the boundaries of traditional education and inspires curiosity that leads individuals to contribute to the ever-expanding field of human understanding. Without research, the transfer of established knowledge from schools is incomplete; students must be reflective of the spirit of exploration in order to apply and search for new knowledge effectively. Teachers and students must take risks and maintain an inquisitive mindset in order to truly personalize the learning experience. Finally, challenges serve as a catalyst for growth in a personalized learning environment. Contrary to a comfortable comfort zone, personalized learning requires an environment where students are continuously expelled beyond their limits. In this process, teachers play an essential role by guiding students while setting ambitious goals to promote individual and social development. In essence, personalized learning is based on interaction between creativity, research and challenges, which not only shapes students' minds, but also shapes the future of society.

PRACTICING PERSONALIZED LEARNING WITH GENERATIVE AI

All personal learning activities focus on students' needs, challenges, abilities, emotions, motivation and learning abilities. Many guidelines and recommendations relate to how to implement personalized learning activities in educational environments and what teachers can do with students. However, there are no concrete examples teachers can use with students. Examples of exercises are difficult to find online, and teachers are themselves in the process of developing activities for personalized learning. This takes time and costs time to study and find the best way to integrate activities into classrooms and teaching materials. Artificial intelligence is one of the ways teachers can use personal learning in classrooms. To test and determine the possibilities of generative AI, which is in the spotlight in almost all sectors of society, education and business, tests were conducted using Google's generative AI Gemini and ChatGPT 3.5. Both artificial intelligence tools were chosen because they are free and anyone with Internet access can use them. The main objective was to examine the quality and utility of the activities offered and the impact on teaching and learning. Gemini prompts are based on generative AI training and Google support, Tips for writing prompts for Gemini. The recommendations include five elements, including the use of natural languages, clear and concise communication, context-based communications, the use of specific and relevant keywords, and the separation of complex tasks into separate prompts.

The analysis began with a general inquiry into personalized learning in primary schools and gradually developed into more specific learning units and more specific groups of learners. The aim is to observe the structure and type of activity generated by generative AI, Gemini and ChatGPT based on commands. Another objective of research is also to analyze how prompts are suitable for developing personalized learning activities in order for teachers to benefit most from generative AI tools. W3Schools defines prompt as a process that develops inputs, usually in the form of text, to guide a generative AI to produce the desired output. In other words, prompting is a way of telling AI what to do. According to W3Schools, a well-designed prompt should be personalized to generate the specific response you want and should be tailored to the characteristics of the specific generated AI used. W3Schools defines four different types of prompts, including instructions, questions, data and examples. This research will be based on text-to-text generative AI, which means that AI generates texts based on text inputs. The text generation is based on machine learning techniques, existing datasets and inputs from previous users to generate responses. By using these elements, text generation algorithms can understand contexts, learn patterns from existing data, and incorporate user feedback into coherent and relevant responses. This process allows text generation systems to continuously improve and adapt to better meet user needs and preferences over time.

W3Schools lists rules and recommendations for prompt writing which refers that user could start with the simple prompt and then build their way up, use call to action recommendation which means that user need to start the prompt with an action word like "Write", "Create", or "Summarize" instead of "Can you". Furthermore, user needs to add a context to the prompt, which means to dd specific and relevant context to the task user want to perform and the last recommendation is to add expectations, clear and direct expectations for the content, like how long it should be and what needs to be included in the answer.

Creating Personalized Learning Materials by Using Prompting

The prompting was conducted based on W3Schools general rules for prompt writing. Each generative AI, Gemini and ChatGPT used the same seven prompts:

1. *Write me examples for personalized learning activities in primary school.*
2. *Write me examples of personalized learning activities for learning English in primary school.*
3. *Write me examples of personalized learning activities for learning English in primary school with use of Gemini.*
4. *Write me examples of personalized learning activities for learning pronouns in English in primary school for the 5th grade students with use of Gemini.*
5. *Write me exercises for learning pronouns for the students who need extra challenge in 5th grade of primary school.*
6. *Create materials for learning relative pronouns and relative adverbs for fifth-grade literacy in primary school. The exercises need to be for the students who need more support.*
7. *Create materials for learning relative pronouns and relative adverbs for fifth-grade literacy in primary school. The exercises need to be for the students who need extra challenges.*

The goal of this part of the research was to analyze what are the differences in the Gemini and ChatGPT responses, and which from the aforementioned prompts can give teachers the best solution and results for developing and conducting personalized learning materials. The prompts were used from more general to more specific ones regarding personalized learning. The key word in the first four prompts was personalized learning and later based on the results of generative AI the specific group of learners was included. For the purposes of the research the prompts were about learning English language in primary schools, more specific for 5th grade students.

GEMINI PROMPTS

First Prompt

The first prompt was general, and it was about activities for personalized learning in primary schools. The prompt was constricted as follows: *Write me examples for personalized learning activities in primary school.* The response was generated and included four categories of learners, students who need extra challenge, students who need more support, kinesthetic learners and visual learners.

The example of activities generated by Gemini.

For Students Who Need Extra Challenge

- **Tiered Activities:** Provide tasks with different complexity levels based on the student's understanding. For example, in a reading activity, offer multiple texts with varying difficulty or ask students to create a more complex product (e.g., a video instead of a drawing) to demonstrate their learning.
- **Open-Ended Projects:** Give students more choice and control in their projects. Let them choose a topic related to the main concept and design their own way to present the information (e.g., building a model, writing a song, creating a comic strip).
- **Enrichment Activities:** Offer additional activities that go beyond the core curriculum but reinforce the same skills. This could be puzzles, logic problems, or creative writing prompts related to the topic.

For Students Who Need More Support

- **Graphic Organizers**: Provide visual aids like charts, diagrams, or mind maps to help students organize information and understand concepts.
- **Differentiated Instruction**: Break down complex tasks into smaller, more manageable steps. Offer additional explanation or one-on-one support for challenging concepts.
- **Choice Boards**: Present students with a variety of activities related to the same learning objective, allowing them to choose tasks that best suit their learning style or interests (e.g., drawing, writing, building with blocks).
- **Assistive Technologies**: Utilize tools like audiobooks, text-to-speech software, or manipulatives (counting blocks, letter tiles) to cater to different learning styles and overcome potential barriers.

For Kinesthetic Learners

- **Movement Breaks:** Integrate short physical activities into the lesson to help students release energy and stay focused.
- **Learning Games:** Design games that involve movement and interaction, such as vocabulary charades or following directions to complete a task.
- **Hands-on Activities:** Incorporate activities that involve building, manipulating objects, or role-playing to solidify concepts.

For Visual Learners

- **Visual Aids:** Use pictures, diagrams, videos, or graphic organizers to illustrate concepts and vocabulary.
- **Color Coding:** Use color-coding to categorize information or highlight key points.
- **Mind Mapping:** Encourage students to create mind maps to visually represent their understanding of a topic.

The response is general as the prompt, but it can give a teacher an overview of basic activities that can be included in the teaching process. In addition, these activities do not include the use of technology so we can see that personalized learning can be conducted without the use of ICT tools.

Second Prompt

The second prompt was more direct and included additional information about the subject that the teacher is teaching. For the purpose of the research the subject of English language was used in search. The prompt was constricted as follows: *Write me examples of personalized learning activities for learning English in primary school.*

This time Gemini once again provided the four categories of learners, students who need extra challenge, students who need more support, kinesthetic learners, and visual learners but this time the activities were different and more focused on language learning. Under each category of learners, the specialized activities were listed.

The example of activities generated by Gemini:

For Students Who Need Extra Challenge:

- **Creative Storytelling**: After reading a simple story, have students create an alternate ending or write the story from a different character's perspective.

- **Word Detective:** Present a list of vocabulary words with definitions. Students create riddles, draw pictures, or use the words in a short story to demonstrate their understanding.
- **DIY Board Games:** Students design a board game related to the target grammar point (e.g., plurals, present tense verbs) and have classmates play it.

For Students Who Need More Support:

- **Matching Games:** Create picture-word or word-word matching games to reinforce new vocabulary or phonics sounds.
- **Interactive Flashcards:** Use online tools to create flashcards with audio recordings of the word and its pronunciation.
- **Sentence Builders:** Provide students with word banks to build simple sentences. Start with basic sentence structures and gradually increase complexity.

For Kinesthetic Learners:

- **Action Verbs Charades:** Students act out verbs related to a specific topic (e.g., classroom objects, daily routines) and classmates guess the word.
- **Simon Says:** Play "Simon Says" with instructions in English, incorporating movements related to the vocabulary being learned.
- **Sing Along!:** Use catchy English songs to introduce new vocabulary or practice pronunciation. Students can act out the lyrics or create simple choreography.

For Visual Learners:

- **Comic Strip Creation:** After reading a short story, have students create a comic strip summarizing the key events. Encourage them to use dialogue bubbles with simple English phrases.
- **Vocabulary Posters:** Students design posters with pictures and definitions for new vocabulary words.
- **Interactive Picture Dictionary:** Create a class picture dictionary where students contribute drawings and short descriptions for learned words.

Third Prompt

The third prompt was even more specialized and include the use of Gemini for conducting personalized learning activities for primary school students for learning English. The four same categories of learners were still the same, but this time activates were more concrete. The prompt was constricted as follows: *Write me examples of personalized learning activities for learning English in primary school with use of Gemini.*

The example of activities generated by Gemini:

For Students Who Need Extra Challenge:

- Storytelling with Variations: Use Gemini to generate a simple story with basic vocabulary and grammar. Students can then use Gemini to:
  - Change the story setting or characters.
  - Create an alternate ending with different choices.
  - Write the story from a different character's perspective.
  - Add more details and descriptive language to the story using prompts from Gemini.
- Vocabulary Expansion Game: Gemini can generate a list of vocabulary words related to a specific topic. Students can then:
  - Use Gemini to find synonyms or antonyms for the words, creating a personalized vocabulary list.
  - Ask Gemini to create sentences using the words, focusing on specific grammar points the student is learning.
  - Play a "definition match" game where Gemini gives definitions and students have to guess the corresponding word.

For Students Who Need More Support:

- Interactive Phonics Practice: Use Gemini for phonics practice by:
  - Asking Gemini to pronounce a specific word and having the student identify the sound or letter combination.
  - Providing a sound and having Gemini generate a list of words containing that sound.
  - Creating a simple fill-in-the-blank activity with missing letters or sounds, prompting Gemini for suggestions.
- Personalized Flashcard Creation: Students can choose a topic or specific vocabulary words they want to learn. Then, they can use Gemini to:
  - Generate definitions or example sentences for the chosen words.
  - Create flashcards with pictures and text prompts.
  - Record themselves saying the words using Gemini's text-to-speech feature, allowing them to practice pronunciation.

For Kinesthetic Learners:

- Action Verb Charades with Feedback: Students can act out verbs related to a specific topic. Gemini can then be used to:
  - o Provide a list of possible verbs based on the student's movements, helping them refine their charade.
  - o Offer synonyms or related verbs to expand their vocabulary.
  - o Generate a short sentence using the guessed verb, encouraging students to use the word in context.
- "Simon Says" with a Twist: Play "Simon Says" with instructions in English using Gemini. Gemini can then:
  - o Offer different levels of difficulty for the instructions, catering to various skill levels.
  - o Provide pictures or animations to visually represent the actions in the instructions.
  - o Give positive reinforcement or suggest alternative actions if the student makes a mistake.

For Visual Learners:

- Image-based Storytelling: Use Gemini to generate images related to a specific topic or story prompt. Students can then use the image as a starting point to:
  - o Write a short story or description using Gemini's text generation capabilities for inspiration.
  - o Create a dialogue between characters in the image, prompting Gemini for suggestions.
  - o Label the different objects or people in the image with English vocabulary words.
- Personalized Illustrated Dictionary: Students can choose a theme or vocabulary set. Gemini can then be used to:
  - o Generate a list of related words.
  - o Find images for each word.
  - o Help students write simple definitions or sentences using the words.

Fourth Prompt

The fourth prompt was directed on the learning pronouns in English language for the students in 5th grade. This time the four categories remained the same, but the activities were even more concrete and detailed. The prompt was constricted as follows: *Write me examples of personalized learning activities for learning pronouns in English in primary school for the 5th grade students with use of Gemini.*

The example of activities generated by Gemini:

For Students Who Need Extra Challenge:

- **Pronoun Puzzle Party:**

1. Students choose a short story they've read and identify all the pronouns.
2. Use Gemini to rewrite the story with pronouns replaced by blanks.
3. Students work in pairs or small groups to fill in the blanks with the correct pronouns, justifying their choices using grammatical rules.
4. Gemini can be used to verify answers or provide hints if students get stuck.

- **Who Said What? Game:**

5. Gemini generates a short dialogue with various pronouns used by different characters.
6. Students rewrite the dialogue, replacing pronouns with the characters' names.
7. They can then act out the dialogue, using Gemini's text-to-speech function to practice pronunciation (optional).

For Students Who Need More Support:

- **Interactive Pronoun Chart:**

8. Create a chart with columns for subject pronouns, object pronouns, and possessive pronouns.
9. Students choose a pronoun category and use Gemini to generate a list of words within that category.
10. They can then use Gemini to create example sentences for each pronoun, focusing on proper usage in context.

- **"I Spy" with Pronouns:**

11. Play a modified "I Spy" game where students describe an object in the classroom using a pronoun (e.g., "I spy with my little eye something you write with. It's **it**.")
12. Classmates guess the object and identify the pronoun used.

13. Gemini can be used to generate different prompts with varying pronoun types to keep the game challenging.

For Kinesthetic Learners:

- **Pronoun Charades:**

14. Students choose a pronoun and act it out without speaking.
15. The class guesses the pronoun based on the student's actions.
16. Gemini can offer synonyms or related pronouns as hints if students struggle.
17. Alternatively, students can act out a short scene with various pronouns used, encouraging them to think about pronoun usage in context.

- **"Simon Says" Pronoun Edition:**

18. Play "Simon Says" with instructions incorporating pronouns (e.g., "Simon says touch your **nose**").
19. Gemini can generate different commands with various pronouns, increasing the difficulty level as students progress.
20. Students who make mistakes can use Gemini to find the correct pronoun and practice saying it correctly.

For Visual Learners:

- **Comic Strip Creation with Pronouns:**

21. Students choose a short story with clear pronoun usage.
22. They use Gemini to generate images depicting key moments in the story.
23. Students then create a comic strip using the images and rewrite the story with speech bubbles, ensuring proper pronoun usage.
24. Gemini can help them find synonyms or clarify pronoun choices if needed.

- **"Spot the Pronoun" Activity:**

25. Use Gemini to generate a short passage with highlighted pronouns in different colors based on their type (subject, object, possessive).
26. Students analyze the passage, identifying the pronouns and explaining their function in the sentence.
27. This activity can be adapted to different difficulty levels by adjusting the complexity of the passage and the number of highlighted pronouns.

Based on these results, the teacher can select activities he/she wants to use and adapt them to their content. If teachers want to develop exercises with generative AI, they can select one of the activities that the tool has proposed and create another prompt.

Teachers always can adapt this example to their needs. To compare if there is a difference between the activities that Gemini provides for each of learners' groups that were identified in first prompt the research was conducted for each group and the comparison of each activity was conducted.

First, the target group of learners needs to be selected and then the specific activity. The first activity will be for the students who need extra challenge. The prompt that has given the best result was specified and stated: *Write me exercises for learning pronouns for the students who need extra challenge in 5th grade of primary school.*

The Gemini provided exercise in the form of a story where students need to fill in the blanks with the correct pronoun. Here is an example of the exercise.

The Pronoun Detectives: A Case of Shifting Meanings

Story

Ms. Johnson's class was buzzing with excitement. A famous author, Ms. Wright, was visiting their school, and they were tasked with helping her solve a peculiar case – a missing manuscript! Ms. Wright explained that her latest work, a detective story, was riddled with pronoun errors. These errors completely changed the meaning of the story!

"You see," Ms. Wright explained, "pronouns have to refer back to specific nouns in the sentence. If you get them wrong, the whole story goes haywire!"

The class, now transformed into a team of Pronoun Detectives, eagerly accepted the challenge. Ms. Wright presented them with excerpts from the manuscript, each containing a pronoun that caused confusion.

Challenge 1: The Case of the Misidentified Culprit

"The butler saw ____ (them/him) sneaking around the mansion late at night. ____ (They/He) must be the thief!"

Challenge students to identify the correct pronoun and explain how it changes the suspect in the story. (Who is the butler accusing – one person or multiple people?)

Challenge 2: The Case of the Missing Motive

"The detective noticed ____ (their/its) nervous behavior. ____ (They/It) must be hiding something!"

Challenge students to identify the correct pronoun and explain how it changes the reason for the character's nervousness. (Is the character hiding something themself, or is something else hidden?)

Challenge 3: The Case of the Disappearing Clue

"The inspector found a secret passage behind ____ (the/their) bookshelf. ____ (The/They) must lead to the hidden treasure!"

Challenge students to identify the correct pronoun and explain how it changes the location of the secret passage. (Does the passage belong to the bookshelf, or does it lead to something else?)

Bonus Challenge

Ms. Wright offered an additional challenge. Can the Pronoun Detectives rewrite the incorrect sentences with the correct pronouns, making the story flow smoothly and identify the real culprit?

This activity encourages students to think critically about pronoun usage and how it affects the overall meaning of a sentence. It also introduces them to the concept of pronoun agreement (singular vs. plural).

Extension Activities

- Have students write their own short detective stories, incorporating different types of pronouns and challenging their classmates to identify any pronoun errors.
- Play a "Pronoun Charades" game where students act out sentences with missing pronouns, and their classmates guess the correct pronoun based on the context.

The fifth prompt was created based on the *curriculum for the School District of Clayton* in USA for the fifth-grade students. Based on *School District of Clayton* fifth-grade literacy learning objectives the use of relative pronouns and relative adverbs were selected for creating prompts. All examples from generative AI are about learning materials and activities for teaching and learning about relative pronouns and relative adverbs. The prompt was constricted as follows: *Create materials for learning relative pronouns and relative adverbs for fifth-grade literacy in primary school. The exercises need to be for the students who need more support.*

Relative Pronoun and Adverb Detectives: A Matching Mission

This activity provides a fun and engaging way for fifth graders who need more support to practice identifying and using relative pronouns and adverbs.

- Materials:
  - **Sentence Strips:**
    - Prepare several sentence strips with blanks where a relative pronoun or adverb should be used.
    - Include some sentences with missing relative pronouns (who, which, that, whose) and others with missing relative adverbs (when, where, why, how).
- Example Sentences (modify difficulty as needed):
  - The student _______ (who/whose) locker is open needs to close it. (Relative Pronoun)
  - We went to the park _______ (where/when) we had a picnic. (Relative Adverb)
  - The book _______ (that/which) I'm reading is about robots. (Relative Pronoun)
  - She practiced piano _______ (how/why) she could impress everyone. (Relative Adverb)
  - **Word Cards:** Create separate word cards with all the possible relative pronouns ("who," "which," "that," "whose") and relative adverbs ("when," "where," "why," "how").
  - **Matching Sheet:** Prepare a worksheet with two sections: "Relative Pronoun Roundup" and "Relative Adverb Roundup." Each section will have a blank space for each sentence strip.
- Step 1: Introducing the Mission
  - Explain that students are now "Relative Pronoun and Adverb Detectives" on a mission to find the missing words in different sentences. These missing words will help complete the sentences and make sense of the story.
- Step 2: Matching the Clues
  - Distribute the sentence strips face down and the word cards face up.
  - Instruct students to pick a sentence strip and read it silently.
  - Ask them to identify the type of missing word (relative pronoun or relative adverb) based on the context of the sentence.
  - Students then need to find the matching word card from the pile that best completes the sentence.

- Step 3: Checking the Evidence
  - o Once students have matched all the sentence strips with word cards, have them work in pairs or small groups.
  - o Each group takes turns reading their completed sentence aloud and explaining why they chose the particular relative pronoun or adverb.
- Step 4: Reinforcing the Learning
  - o As a class, discuss the completed sentences and the role of relative pronouns and adverbs in connecting information within the sentence.
  - o You can also challenge students to rewrite some of the sentences without using relative pronouns or adverbs and discuss how the meaning might change.
- Differentiation:
  - o Start with a smaller set of sentence strips and word cards, focusing on one type of relative pronoun or adverb at first.
  - o Provide students with a reference sheet listing the different relative pronouns and adverbs and their uses.
  - o Allow students to draw pictures to illustrate their completed sentences, further solidifying the meaning.
- Extension Activities:
  - o Students can create their own sentences with blanks for relative pronouns and adverbs, challenging their classmates to find the matching words.
  - o Play a "Relative Pronoun and Adverb Charades" game, where one student acts out a sentence with a missing relative pronoun or adverb, and the others guess the missing word and complete the sentence.

This activity allows students to learn by doing, practicing matching the correct relative pronoun or adverb based on context. The collaborative element and discussion encourage deeper understanding for students who need more support.

The second prompt was for the students who need extra challenge. The prompt was constricted as follows: *Create materials for learning relative pronouns and relative adverbs for fifth-grade literacy in primary school. The exercises need to be for the students who need extra challenges.*

The Relative Pronoun and Adverb Challenge: Building Sentences, Unveiling Meanings

This activity caters to fifth-grade students who need an extra challenge in mastering relative pronouns and adverbs. It focuses on sentence building and analyzing how these words affect the meaning.

- Materials:
  - o **Sentence Starters:** Prepare a set of cards with sentence starters that leave room for both a relative pronoun and an adverb clause.
- Example Sentence Starters:
  - o The teacher praised the student _______ (who/which) _______ (always completes homework on time).
  - o We visited the museum _______ (where/when) _______ (they had a dinosaur exhibit).
  - o The author, _______ (whose/who) books I love, _______ (just released a new novel).
  - o **Relative Pronoun and Adverb Cards:** Create separate sets of cards with various relative pronouns ("who," "which," "that," "whose") and relative adverbs ("when," "where," "why," "how").
  - o **Blank Sentence Strips:** Provide each student with several blank sentence strips.
  - o **Challenge Sheet:** Prepare a worksheet with two sections: "Relative Pronoun Power Play" and "Relative Adverb Agility." Each section has a blank table with three columns: Sentence Starter, Relative Pronoun/ Adverb Choice, and Completed Sentence.
- Step 1: Building Sentences
  - o Briefly review the functions of relative pronouns and adverbs. Remind students that relative pronouns connect to a noun or pronoun, while relative adverbs connect to a verb, adjective, or adverb.
  - o Distribute the sentence starters and relative pronoun/adverb cards face down.
  - o Students work in pairs or small groups. Each group takes a sentence starter card and flips over two cards: one from the relative pronoun pile and one from the relative adverb pile.
- Step 2: Creating Variations
  - o The challenge is to combine the chosen relative pronoun and adverb with the sentence starter to create a grammatically correct and meaningful sentence on their blank strip.
  - o Encourage students to discuss and explore different combinations to see how the meaning of the sentence changes with different choices.
  - o For example, with the sentence starter "The teacher praised the student _______ (who/which) _______ (always completes homework on time)," students could choose "who" and "always" to create "The teacher praised the student **who always** completes homework on time" (identifying a specific student).

    - Alternatively, they could choose "which" and "always" to create "The teacher praised the student **which always** completes homework on time" (referring to any student who fulfills this condition).
- Step 3: Recording and Analysis
    - Instruct students to record their completed sentences in the "Relative Pronoun Power Play" and "Relative Adverb Agility" sections of the challenge sheet, along with the chosen relative pronoun and adverb.
    - Once they have completed a few sentences, facilitate a class discussion.
    - Ask students to share their sentences and explain the meaning they convey based on the chosen relative pronoun and adverb.
    - Discuss how even a slight change in these words can significantly alter the focus and meaning of the sentence.
- Step 4: Going Beyond
    - For an additional challenge, students can rewrite some of the sentences without using relative pronouns or adverbs. Discuss how this might affect clarity and sentence structure.
    - Encourage students to write their own original sentences using both relative pronouns and adverbs, showcasing their understanding.
- Differentiation:
    - Provide sentence starters with varying levels of complexity to cater to individual needs.
    - For students who need more support, start with simpler sentence structures that focus on a specific relative pronoun or adverb.
    - Offer a word bank containing relevant relative pronouns and adverbs for students who struggle with recall.

This activity encourages critical thinking and analysis by challenging students to build sentences and explore how relative pronouns and adverbs influence the meaning. It caters to advanced learners who are ready to delve deeper into the nuances of these grammatical elements.

CHATGPT 3.5 PROMPTS

The second half of the research was conducted using the generative AI ChatGPT 3.5. During this analysis the same prompts were used as with the Gemini. The aim was to research what are the differences between these two AI tools based on their responses and which is more suitable for developing personalized learning units.

Prompt 1: Write Me Examples for Personalized Learning Activities In Primary School

ChatGPT Response:

1. **Interest-Based Projects:** Allow students to choose topics of interest for research projects or presentations. For instance, if a student loves animals, they could research and present on a specific animal species.
2. **Learning Stations:** Set up different learning stations in the classroom where students can engage with material in various ways based on their preferences. For example, one station might involve hands-on activities, another could be a reading corner, and another might incorporate technology-based learning.
3. **Choice Boards:** Provide students with a choice board containing a variety of activities related to a topic or skill. Students can select which activities they want to complete based on their learning style and interests.
4. **Peer Teaching:** Allow students to teach each other based on their strengths and interests. For example, a student who excels in math could help teach a small group of peers a challenging concept.
5. **Goal Setting and Reflection:** Have students set learning goals for themselves and regularly reflect on their progress. Encourage them to identify areas where they need additional support and resources.
6. **Differentiated Assignments:** Offer students different assignment options that cater to their individual strengths and preferences. For example, students could choose to write a story, create a visual representation, or give an oral presentation to demonstrate their understanding of a concept.
7. **Flexible Grouping:** Group students based on their learning needs rather than their grade level. This allows students to work with peers who are at a similar level and receive targeted instruction.
8. **Student-Led Conferences:** Instead of traditional parent-teacher conferences, allow students to take the lead in discussing their progress with their parents. They can showcase their work, reflect on their learning, and set goals for the future.
9. **Learning Contracts:** Collaborate with students to create personalized learning contracts that outline their learning goals, strategies for achieving them, and criteria for success. This gives students ownership of their learning process.
10. **Self-Paced Learning:** Provide students with opportunities to learn at their own pace, allowing them to move ahead when they're ready or spend more time on concepts that require additional practice.

Based on the results the first difference in the approach of these two tools can be spotted. ChatGPT did not divided learning activities based on the different groups of learners like Gemini. ChatGPT provided general activities which can be conducted with students. This response is more general, and it is not focused on different aspects of personalized learning.

Prompt 2: Write Me Examples of Personalized Learning Activities for Learning English in Primary School

ChatGPT Response:

1. **Interactive Language Games:** Engage students in fun and interactive language games that cater to their interests and language proficiency levels. For example, word bingo, vocabulary puzzles, or language-based scavenger hunts.
2. **Language Journals:** Encourage students to keep language journals where they can write about their daily experiences, thoughts, and feelings in English. This allows them to practice writing skills while expressing themselves in a personal way.
3. **Reading Buddies:** Pair students with reading buddies who are at a similar language level but have different interests. They can take turns reading aloud to each other and discussing the text, fostering both language development and social skills.
4. **Digital Language Learning Platforms:** Introduce students to age-appropriate digital language learning platforms that adapt to their individual learning needs and provide personalized feedback. These platforms can offer activities such as interactive lessons, quizzes, and games.
5. **Role-Playing Activities:** Create role-playing scenarios based on real-life situations that students might encounter, such as ordering food at a restaurant or asking for directions. This allows them to practice language skills in a meaningful context while also building confidence.
6. **Individualized Vocabulary Lists:** Work with students to create personalized vocabulary lists based on their interests and learning goals. Encourage them to add new words they encounter in their reading or daily life to their lists and practice using them in context.
7. **Peer Editing and Feedback:** Pair students up for peer editing and feedback sessions where they can review each other's writing or speaking assignments. This promotes collaboration, critical thinking, and language development.

8. **Language Exploration Centers:** Set up language exploration centers in the classroom with different activities related to listening, speaking, reading, and writing in English. Students can choose activities based on their interests and learning preferences.
9. **Flipped Classroom Activities:** Assign short videos or audio recordings for students to watch or listen to at home, covering language concepts or skills. Then, use class time for hands-on activities, discussions, or practice exercises related to the material.
10. **Cultural Exchange Projects:** Facilitate cultural exchange projects where students can learn about English-speaking countries and cultures while practicing language skills. This can involve researching, creating presentations, or even engaging in virtual exchanges with students from other countries.

Prompt 3: Write Me Examples of Personalized Learning Activities for Learning English in Primary School With Use of ChatGPT

ChatGPT Response:

1. **Language Quizzes and Trivia:** Students can engage in interactive quizzes and trivia games with ChatGPT to test their vocabulary, grammar, and comprehension skills. ChatGPT can generate questions tailored to each student's proficiency level and areas of interest.
2. **Writing Prompts and Feedback:** Students can receive writing prompts from ChatGPT and submit their compositions for feedback. ChatGPT can provide constructive criticism, suggestions for improvement, and explanations of grammar rules, helping students refine their writing skills.
3. **Story Starters and Creative Writing:** ChatGPT can generate story starters or writing prompts to inspire students' creativity. Students can use these prompts as a springboard for writing their own stories, poems, or dialogues in English.
4. **Language Practice Conversations:** Students can engage in simulated conversations with ChatGPT to practice their spoken English skills. ChatGPT can act as a conversation partner, asking questions, providing responses, and offering corrective feedback on pronunciation and fluency.
5. **English Language Research Assistant:** Students can ask ChatGPT questions about English language concepts, grammar rules, vocabulary definitions, and more. ChatGPT can provide clear explanations and examples to help students deepen their understanding of the language.

6. **Language Learning Challenges:** ChatGPT can create personalized language learning challenges for students based on their interests and learning goals. For example, students can compete in vocabulary quizzes, grammar puzzles, or pronunciation challenges generated by ChatGPT.
7. **Virtual Language Immersion:** ChatGPT can simulate immersive language environments where students interact with virtual characters in English. Students can engage in role-playing scenarios, simulations, and virtual tours guided by ChatGPT, practicing their language skills in context.
8. **English Language Games and Activities:** ChatGPT can suggest fun and educational language games and activities for students to play individually or in groups. For example, students can play word association games, language puzzles, or storytelling games with ChatGPT's guidance.
9. **Personalized Reading Recommendations:** Students can receive personalized reading recommendations from ChatGPT based on their interests and reading level. ChatGPT can suggest English-language books, articles, websites, and other resources for students to explore independently.
10. **English Language Tutoring Sessions:** Students can schedule one-on-one tutoring sessions with ChatGPT for personalized instruction and support in English language learning. ChatGPT can provide tailored lessons, practice exercises, and feedback to help students improve their language skills.

Prompt 4: Write Me Examples of Personalized Learning Activities for Learning Pronouns in English in Primary School for the 5th Grade Students With Use of ChatGPT

ChatGPT Response:

1. **Interactive Pronoun Quiz:** ChatGPT can generate a personalized pronoun quiz for each student based on their current understanding and learning goals. The quiz could include multiple-choice questions, fill-in-the-blank exercises, and matching activities to reinforce pronoun usage.
2. **Pronoun Practice Conversations:** Students can engage in simulated conversations with ChatGPT where they practice using pronouns in context. ChatGPT can provide prompts for dialogue exchanges, allowing students to practice using pronouns in various situations such as introducing themselves, talking about their hobbies, or describing their family members.

3. **Personalized Pronoun Stories:** ChatGPT can assist students in creating personalized stories that incorporate pronouns. Students can provide ChatGPT with information about themselves, their interests, and their experiences, and ChatGPT can generate a customized story using pronouns to reflect the student's input.
4. **Pronoun Puzzles and Games:** ChatGPT can suggest pronoun-themed puzzles and games for students to play, such as pronoun crossword puzzles, word searches, or scavenger hunts. Students can work independently or in groups to solve the puzzles while reinforcing their understanding of pronouns.
5. **Pronoun Role-Playing Activities:** ChatGPT can facilitate role-playing activities where students take on different roles and practice using pronouns appropriately. For example, students can role-play scenarios such as ordering food at a restaurant, planning a party, or resolving a conflict, with ChatGPT providing guidance and feedback on pronoun usage.
6. **Pronoun Sorting and Categorization:** ChatGPT can suggest interactive activities where students sort pronouns into categories based on their function or usage. For instance, students can categorize pronouns as subject pronouns, object pronouns, possessive pronouns, or reflexive pronouns, with ChatGPT providing explanations and examples to reinforce learning.
7. **Pronoun Challenges and Competitions:** ChatGPT can create personalized pronoun challenges and competitions for students to participate in. Students can compete against each other or work individually to complete pronoun-related tasks and earn rewards or recognition for their achievements.
8. **Pronoun Hunt:** ChatGPT can guide students in a pronoun scavenger hunt where they search for pronouns in texts, advertisements, or real-world objects. Students can identify pronouns, categorize them by type, and discuss their findings with ChatGPT to reinforce their understanding of pronoun usage.
9. **Pronoun Riddles and Brain Teasers:** ChatGPT can generate pronoun-themed riddles and brain teasers for students to solve. These challenges can be designed to encourage critical thinking and problem-solving skills while reinforcing pronoun usage in a fun and engaging way.
10. **Pronoun Reflection and Feedback:** ChatGPT can provide personalized feedback to students based on their pronoun usage in written assignments or spoken interactions. Students can submit their work to ChatGPT for review, and ChatGPT can offer constructive feedback, suggestions for improvement, and explanations of pronoun-related concepts.

Prompt 5: Write Me Exercises for Learning Pronouns for the Students Who Need Extra Challenge in 5th Grade of Primary School

ChatGPT Response:

1. **Pronoun Identification:** Provide a passage or a series of sentences where pronouns are used in complex ways. Students must identify each pronoun and categorize them based on their type (subject pronoun, object pronoun, possessive pronoun, reflexive pronoun).
2. **Pronoun Transformations:** Give sentences with simple pronouns and ask students to rewrite them using more complex pronoun forms. For example:
3. **Original:** "She likes ice cream." Rewrite: "The girl who lives next door likes ice cream."
4. **Pronoun Agreement:** Present sentences with incorrect pronoun-antecedent agreement and ask students to correct them. For instance:
5. **Incorrect:** "Each of the boys brought their lunch." Correct: "Each of the boys brought his lunch."
6. **Pronoun Case:** Provide sentences where pronoun case is crucial for clarity, and ask students to identify and correct any errors. For example:
7. **Original:** "Me and my friend went to the park." Correct: "My friend and I went to the park."
8. **Pronoun Ambiguity:** Present sentences with ambiguous pronouns and ask students to rewrite them to clarify the intended meaning. For example:
9. **Ambiguous:** "She gave her sister her book." Clarified: "She gave her book to her sister."
10. **Pronoun Review:** Create a pronoun review worksheet with a mix of exercises covering various pronoun concepts, including personal, possessive, demonstrative, relative, and indefinite pronouns.
11. **Pronoun Usage in Context:** Provide short passages or paragraphs where students must identify pronouns and explain their function within the context of the text. Encourage them to analyze how pronouns contribute to the overall meaning and coherence of the passage.
12. **Pronoun Relationships:** Give students sentences with multiple pronouns referring to different antecedents, and ask them to clarify the relationships between the pronouns and their referents. For example:
13. "They said she would bring it, but she forgot."

14. **Pronoun Substitution:** Provide sentences with repetitive noun phrases and ask students to replace them with pronouns to improve clarity and cohesion. For example:
15. **Original:** "The girl with the long hair and the blue dress won the race." Substituted: "She won the race."
16. **Pronoun Challenges in Writing:** Assign creative writing tasks that require students to incorporate a variety of pronouns effectively. Encourage them to experiment with different pronoun forms and structures to convey meaning and create engaging narratives.

Prompt 6: Create Materials for Learning Relative Pronouns and Relative Adverbs for Fifth-Grade Literacy in Primary School. The Exercises Need to be for the Students Who Need More Support

ChatGPT Response:

- **Lesson Materials:**

1. **Introduction to Relative Pronouns and Relative Adverbs**: Start by introducing students to the concept of relative pronouns and relative adverbs. Provide simple definitions and examples to illustrate how these words are used to connect clauses and provide additional information.
2. **Visual Aids**: Use visual aids such as posters, diagrams, or anchor charts to reinforce the key concepts of relative pronouns and relative adverbs. Include examples and visual cues to help students understand how these words function in sentences.
3. **Guided Practice**: Provide guided practice activities where students can identify relative pronouns and relative adverbs in sentences. Offer support and feedback as students work through the exercises to ensure comprehension.
4. **Interactive Activities**: Incorporate interactive activities such as games, puzzles, or online quizzes to engage students and reinforce learning. These activities can provide opportunities for students to practice using relative pronouns and relative adverbs in context.
5. **Modeling and Examples**: Model how to use relative pronouns and relative adverbs in sentences and provide plenty of examples for students to analyze and discuss. Break down complex sentences into smaller parts to help students identify the relative clauses and the words that connect them.

- **Exercise Materials:**

1. **Fill in the Blank**: Provide sentences with missing relative pronouns or relative adverbs and ask students to fill in the blanks with the correct words. For example:
   a. The book _______ I borrowed from the library is due tomorrow.
   b. I don't remember the day _______ we went to the zoo.
2. **Matching Activity**: Create a matching activity where students match sentences with their corresponding relative pronouns or relative adverbs. Provide sentence strips and word cards for students to match together. For example:
   a. Sentence: The house _______ is painted blue is mine.
   b. Word Card: where
3. **Sentence Building**: Give students sentence fragments containing relative clauses and ask them to combine them using relative pronouns or relative adverbs. For example:
   a. Fragment 1: The movie theater
   b. Fragment 2: We saw the latest blockbuster
   c. Combined Sentence: The movie theater where we saw the latest blockbuster.
4. **Sentence Analysis**: Provide sentences containing relative clauses and ask students to identify the relative pronouns or relative adverbs and the clauses they connect. Encourage students to explain how the relative pronouns or relative adverbs function within the sentence.
5. **Creative Writing Prompts**: Offer creative writing prompts that encourage students to incorporate relative pronouns and relative adverbs into their writing. Provide starter sentences or story prompts to inspire students' creativity and encourage them to use these words to add detail and depth to their writing.

Prompt 7: Create Materials for Learning Relative Pronouns and Relative Adverbs for Fifth-Grade Literacy in Primary School. The Exercises Need to be for the Students Who Need Extra Challenges

ChatGPT Response:

- **Lesson Materials:**

1. **Advanced Explanation**: Provide a more in-depth explanation of relative pronouns and relative adverbs, including their functions and different types. Use examples that demonstrate complex sentence structures and relationships between clauses.
2. **Comparative Analysis**: Compare and contrast relative pronouns and relative adverbs with other types of pronouns and adverbs. Highlight the unique roles and functions of relative words in connecting clauses and providing additional information.
3. **Advanced Examples**: Include advanced examples of sentences containing relative clauses with complex structures and nuances. Break down these examples step-by-step to help students understand how relative pronouns and relative adverbs contribute to the meaning of the sentence.
4. **Extended Activities**: Offer extended activities such as research projects or writing assignments that require students to use relative pronouns and relative adverbs in more sophisticated ways. Encourage students to explore how these words are used in literature, academic writing, and real-world contexts.
5. **Critical Thinking Questions**: Pose critical thinking questions that prompt students to analyze and evaluate the use of relative pronouns and relative adverbs in different contexts. Encourage students to consider the effectiveness and impact of these words on the clarity and coherence of a sentence.

- **Exercise Materials:**

1. **Sentence Transformation**: Provide sentences with relative clauses and ask students to rewrite them using different relative pronouns or relative adverbs. Encourage students to experiment with word choice and sentence structure to convey the same meaning in alternative ways.

2. **Complex Sentence Construction**: Challenge students to create complex sentences containing multiple relative clauses using a variety of relative pronouns and relative adverbs. Provide prompts or sentence starters to guide students in their sentence construction.
3. **Contextual Usage**: Present passages or paragraphs with missing relative pronouns or relative adverbs and ask students to choose the most appropriate word based on the context. Encourage students to justify their choices by explaining how each word contributes to the meaning of the sentence.
4. **Literary Analysis**: Provide excerpts from literature or informational texts that contain examples of relative pronouns and relative adverbs and ask students to analyze their usage within the context of the passage. Encourage students to consider the author's intent and the effect of these words on the reader's understanding.
5. **Creative Writing Challenges**: Offer creative writing challenges that require students to incorporate relative pronouns and relative adverbs into their writing in imaginative and inventive ways. Encourage students to experiment with sentence structure and language usage to create engaging and sophisticated narratives.

COMPARISON OF GEMINI AND CHATGPT

Each generative AI, Gemini and ChatGPT used the same seven prompts:

1. *Write me examples for personalized learning activities in primary school.*
2. *Write me examples of personalized learning activities for learning English in primary school.*
3. *Write me examples of personalized learning activities for learning English in primary school with use of Gemini.*
4. *Write me examples of personalized learning activities for learning pronouns in English in primary school for the 5th grade students with use of Gemini.*
5. *Write me exercises for learning pronouns for the students who need extra challenge in 5th grade of primary school.*
6. *Create materials for learning relative pronouns and relative adverbs for fifth-grade literacy in primary school. The exercises need to be for the students who need more support.*
7. *Create materials for learning relative pronouns and relative adverbs for fifth-grade literacy in primary school. The exercises need to be for the students who need extra challenges.*

The goal of the research was to determine which AI tools are more appropriate for the development of teaching units for personalized learning. A comparison of ChatGPT and Gemini for use in personal learning, highlighting both their positive and negative impacts and other characteristics that will be presented in this section. During the analysis of these two generative AI tools, 4 categories have emerged and been researched, content (1), pedagogical strategies and instructional design (2), prompt responsiveness (3) and technological integration and interactivity (4). Each response from ChatGPT and Gemini was analyzed based on the provided content, e. g. what are the similarities and differences between the content provided by the AI tools, what kind of exercise tools were developed for teachers based on prompts that were used, etc. The second category that was examined is related to pedagogical strategies and instructional design that AI tools provided and used in their exercises and learning materials. The third category is prompt responsiveness that refers to accuracy of provided content based on the prompt that was given to the AI tools. The fourth category refers to technological integration and interactivity and examines in what measure the generative AI tools provided learning materials and content that have the integration of technology, e.g. which tool provides more technology integration and which provides less. ChatGPT and Gemini both use advanced language models to generate responses. However, their outputs and the nature of their personalized learning materials can vary significantly based on the prompt structure.

Content Customization and Adaptability (1)

In terms of content customization and adaptability, ChatGPT and Gemini exhibit distinct characteristics. ChatGPT often produces more generalized responses that can be adapted to various learning scenarios, while Gemini provides more structured and specific content tailored to different learner needs. For example, when asked about learning activities, ChatGPT might suggest broad strategies like "use interactive games" without specifying which games or how they cater to different learning styles. Its outputs are highly dependent on the detail of the prompts it receives. More detailed prompts yield more targeted suggestions, but educators still need to interpret and apply them in their specific educational contexts. Gemini often provides more detailed and context-specific responses, particularly when prompts are precise. It includes examples like tiered activities, open-ended projects, and specific tools like graphic organizers for different types of learners. ChatGPT can generate creative and varied educational content, but its effectiveness depends on the clarity and specificity of the prompt. It consistently categorized its outputs based on the needs of different learner types—such as those requiring extra support or challenge, kinesthetic learners, and visual learners. This categorization helps educators quickly identify and apply the most relevant activities for diverse educational needs in a structured way. Gemini's responses included detailed descriptions and examples of activities. For instance, it suggested specific games like “Pronoun Detectives” or using “graphic organizers” to help visual learners understand grammar concepts. These specific activities can be directly implemented with minimal modification.

ChatGPT often produced generalized responses, which can be adapted to various learning scenarios but may lack the precise tailoring needed for specific learner needs. For instance, when asked about learning activities, ChatGPT might suggest broad strategies like “use interactive games” without specifying which games or how they cater to different learning styles.

Prompt Responsiveness (2)

Figure 1 shows several key terms and description regarding the prompt responsiveness that have emerged during this research.

Figure 1. Structure and specificity of responses from ChatGPT and Gemini

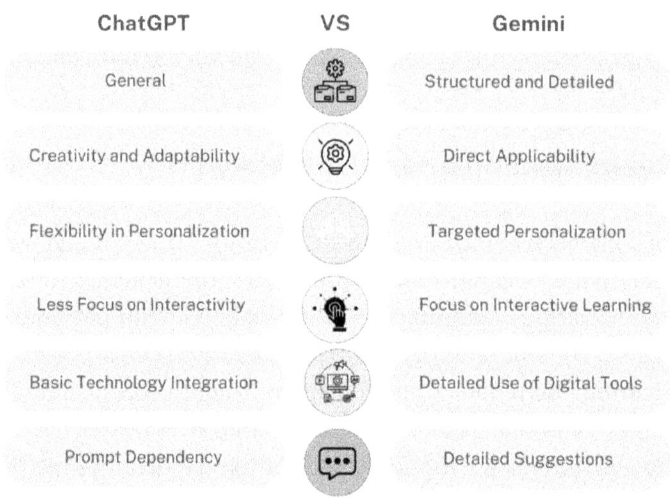

In the context of generative AI models such as ChatGPT and Gemini, the ability to respond quickly refers to the effective and effective response of AI to user inputs and responses. It includes several factors that contribute to the speed and quality of AI responses. One of the most obvious aspects of quick response is the speed at which AI reacts, also known as latency. This is the time when AI processes prompts and generates answers. Reduced latency leads to faster response times, allowing interaction to feel smoother and more conversational. In generative AI, speed alone is not enough; the response must be contextually appropriate and coherent, and this segment has been analyzed. High responsiveness means that AI can quickly generate relevant input answers, coordinate with user requests and be coherent within the ongoing conversation. Another key factor is the ability to adapt to the wide range of inputs of AI. Reaction models must be able to effectively handle simple and complex prompts. Whether it's a real question, solving a problem, or creating creative content, AI needs to respond accurately and reliably to user expectations. This adaptability is closely linked to the quality of interaction.

The AI must maintain accuracy and relevance across different types of prompts, ensuring that the information provided is not only fast but also valuable. Maintaining the flow of conversation is also an essential aspect of prompt responsiveness in AI systems like ChatGPT and Gemini. For dialogue-based interactions to feel natural and engaged, AI must generate responses that follow the context, tone and direction of the conversation. This allows seamless and intuitive experiences, making AI feel more human-like in interactions. Prompt responsiveness in generative AI is about balancing the speed of responses with their relevance, coherence, and accuracy. The goal is to ensure that the AI meets user needs effectively, delivering timely, high-quality outputs in a way that feels natural and fluid during real-time interactions.

Gemini is noted for its structured responses, categorizing learners by needs such as those requiring extra challenges or support, and tailoring activities accordingly. For instance, it provides specific examples for kinesthetic and visual learners. Gemini offered more concrete and detailed activities, particularly as prompts became more specific. For example, activities were tailored to learning pronouns and relative pronouns/adverbs in English. Gemini consistently categorized activities into four types of learners: students needing extra challenge, students needing more support, kinesthetic learners, and visual learners. This structure provided clearer guidance for teachers.

ChatGPT tends to offer more generalized suggestions and may not automatically categorize learners unless explicitly asked. The quality and specificity of ChatGPT's responses are highly dependent on the prompt detail. More detailed prompts result in more targeted suggestions, but still require educators to interpret and implement them within a specific educational context. ChatGPT's responses could be adapted by teachers but required more interpretation to tailor to specific learning needs.

Pedagogical Strategies and Instructional Design (3)

ChatGPT offers a wide range of educational strategies, including interactive learning, project-based learning and collaboration tasks. This creative flexibility is especially useful for experienced educators, who can take a broad idea and creatively adapt it to teaching styles and student needs. ChatGPT's suggestions serve often as a starting point for innovative lesson planning, allowing teachers to experiment with new and engaging teaching methods. Gemini places a strong emphasis on differentiated teaching and offers different activities tailored to students' needs. Its responses include specific strategies for kinesthetic learners, visual learners, and students requiring additional support or challenges. By offering tiered activities and concrete examples, Gemini helps educators address the diverse proficiency levels within a classroom, ensuring that each student receives the appropriate level of instruction and support. ChatGPT offers a variety of pedagogical strategies, such as interactive learning, project-based learning and collaboration tasks. These strategies require educators to design the specific characteristics of each activity. Gemini emphasizes differentiated instruction by tailoring activities to various student needs, providing tiered activities, and concrete actionable examples that support learning objectives.

ChatGPT offered a range of pedagogical strategies, such as interactive learning, project-based learning, and collaborative tasks. However, these strategies were often presented in a general format, requiring educators to design the specifics of each activity. The tool provides a creative base that teachers can build upon, offering room for innovation in how lessons are delivered. This flexibility is beneficial for experienced educators who can take broad ideas and adapt them creatively to their teaching style and student needs. Gemini emphasized differentiated instruction by tailoring activities to various student needs. For example, it provided tiered activities—simplified tasks for those needing more support and complex ones for advanced learners. This differentiation is crucial for addressing the varied proficiency levels in a classroom. The platform often provided concrete, actionable examples. For instance, when focusing on pronouns, Gemini suggested specific exercises like sorting activities for kinesthetic learners and color-coded charts for visual learners, which directly support the learning objectives.

Technological Integration and Interactivity (4)

Both tools can suggest activities with or without the integration of technology, offering flexibility depending on the educational environment's resources. ChatGPT's suggestions sometimes include technology use, but they are less specific, often suggesting the possibility of using technology without detailed guidance. In contrast, Gemini frequently incorporates technology into its suggestions, advocating for the use of digital tools and providing specific guidance on using these tools effectively.

ChatGPT's approach to integrating technology into learning is more generalized. While it suggests the use of digital tools, such as digital flashcards or interactive online platforms, it often leaves the specifics to the educator’s discretion. This can be advantageous for teachers who prefer to have flexibility and control over the integration process. However, it may require additional effort from educators to determine the most effective way to implement these technological suggestions.

On the other hand, Gemini frequently emphasizes the integration of technology and provides detailed guidance on using specific digital tools. For example, Gemini might recommend creating interactive quizzes or digital storyboards, providing step-by-step instructions on how to utilize these tools effectively. This detailed approach not only facilitates the incorporation of technology into the classroom but also ensures that it enhances the learning experience through structured, interactive elements. Both ChatGPT and Gemini contribute to creating interactive learning experiences in different ways. ChatGPT's broad and flexible suggestions allow educators to design interactive activities that can be tailored to various learning contexts. For instance, it might suggest role-playing scenarios or collaborative projects that encourage student participation and engagement. Gemini, however, provides more specific interactive activities, such as using virtual reality simulations or online discussion boards, ensuring that these experiences are directly aligned with the learning objectives. Both tools can suggest activities with or without the integration of technology, offering flexibility depending on the educational environment's resources. ChatGPT suggestions occasionally included the use of technology but were less specific about how to integrate these tools compared to Gemini. Gemini often suggested specific uses of technology, such as using its own capabilities to generate or refine content, providing a clear pathway for digital integration in learning.

Similarities and Overlapping Areas

The research has identified 4 similarities and overlapping themes that have emerged in use of ChatGPT and Gemini for personalized learning that can be seen in Figure 2.

Figure 2. Similarities and overlapping themes of ChatGPT and Gemini for personalized learning

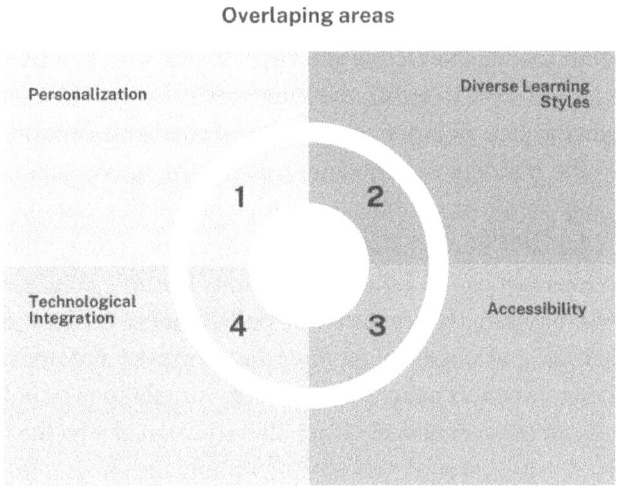

The four categories of overlapping are personalization and differentiation (1), support for diverse learning styles (2), technological integration (3) and accessibility and teacher support (4). (1) ChatGPT and Gemini are designed to enhance personalized learning by adapting educational content to student needs. They achieve this through a differentiated instruction strategy that ensures that activities and materials are adaptable to various learning styles, abilities, and individual requirements. This emphasis on personalization helps to meet the unique needs of each student and promotes a more effective and engaging learning experience. Both tools seek to adapt learning experiences to the needs of individual students and recognize the importance of considering different learning styles. (2) ChatGPT and Gemini provide resources and suggestions to accommodate different learning styles such as visual, auditory, and sensory learners. This tool offers a variety of activities and examples adapted to these different modes, and helps educators create a more inclusive and supportive learning environment. This adaptability ensures that all students, regardless of their learning style, have access and benefit from educational content. (3) Both tools promote the integration of technology into classrooms to improve learning experiences. They suggested using digital tools and resources, such as interactive games, online platforms, and virtual simulations, to create engaging and interactive activities. This emphasis on technology not only enhances the learning process, but also helps students develop important digital literacy skills that are crucial in today's technological-driven world. (4) ChatGPT and Gemini are aimed at democratizing access to high-quality educational resources by providing tools in free versions. This accessibility allows educators and learners from various backgrounds to benefit from advanced AI technologies. Both tools also support teachers by providing concrete examples, structured learning activities and detailed guidance to help teachers save time and effort in preparing and teaching lessons. This support enables teachers to focus more on students' participation and interaction and to improve the overall learning experience.

Both ChatGPT and Gemini share several similarities and overarching themes in their approach to enhancing education. One key similarity is their commitment to personalization. Both tools are designed to accommodate different learning styles and needs, acknowledging the significance of tailored educational experiences. This focus on personalization ensures that students receive learning activities that are best suited to their individual preferences and abilities.

Another common theme is their emphasis on engagement and motivation. Both AI systems offer dynamic and motivating learning activities, which are essential for keeping students interested and actively participating in the learning process. By providing engaging content, they help sustain students' attention and foster a positive attitude toward learning. Additionally, both ChatGPT and Gemini function as valuable resources for educators. They provide a wealth of ideas and adaptable frameworks that can be utilized in diverse educational settings. This support allows teachers to design more effective and personalized lesson plans, leveraging the AI systems to enhance their teaching strategies.

Both ChatGPT and Gemini responded to the same set of prompts, which ranged from general to highly specific requests for personalized learning activities in primary schools, particularly focused on learning English for fifth-grade students.

Positive and Negative Characteristics

Analysis shows positive and negative impacts that both AI tools have in process of developing and generating personalized learning materials. Additionally, they support teachers by providing concrete examples and structured learning activities, helping to develop personalized learning plans more efficiently. The following analysis delves into these positive and negative impacts, exploring how ChatGPT and Gemini shape personalized learning environments. Figure 15 categorizes these implications, focusing on both their potential to enhance and their limitations in the educational process.

Research has provided insight into the positive and negative impacts that ChatGPT and Gemini have on personal learning. The Figure XX shows categorization of positive and negative implications of their use in creating personalized learning materials. Positive impacts are related to diversity (1), personalization (2), accessibility (3) and support (4) while negative impacts are related to technology dependence (5), quality (6), depersonalization (7) and inconsistencies (8).

Figure 3. Positive and negative characteristics of ChatGPT and Gemini

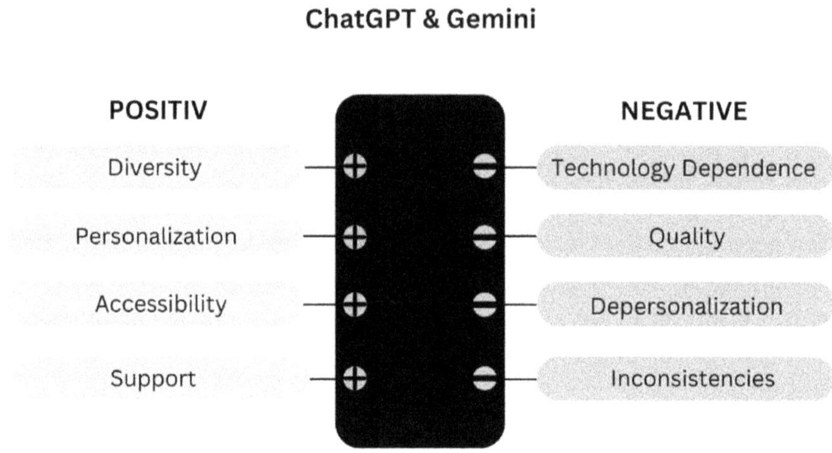

Both tools can provide diverse learning resources based on a wide array of activities and resources that cater to different learning styles, enhancing engagement and comprehension. The quality and relevance of the generated content heavily depend on the quality of the prompts, poorly constructed prompts can result in irrelevant or low-quality outputs, hindering learning. More detailed prompts result in more targeted suggestions, but educators still need to interpret and implement them within a specific educational context. (1). They enable the creation of tailored educational experiences by generating content that can be adjusted for varying difficulty levels and learner needs (2). As both tools have free versions, they democratize access to personalized learning materials, allowing educators and learners worldwide to benefit from advanced AI technologies (3). By providing concrete examples and structured learning activities, these tools assist teachers in developing personalized learning plans more efficiently, saving time and effort (4).

The integration of AI tools such as ChatGPT and Gemini poses significant concerns as to the possibility of excessive dependence on technology. There is a risk that educators will overly rely on content generated by AI, which could lead to a decrease in their creativity and their development of teaching skills. Educators should use these tools as a complement rather than a replacement for their expertise and judgment (5). The effectiveness of the content generated depends heavily on the quality of the prompt. Insufficiently constructed prompts may lead to an irrelevant or low-quality output and potentially impede learning. While AI provides tools to externalize tasks like content generation and performance monitoring, there are concerns about dehumanization, loss of critical thinking skills, and reliance on technology over human judgment (Cukurova, 2024).

This necessitates a degree of prompt engineering skill among educators to ensure that the AI responses meet the desired educational standards and objectives. (6). Despite their ability to tailor content, ChatGPT and Gemini might lack the nuanced understanding of students' needs that a human teacher possesses. This can sometimes result in impersonal interactions, as AI lacks the emotional intelligence and contextual awareness that human educators bring to the classroom. Educators must therefore ensure that AI-generated content is supplemented with personal interaction and understanding to maintain a holistic educational experience (7). AI models, including ChatGPT and Gemini, can occasionally produce inconsistent or incorrect information. Such inconsistencies could mislead learners if not carefully reviewed and vetted by educators. It's crucial for teachers to critically assess AI-generated content and make necessary adjustments to ensure accuracy and relevance (8). While both ChatGPT and Gemini provide tools for conducting personalized learning, they should be used as supplements to, rather than replacements for, traditional teaching methods and teachers. The choice between ChatGPT and Gemini ultimately depends on the educator's needs and preferences. Those who value flexibility and creativity might lean towards ChatGPT, while those who prefer structured, detailed guidance might find Gemini more suitable. Regardless of the choice, both tools serve as additional resources in conducting personalized learning and supporting teachers in creating engaging, effective educational experiences.

ChatGPT and Gemini represent significant advancements in the realm of personalized learning, offering diverse, accessible, and adaptable resources that enhance both student engagement and educator efficiency. Their ability to tailor content to individual learning styles and needs makes them valuable tools in modern education. However, reliance on these artificial intelligence tools also poses challenges, including risks related to excessive dependence, content quality, depersonalization and occasionally inaccuracies. These AI-based solutions provide a meaningful support to the education process but should be seen as additional resources to improve teachers' critical roles rather than replace them. A balanced approach to integrate AI capabilities with teachers' expertise and judgment is essential to maximize the benefits of these technologies and reduce their limitations.

EXAMPLES OF PROMPTS FOR CHATGPT AND GEMINI

Based on the research in Table 1 there are examples of prompts that can be used for creating and generating personalized learning materials for teachers. During the analysis of the prompts generated by generative AI tools the 4 categories emerged, general prompts, subject-specific, learner-centered and prompts for fostering creativity and engagement during the class. These examples always can be altered and modified based on the students' specific needs, backgrounds, and capabilities. Teachers can and must adjust the prompts for the structure of their students. The first step is to identify the capabilities of their students and based on the results teachers need to provide and develop personalized learning materials. The generative AI tools can be additional supplements and help teachers in the preparation, but they cannot solely depend on it.

Table 1. Categorization of prompts

CATEGORIES	GENERAL	SUBJECT-SPECIFIC	LEARNER-CENTRED	CREATIVITY AND ENGAGEMENT
PROMPTS	Write me examples of personalized learning activities for primary school students	Create personalized learning activities for teaching English in primary school that support students with varying abilities	Write an exercise for teaching relative pronouns and relative adverbs that challenges advanced 5th-grade students.	Develop personalized learning materials that encourage students to explore English through creative storytelling or visual aids.
	Design activities that cater to students with different learning needs (e.g., students who need extra challenge, students who need more support	Design an English language learning activity for visual learners and kinesthetic learners in the 5th grade.	Create a literacy exercise focusing on relative pronouns for 5th graders who need extra support in language learning.	Create hands-on activities for kinesthetic learners to reinforce English vocabulary through interactive games.

Table 2 and Table 3 provide additional examples how ChatGPT and Gemini can be used for development of personalized learning materials. These examples have been created based on 7 prompts that have been used for initial testing and analysis of AI tools. Based on the ChatGPT and Gemini responses the two tables have been created to help teachers in their use of generative AI tools during the process of adjusting and adapting teaching materials to the needs of their students.

Table 2. Prompts for ChatGPT

EXAMPLE	PROMPT	OUTPUT
Interactive Pronoun Quiz	Create a personalized pronoun quiz for 5th-grade students learning English. Include a mix of multiple-choice questions, fill-in-the-blank exercises, and matching activities.	ChatGPT generates a quiz tailored to the student's level, testing their understanding of pronouns in various contexts.
Pronoun Practice Conversations	Facilitate a simulated conversation practice for students to use pronouns. Include prompts for dialogue exchanges on topics like hobbies or family.	Students engage in conversations, practicing pronoun usage with feedback from ChatGPT.
Personalized Pronoun Stories	Help students create personalized stories that focus on pronoun usage. Use information about the students' interests and experiences.	ChatGPT generates stories incorporating personal details, enhancing the learning of pronouns in context.
Pronoun Puzzles and Games	Suggest pronoun-themed puzzles and games suitable for 5th graders.	Includes crossword puzzles, word searches, and scavenger hunts that reinforce pronoun learning.
Pronoun Role-Playing Activities	Create role-playing scenarios for students to practice using pronouns in various situations.	Scenarios such as ordering food or planning a party, with ChatGPT guiding and providing feedback.

Table 3. Prompts for Gemini

EXAMPLE	PROMPT	OUTPUT
Storytelling with Variations	Generate a basic story using simple vocabulary and grammar. Then provide prompts for students to modify the story, such as changing the setting or characters.	Students can explore different narrative elements and enhance the story, which helps in practicing language skills.
Interactive Phonics Practice	Use Gemini to practice phonics with 5th graders. Include activities like identifying sounds or filling in blanks with missing letters.	Activities are tailored to the phonics needs of students, with options to practice pronunciation and spelling.
Action Verb Charades with Feedback	Design an action verb charades game where students act out verbs, and Gemini provides feedback or suggests synonyms.	This kinesthetic learning approach helps students learn verbs through physical activity and immediate feedback.
Image-based Storytelling	Use images to prompt storytelling. Students create stories or dialogues based on the images provided by Gemini.	Visual stimuli are used to inspire creative writing and vocabulary usage.
Personalized Illustrated Dictionary	Create a personalized illustrated dictionary for a specific vocabulary set. Include definitions, sentences, and related images.	Students compile a dictionary that helps them understand and remember vocabulary through visual association.

These prompts illustrate how ChatGPT and Gemini can be utilized to create diverse and engaging educational materials tailored to individual learning needs. The differences in the responses highlight each tool's unique capabilities in facilitating personalized learning.

REFERENCES

Ayeni, O. O., Al Hamad, N. M., Chisom, O. N., Osawaru, B., & Adewusi, O. E. (2024). AI in education: A review of personalized learning and educational technology. *GSC Advanced Research and Reviews*, 18(2), 261–271. DOI: 10.30574/gscarr.2024.18.2.0062

Bernacki, M. L., Greene, M. J., & Lobczowski, N. G. (2021). A systematic review of research on personalized learning: Personalized by whom, to what, how, and for what purpose (s)? *Educational Psychology Review*, 33(4), 1675–1715. DOI: 10.1007/s10648-021-09615-8

Brass, J., & Lynch, T. L. (2020). Personalized learning: A history of the present. *Journal of curriculum theorizing, 35*(2).

Chen, S. Y., & Wang, J. H. (2021). Individual differences and personalized learning: A review and appraisal. *Universal Access in the Information Society*, 20(4), 833–849. DOI: 10.1007/s10209-020-00753-4

Cheung, S. K. S., Fu, L. W., Kwok, L. F., & Poulova, P. (2021). In search of the good practices of personalized learning. *Interactive Learning Environments*, 29(2), 179–181. DOI: 10.1080/10494820.2021.1894830

Cukurova, M. (2024). The interplay of learning, analytics and artificial intelligence in education: A vision for hybrid intelligence. *British Journal of Educational Technology. Gemini*. Retrieved August 15, 2024, from https://gemini.google.com/

Ghimire, A., Prather, J., & Edwards, J. (2024). Generative AI in Education: A Study of Educators' Awareness, Sentiments, and Influencing Factors. *arXiv* preprint *arXiv*:2403.15586.

Google. (2024). *Tips to write prompts for Gemini*. Available at: https://support.google.com/a/users/answer/14200040?hl=en

Gunawardena, M., Bishop, P., & Aviruppola, K. (2024). Personalized learning: The simple, the complicated, the complex and the chaotic. *Teaching and Teacher Education*, 139, 104429. DOI: 10.1016/j.tate.2023.104429

Ifenthaler, D., Majumdar, R., Gorissen, P., Judge, M., Mishra, S., Raffaghelli, J., & Shimada, A. (2024). Artificial Intelligence in Education: Implications for Policymakers, Researchers, and Practitioners. *Tech Know Learn*, 29(4), 1693–1710. DOI: 10.1007/s10758-024-09747-0

Katsamakas, E., Pavlov, O. V., & Saklad, R. (2024). Artificial Intelligence and the Transformation of Higher Education Institutions: A Systems Approach. *Sustainability (Basel)*, 16(14), 6118. DOI: 10.3390/su16146118

Lee, D., Huh, Y., Lin, C. Y., & Reigeluth, C. M. (2018). Technology functions for personalized learning in learner-centered schools. *Educational Technology Research and Development*, 66(5), 1269–1302. DOI: 10.1007/s11423-018-9615-9

Makhambetova, A., Zhiyenbayeva, N., & Ergesheva, E. (2021). Personalized learning strategy as a tool to improve academic performance and motivation of students. *International Journal of Web-Based Learning and Teaching Technologies*, 16(6), 1–17. DOI: 10.4018/IJWLTT.286743

Martinez, M. (2002). Designing learning objects to personalize learning. *The instructional use of learning objects*, 151-171.

Peng, H., Ma, S., & Spector, J. M. (2019). Personalized adaptive learning: An emerging pedagogical approach enabled by a smart learning environment. *Smart Learning Environments*, 6(1), 1–14. DOI: 10.1186/s40561-019-0089-y

Prompt Engineering Guide. (n.d.). Retrieved August 15, 2024, from https://www.promptingguide.ai/

Redding, S. (2013). *A perspective on personalized learning and practice guide for teachers.* Center on Innovations in Learning.

Shemshack, A., Kinshuk, , & Spector, J. M. (2021). A comprehensive analysis of personalized learning components. *Journal of Computers in Education*, 8(4), 485–503. DOI: 10.1007/s40692-021-00188-7

The School District of Clayton. (n.d.). Available at: https://www.claytonschools.net/Page/13457

UNESCO International Bureau of Education. (2017). Personalized learning. Available at: https://unesdoc.unesco.org/ark:/48223/pf0000250057

W3schools. (n.d.). Retrieved August 15, 2024, from https://www.w3schools.com/gen_ai/gen_ai_prompt_intro.php

Wolf, M. A. (2010). *Innovate to educate: System [re] design for personalized learning, a report from the 2010 symposium.* Software and Information Industry Association.

Chapter 5
Case Study of Using AI Tools in Higher Education

ABSTRACT

This chapter offers an overview of a case study conducted in higher education settings, focusing on students' engagement with AI tools. The research analyzed students' perspectives and motivations concerning the integration of AI tools for task completion and assignment management. Furthermore, it explores how students used AI tools for learning new materials and navigating complex teaching concepts. By examining the student experience, this chapter provides valuable insights into the implications of AI tools in higher education contexts.

OVERVIEW OF THE RESEARCH

The main objective of this research was to explore and analyze how students use generative AI tools for learning, as well as to assess their experiences with these tools in a classroom setting. The study was conducted during the second semester of the 2023/2024 academic year at the University of Zagreb, involving a sample of 89 students enrolled in the facultative subject *Computer Science*. The aim of this study was to understand how generative AI supports or challenges the learning processes of students and how they perceive the integration of these tools into the academic environment. The study investigated students' experiences using AI tools for learning and aims

DOI: 10.4018/979-8-3693-3474-4.ch005

to provide interpretation of the role of AI in education. In this study, students received instructions and guidelines on how to use generative AI tools for learning, but the teaching process itself was structured around self-directed learning at home. Instead of traditional classroom instruction, students were tasked with using the AI tools to learn new material and complete exercises individually at home. The absence of teacher supervision during this phase meant that students had to rely on the AI tools as their primary resource for understanding the material and solving tasks.

The research questions in this chapter are:

1. To what extent do AI tools improve the understanding of new concepts compared to traditional learning methods?
2. What are the benefits, challenges, and limitations students experience when using AI tools independently for learning?
3. How does using AI tools impact students' confidence and self-efficacy in learning?
4. Can AI tools effectively supplement traditional learning models?

The research assesses several aspects, including how students engaged with the AI tools (1), including the strategies they developed to effectively use the tools for learning, the extent to which these tools facilitated the understanding of new concepts (2), and the students' experiences, including perceived benefits, challenges, and any limitations they encountered while learning independently with AI (3). By analyzing student interactions with generative AI, the research analyzes how such tools could support autonomous learning, particularly in technical subjects like computer science. The goal was to gain insights into whether generative AI could be an effective supplement or even an alternative to traditional learning models, and how it could be integrated into educational settings. The study also aimed to provide feedback on students' attitudes towards the use of AI for learning, including their levels of confidence, self-efficacy, and the impact on their learning outcomes.

METHODOLOGY

This research used a mixed-methods approach, combining quantitative and qualitative data collected with aim of exploring how students independently used generative AI tools for learning and to assess their experiences with these tools. The methodology involved two components, autonomous student assignments using AI tools, followed by a survey to gather detailed feedback on their experiences.

The research was conducted during the second semester of the 2023/2024 academic year and involved 89 students from the University of Zagreb, enrolled in the facultative *Computer Science* course. These students were selected as they were already familiar with basic AI concepts, which made them suitable candidates for evaluating the use of generative AI in independent learning. The knowledge about AI tools students gained during the classes of *Computer Science* course at university. The research was carried out in two phases, autonomous learning assignments (1) and post-assignment survey (2). During the autonomous learning assignments (1), students were assigned to independently learn new material using generative AI tools without direct teacher intervention. Prior to the assignment, students were given guidelines on how to use the AI tools, including instructions on how to interact with the AI to optimize learning outcomes, such as how to structure prompts and engage in effective dialogue with the tools. Each student was required to engage with the AI tools at home, using them to learn new topics related to the *Computer Science* course. The assignments were designed to challenge students to apply their knowledge and problem-solving skills, relying solely on the AI-generated content for guidance. The tasks involved a different learning exercise, including reading new concepts, solving problems, and completing exercises provided by teacher. Throughout the process, students were encouraged to document their interactions with the AI, including the prompts used and any feedback or insights they gained from the tool. This phase aimed to assess how well students could autonomously use AI to learn and comprehend new content and complete assignments. Student performance was evaluated based on the completion of these assignments and their ability to demonstrate understanding of the material through written responses and problem-solving tasks. After completing the assignments, the second phase post-assignment survey (2) started, where students participated in a survey designed to capture their experiences with generative AI tools. The survey was structured to collect both quantitative and qualitative data and included questions related to the aspects regarding the use of AI tools, the effectiveness of learning, challenges and limitations regarding the use of tools, autonomy and confidence and level of satisfaction. The complete survey can be found in section Appendix under Appendix A and an example of the used exercise under Appendix E.

Use of AI tools analyze how intuitive and user-friendly students found the generative AI tools. Learning effectiveness researchers students' perceptions of how effectively the AI tools helped them understand new material, compared to traditional learning methods. Challenges and limitations analyze whether were there any difficulties or limitations students encountered while using AI tools, such as technical issues, AI errors, or confusion about the content generated by the AI.

Autonomy and confidence were focused on the students' levels of confidence in using AI tools to learn independently. This set of questions was aimed at level of satisfaction and future use of AI tools where students' satisfaction with the experience and their interest in using generative AI for future learning was analyzed. The survey used a combination of Likert-scale questions, multiple-choice items, and open-ended questions to ensure an understanding of the students' experiences. Likert-scale questions measured students' attitudes and perceptions on a scale from 1 (strongly disagree) to 5 (strongly agree), while open-ended questions allowed students to elaborate on their experiences in greater detail.

DATA ANALYSIS

The data collected from the two phases was analyzed using quantitative and qualitative methods. The survey responses were statistically analyzed to identify trends and patterns in student experiences, such as the overall satisfaction with the AI tools, ease of use, and perceived learning effectiveness. Descriptive statistics, including mean scores and standard deviations, were calculated for Likert-scale responses, while frequency distributions were used for multiple-choice questions. Open-ended responses from the survey were analyzed using thematic analysis. This involved identifying key themes and recurring issues in students' descriptions of their experiences, such as common challenges and perceived benefits of AI. Student assignments were assessed based on predefined criteria, including the accuracy of responses, demonstration of understanding, and the quality of interaction with AI tools. This evaluation helped determine the extent to which students were able to effectively use AI to learn and apply new material.

The research was conducted in accordance with ethical guidelines for academic research. All participants were informed about the purpose of the study, the use of AI tools, and the nature of the data being collected. Participation was voluntary, and students were assured that their performance and survey responses would remain confidential. No sensitive personal data was collected during the study, and students had the option to withdraw from the research at any stage without any impact on their academic standing. While this research provides insights into the use of generative AI for independent learning, it is limited by its focus on a specific group of students within the *Computer Science* field. The results may not be fully generalizable to other subjects or educational contexts where AI tools might be used differently. Additionally, the study relies on self-reported data from students, which may be bias in how they perceive and report their experiences. This research methodology enabled exploration of how generative AI tools can be used for autonomous learning. By combining the evaluation of assignments with detailed survey responses, the study provided both objective and subjective insights into students' experiences and the potential of AI tools to improve and implement independent learning in higher education environment.

EXAMPLE OF EXERCISE

The exercises assigned to the students were designed to improve their understanding of basic Excel functions by using generative AI tools to research and learn about these functions. The tasks required students to independently learn how to use these functions and then apply them in practical examples, thus combining theory with hands-on application. The exercises were divided into two parts:

Part 1: Research and Description of Excel Functions

In the first part of the exercise, students were instructed to use the generative AI tool, according to their choice, to search for and gather information on the following Excel functions: SUM, SUMIF, COUNT, COUNTIF, MIN, MAX, AVERAGE, IF, and MODE. For each function, students were required to complete the following tasks:

- **Function Description**
- Students were asked to write a clear description of each function. This description had to explain what the function does, including its purpose and how it can be used in Excel. For example, the description for the SUM function would explain that it is used to add together a range of numbers or values.
- **Practical Examples**
- Students were then required to provide two practical examples for each function. These examples had to demonstrate real-world applications of the functions. For instance, for the SUM function, one example might be summing up the total sales for a week, and another example might involve calculating the total expenses for a budget.
- **Use of AI tools**
- Students were asked to include a note at the end of the document, indicating which AI tools they used.

Students were instructed to save this document as *functions_name_surname.docx*, ensuring their file was named appropriately for easy identification.

Part 2: Application of Knowledge to Excel Data

In the second part of the exercise, students were required to apply the knowledge they gained from the previous task to a dataset provided in the file *functions_tables.xlsx*. This file contained a set of data that would allow students to use the functions they had researched in practical scenarios.

The tasks for this part included:

- **Applying Functions to Data**

- Students were required to use the Excel functions they researched in the first part of the exercise on the dataset in the *functions_tables.xlsx* file. This could involve using the SUM function to calculate totals, the IF function to implement conditional logic, or the AVERAGE function to find the mean of a set of values, among other tasks.
- **Use of AI Tools for Assistance**
- Students were allowed to use AI tools to help them solve the tasks in this part of the exercise. This included using generative AI tools to generate ideas, troubleshoot, or find additional information on how to implement the functions in Excel.
- **Submission**
- Once students completed the tasks, they were instructed to save their file with the results, ensuring it was correctly formatted and used the Excel functions they had researched. This file had to be named according to the instructions to facilitate grading and feedback.

The combination of these two parts aimed to provide students with both theoretical knowledge and practical experience, reinforcing their learning of Excel functions through self-directed research and application. The exercises also encouraged the use of AI tools to support independent learning and problem-solving, reflecting real-world scenarios where AI can assist in enhancing productivity and understanding.

STUDENT EXPERIENCE IN USING AI TOOLS

Not all students participated in the second phase of the research, a post-assignment survey. Out of 89 students just 34 filled out the questionnaire.

All participants in the dataset belong to the age group of 18-22, making up 100% of the total respondents. In the research participated 94.12% females, 2.94% males and 2.94% clarified as other. Majority of students, 97.06% was at first year of study and 2.94% were at second year of study. The students were asked if they had ever used AI tools before this exercise, 76.47% responded yes and 23.53% responded no. The majority of students (76.47%) that used before this exercise some type of generative AI tools stated that they used it for finding information (73.08%), learning (23.08%) and personal purposes (3.85%).

Figure 1 shows the frequency of AI tool usage with students where it can be seen that the majority of participants, 41.18%, use AI tools once or twice a month. A significant portion, 29.41%, reported never using AI tools. About 20.59% use them once or twice a week, while a smaller group, 5.88%, use them several times a week. Only 2.94% of respondents indicated that they use AI tools every day. This suggests that while a large proportion of participants use AI tools occasionally, frequent daily use is relatively rare.

Figure 1. Frequency of use of AI tools

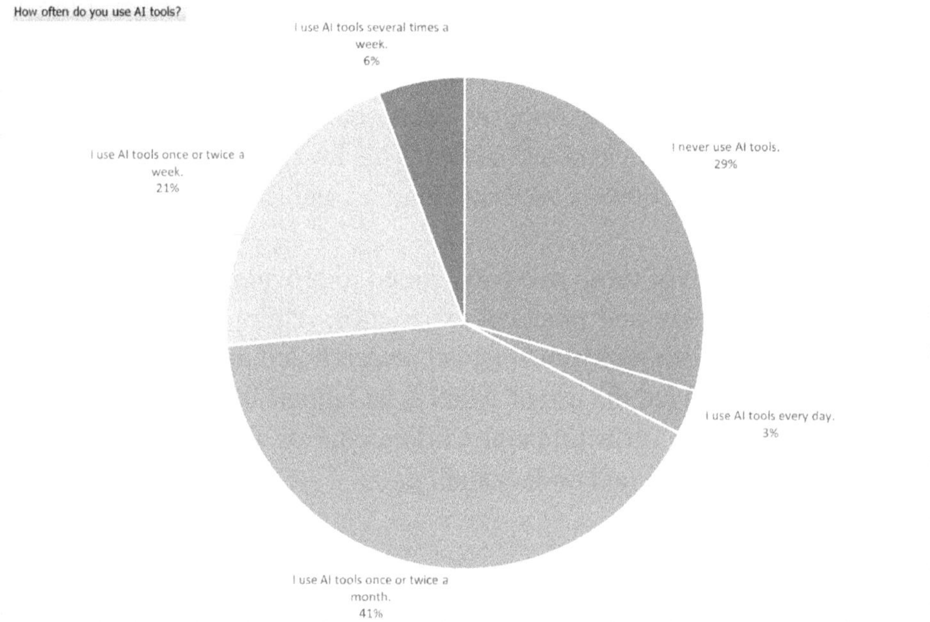

The distribution of AI tools used by participants reveals a strong preference for generative AI tool, ChatGPT. Around 11.76% of participants mentioned ChatGPT, indicating that it is the most popular and widely used tool. A smaller number of participants, approximately 2.94% each, referred to other AI tools such as My AI on Snapchat, Gemini, or Microsoft Copilot. Additionally, about 8.82% of respondents indicated they had not used any AI tools at all. ChatGPT stands out as the most recognized and commonly used AI tool among the participants.

The information gained for participants about success of mastering new material using AI tools shows that 47.06% of participants partially mastered the material. Additionally, 20.59% found some parts unclear, and another 20.59% reported completely mastering the material. However, 11.76% indicated that they did not master the material at all. This result suggests that most participants were able to understand the material to varying degrees, only a smaller portion fully mastered it using AI tools.

Figure 2 presents responses regarding the need for additional help from the teacher during the use of AI tool for learning new materials. The results shows that 67.65% of participants felt they required extra support, while 32.35% did not. This indicates that the majority of participants felt the need for teacher assistance when using AI tools.

Figure 2. Need for additional help from the teacher

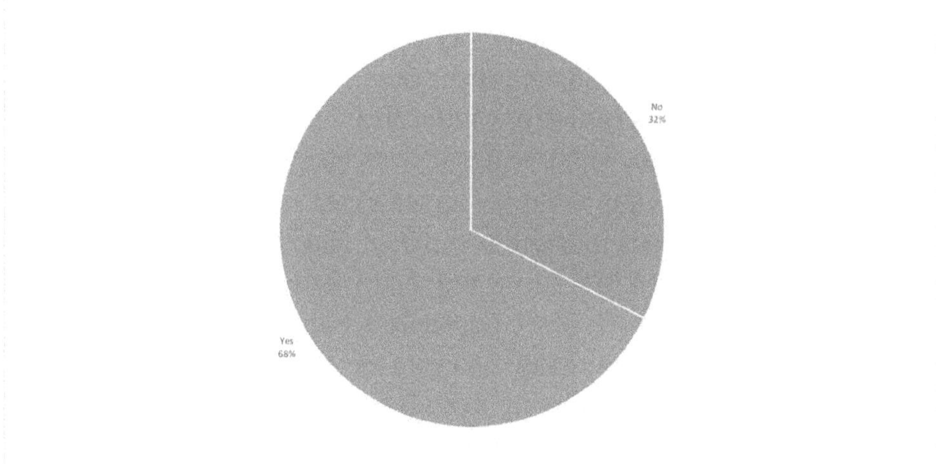

The distribution of responses regarding the clarity of the AI tool's instructions shows that 55.88% of participants found the instructions clear, while 11.76% found them completely clear. Additionally, 20.59% of participants were neutral, finding the instructions neither clear nor unclear. A small percentage, 8.82%, reported that the instructions were completely unclear, and 2.94% found them unclear. This shows that the majority of participants found the AI tool's instructions to be generally clear, with only a small portion expressing difficulty in understanding them. The willingness to use AI tools again for learning reveals that 79.41% of participants would consider using them again, while 20.59% would not. This indicates that a large majority of participants are open to continuing the use of AI tools for learning purposes. The use of AI tools as a helping tool during the process of solving tasks shows that 79.41% of participants would use AI tools again, while 20.59% would not. This indicates that a significant majority of participants are inclined to use AI tools for assistance with solving tasks in the future.

The level of satisfaction with the use of the AI tool for solving tasks shows that 47.06% of participants are satisfied, and an additional 20.59% are completely satisfied. Meanwhile, 20.59% remain neutral, while 5.88% are completely dissatisfied and another 5.88% are dissatisfied. This shows that the majority of participants are generally satisfied with the AI tool for solving tasks, although a small portion of participants expressed dissatisfaction.

The level of satisfaction with the use of the AI tool for mastering new material shows that 41.18% of participants were satisfied, and 17.65% were completely satisfied. Additionally, 29.41% of participants felt neutral about the tool's effectiveness. A smaller percentage, 5.88%, were completely dissatisfied, and another 5.88% were dissatisfied. This indicates that most participants were either satisfied or neutral about the AI tool's ability to help them master new material, with a smaller percentage expressed dissatisfaction.

The level of satisfaction with the explanations provided by the AI tool shows that 50.00% of participants were satisfied, and 26.47% were completely satisfied. Additionally, 14.71% felt neutral about the explanations, while 5.88% were dissatisfied, and 2.94% were completely dissatisfied. This indicates that a majority of participants were satisfied with the AI tool's explanations, with only a small percentage expressing dissatisfaction. The question regarding whether the AI tool helped participants solve tasks more easily shows that 44.12% participants agreed and 32.35% completely agreed. Additionally, 17.65% were neutral, while 5.88% completely disagreed. This indicates that the majority of participants found the AI tool helpful in solving tasks, with only a small part of them expressed disagreement. On the other hand, the question whether the AI tool helped participants better understand new material reveals that 44.12% participants agreed, and 20.59% completely agreed. In addition, 23.53% remained neutral, with 8.82% completely disagreeing and 2.94% disagreeing. This shows that a majority of participants found the AI tool helpful in understanding new material, although a smaller percentage expressed either disagreement or neutrality.

Figure 3 presents responses regarding whether the AI tool saved participants time and effort reveals a strong positive consensus. A combined 82.36% of respondents either completely agreed (41.18%) or agreed (41.18%) that the AI tool was effective in reducing the time and effort needed to complete tasks. This high percentage suggests that most participants found the tool beneficial in streamlining their work processes, potentially improving their productivity and efficiency.

Figure 3. Students' perception regarding the time and effort AI tool saves

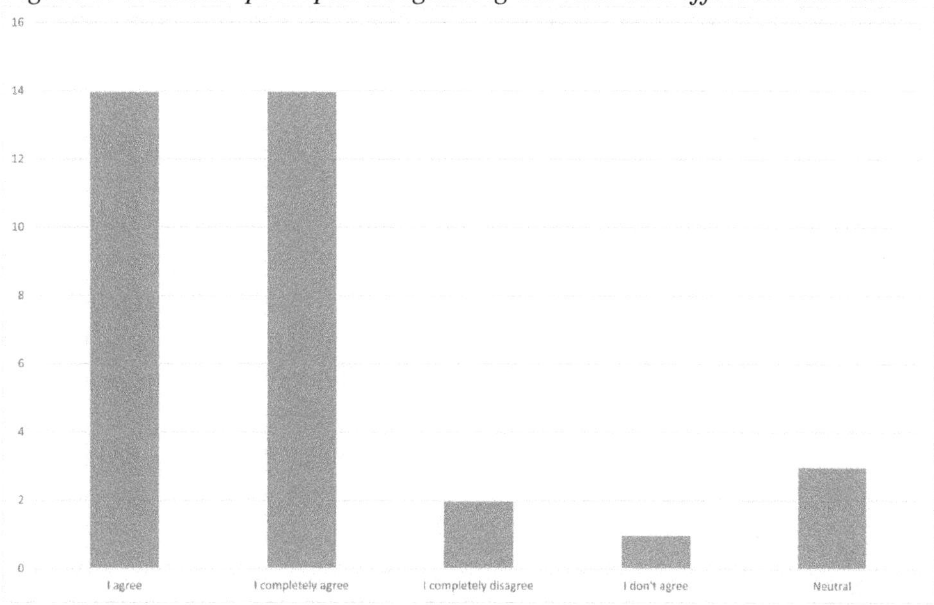

Meanwhile, 8.82% of participants felt neutral about the AI tool's impact on saving time and effort, indicating that while they didn't find the tool particularly time-saving, they also didn't feel it significantly hindered their efforts. On the other hand, a small portion of 5.88% participants completely disagreed and 2.94% disagreed, suggesting that for this subset, the AI tool either did not meet their expectations in terms of time-saving, or may have even required additional time and effort due to factors such as inefficiencies or misunderstandings in the tool's usage. The data shows a strong majority of participants who recognized the AI tool as a valuable resource for saving time and effort, with only a small fraction reporting negative experiences in this regard.

The ease of use of the AI tool shows that 44.12% of participants completely agreed and 41.18% agreed that the tool was easy to use. This means that a vast majority, totaling 85.30%, had a positive experience with the usability of the AI tool, indicating that it was intuitive and user-friendly for most users. A smaller portion, 8.82%, remained neutral, suggesting they neither found the tool particularly easy nor difficult to use, perhaps encountering some challenges but not significant enough to shift their opinion strongly.

Meanwhile, only 5.88% of participants completely disagreed, implying that this group faced considerable difficulties in using the AI tool. This group may have encountered issues such as a steep learning curve, unclear instructions, or technical challenges. The majority of participants found the AI tool easy to use, with only a small fraction of users having a less positive experience, highlighting the general effectiveness of the tool's design and functionality. Whether participants would recommend the AI tool to others shows that 44.12% agreed and 35.29% completely agreed, totaling nearly 80.41% of participants who would recommend the tool. This indicates strong support for the AI tool, with the majority of participants having had positive experiences and being confident enough in the tool's value to suggest it to others. A smaller group, 11.76%, remained neutral, suggesting that while these participants didn't find the tool problematic, they were not strongly compelled to recommend it, possibly due to a lack of standout features or mixed results in their own experience.

Meanwhile, a minor portion of participants, 5.88% disagreed and 2.94% completely disagreed, signaling dissatisfaction and reluctance to recommend the AI tool. These participants may have encountered challenges, technical issues, or found the tool ineffective in addressing their needs.

The majority of participants expressed willingness to recommend the AI tool, reflecting a generally positive perception, while only a small percentage of participants were either neutral or opposed to recommending it.

Figure 19 shows responses regarding whether the AI tool helped participants feel confident in their knowledge. The results shows that 47.06% of participants were neutral on this aspect, suggesting that nearly half of the respondents did not experience a significant shift in their confidence due to the AI tool.

However, 20.59% agreed that the AI tool helped them feel more confident, and 8.82% completely agreed, indicating that nearly 30% of participants did feel an increase in confidence after using the tool. On the other hand, 14.71%

disagreed, and 8.82% completely disagreed, suggesting that around 23.53% of participants felt that the AI tool did not contribute to their confidence in their knowledge, possibly due to challenges in understanding or relying on the tool's output.

While some participants experienced increased confidence in their knowledge thanks to the AI tool, a significant portion remained neutral, indicating that the tool's impact on confidence was not strongly felt by many.

Figure 4. Level of confidence in students' knowledge

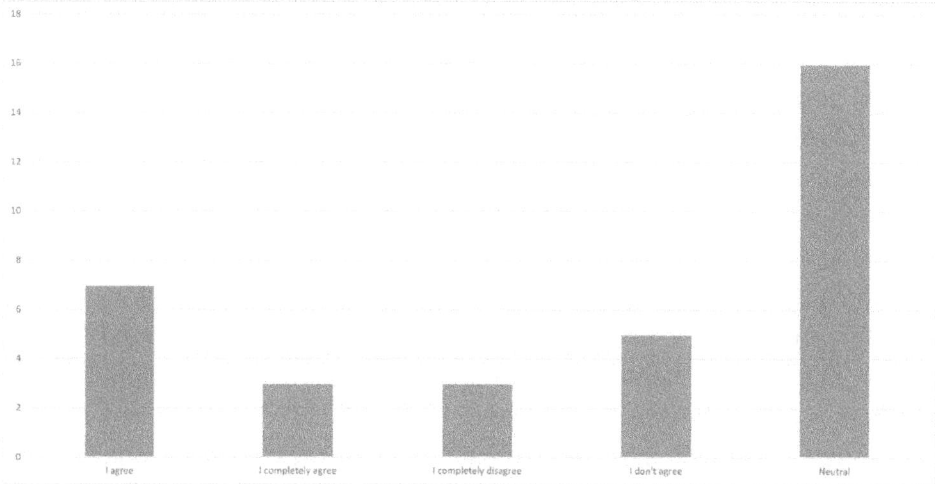

Whether the AI tool helped participants understand the concept of tasks shows that 52.94% agreed, and an additional 11.76% completely agreed, indicating that a combined 64.7% of participants found the tool helpful in grasping task concepts. This suggests that the majority of participants benefited from the AI tool in understanding the tasks they were working on.

A smaller portion, 20.59%, remained neutral, suggesting that while these participants did not find the AI tool unhelpful, they also did not find it significantly impactful in enhancing their understanding.

On the other hand, 8.82% completely disagreed and 5.88% disagreed, making up about 14.7% of participants who felt that the AI tool did not assist them in understanding the task concepts.

The majority of participants found the AI tool helpful for understanding tasks, while a smaller group either felt neutral or disagreed with this sentiment.

The distribution of responses regarding the intention to use AI tools for solving tasks in the future shows that 38.24% of participants agreed and 26.47% completely agreed, meaning that a combined 64.71% are inclined to continue using AI tools for task-solving. This reflects a strong interest among the majority of participants in relying on AI tools for future tasks.

Meanwhile, 17.65% of participants expressed neutrality, indicating they may be undecided or indifferent about using AI tools in the future.

On the other hand, 14.71% completely disagreed and 2.94% disagreed, representing a smaller group, about 17.65%—who do not plan to use AI tools for solving tasks in the future, possibly due to unsatisfactory experiences or a preference for other methods.

The majority of participants are open to using AI tools for solving tasks in the future, though a smaller group remains neutral or disagrees with this approach. Whether the AI tool helped participants develop problem-solving skills shows a mixed range of opinions. A significant portion, 35.29%, remained neutral, suggesting that many participants did not have a strong opinion on the AI tool's impact on their problem-solving skills. Meanwhile, 26.47% agreed and 11.76% completely agreed, indicating that around 38.23% of participants felt the AI tool had a positive impact on developing their problem-solving abilities. On the other hand, 14.71% disagreed and 11.76% completely disagreed, making up about 26.47% of respondents who felt that the AI tool did not help them improve their problem-solving skills.

The responses show that opinions are somewhat divided, with a considerable portion feeling neutral, while others either positively or negatively assessed the AI tool's influence on their problem-solving skills. Whether the AI tool allowed participants to customize their learning approach shows a range of perspectives. While 26.47% agreed and 17.65% completely agreed, together accounting for 44.12% of participants who found the tool helpful in tailoring their learning to their needs, 32.35% participants remained neutral. This suggests that many participants did not feel strongly one way or the other about the tool's ability to support personalized learning. On the other hand, 14.71% disagreed and 8.82% completely disagreed, meaning that about 23.53% of respondents felt that the AI tool did not effectively help them customize their learning approach. While a part of participants found the AI tool useful for personalizing their learning experience, a significant number were neutral, and a smaller group expressed disagreement, reflecting a diversity of opinions on the tool's ability to meet individual learning needs.

Regarding the correct and incorrect information gained from AI tools shows that most participants did not believe this was an issue. A combined 44.12% disagreed and 17.65% completely disagreed, indicating that over 61.77% of participants felt the AI tool generally provided correct examples. However, 23.53% of participants remained neutral, suggesting that a one part of the participants were unsure or indifferent about the accuracy of the examples provided by the tool. On the other hand, 11.76% agreed and 2.94% completely agreed, meaning that around 14.7% of participants encountered incorrect examples from the AI tool. The majority of participants did not experience issues with incorrect examples, though a smaller portion expressed neutrality or agreement that inaccuracies occurred.

The percentage breakdown of responses to the statement "Additional interpretation of information was needed for clearer understanding of AI content" reveals that 32.35% agreed, indicating that about a third of participants felt the AI content required further interpretation for clarity. Additionally, 14.71% strongly agreed, bringing the total to nearly 47.06% of respondents who believed more interpretation was necessary. On the other hand, 23.53% disagreed, and 8.82% strongly disagreed, totaling 32.35% of participants who felt that the AI content was sufficiently clear without the need for extra explanation. Meanwhile, 20.59% remained neutral, suggesting that this group did not have a strong opinion on whether additional interpretation was necessary. While nearly half of the respondents felt that further interpretation was needed to better understand the AI content, a significant portion either disagreed or were neutral on the matter.

The response distribution reflects a strong overall confidence in the AI tool's accuracy. Around 76.47% participants, did not believe the tool provided incorrect information, with a significant portion actively disagreeing (44.12%) and strongly disagreeing (32.35%) with the idea that the AI generated errors. This suggests that, for most users, the AI tool was seen as a reliable source of information. However, a smaller segment of users had different experiences. Approximately 11.76% agreed that the AI tool gave them incorrect information. This group likely encountered errors in the content generated by the tool, such as factual inaccuracies or misleading outputs. Another 11.76% of participants were neutral, which could indicate uncertainty about the AI's accuracy or infrequent use of the tool, making it difficult for them to assess whether the information was reliable. While most participants trusted the AI tool and felt it provided accurate information, a small portion either experienced issues with incorrect outputs or were uncertain about its reliability. This suggests that while the AI tool is generally effective, there may still be occasional inaccuracies that affect a minority of participants' experiences.

The data shows that 61.76% of participants did not need to use additional sources to interpret the answers and guidelines provided by the AI tool, indicating that for the majority, the AI's explanations were clear and sufficient on their own. However, a 38.24% of respondents found it necessary to consult other sources to better understand the AI's output. This suggests that while the AI tool was generally effective in providing understandable guidance, a significant portion of participants felt that it lacked clarity or completeness at times, prompting them to seek further information elsewhere. This group may have encountered explanations or guidelines from the AI that were either too vague, technical, or incomplete, necessitating additional support to fully comprehend the material.

While most participants could rely on the AI tool without outside help, a minority needed supplementary resources to make sense of the AI's responses, highlighting room for improvement in the clarity of its outputs. The unique reasons provided by respondents for using other sources to interpret the AI tool's responses highlight several recurring issues (Table 1). A significant number of participants cited unclear or vague responses from the AI, leading them to seek additional clarification. Some felt the AI tool's explanations were either overly complex or not specific enough for their needs, prompting them to turn to other resources, such as Google, for clearer or more straightforward guidance.

Accuracy concerns also played a role, with several users indicating that the AI provided incorrect or imprecise answers, which required verification through other sources. In some cases, respondents used additional resources to check the correctness of the AI's outputs, reflecting a lack of full trust in the tool's reliability. Translation issues, particularly with AI tools not fully developed in the Croatian language, such as Gemini, were another factor. Some participants noted that poor translations made it difficult to understand the AI's responses, compelling them to seek alternative explanations. The main reasons for using other sources were related to the AI tool's limitations in clarity, accuracy, and language translation, all of which linger participants' ability to fully rely on the tool without external assistance.

Table 1. Participants comments about using additional tools for better interpretation of the generative AI responses

Question: Did you have to use other sources to interpret the AI tool's answers and guidance? If yes, what is the reason for using other sources?
RESPONSES
Sometimes unclear responses from the AI tool.
Because the AI tool didn't provide accurate answers.
Unclear explanation.
More specific explanation.
Uncertainty
Used other sources when the AI tool's guidance was unclear or presented a more complicated way of solving the task.
Poor translation into Croatian by AI tools that aren't fully developed (e.g., Gemini).
Inaccurate or unclear response.

Future use of AI tools in this part shows that 76.47% of participants expressed a willingness to use the AI tool in the future, indicating strong overall interest in continuing to rely on the tool. This significant majority reflects positive experiences or perceptions of the AI tool's usefulness in tasks or learning. Meanwhile, 11.76% of participants were unsure, suggesting that this group may have had mixed experiences with the tool, leading to uncertainty about its future value for them. Similarly, 11.76% stated that they would not use the tool again, likely due to dissatisfaction with its performance, accuracy, or ease of use. The majority of participants are inclined to use the AI tool moving forward, although a small portion remains undecided or unwilling, likely based on varying levels of satisfaction with the tool's functionality.

It is evident that most participants used the AI tool with moderate frequency. Both "Sometimes" and "Often" received equal responses at 32.35% each, indicating that a large portion of respondents relied on the AI tool fairly regularly while solving tasks.

Meanwhile, 23.53% reported using the tool "Rarely," suggesting occasional use, while 8.82% never used the tool, and only 2.94% always used it. This indicates that while the AI tool was a useful resource for many, continuous or consistent reliance on it was less common, with most participants turning to the tool on a periodic basis. The majority of participants used the AI tool with moderate regularity, with only a small percentage either never or always using it. This suggests that while the tool was integrated into task-solving for many, it was not an indispensable part of their process for all users. A significant majority of participants found the AI tool to be reliable in solving tasks. Specifically, 61.76% indicated that the AI tool was "Mostly accurate," while an additional 17.65% found it "Often accurate," and 14.71% reported it to be "Always accurate." This means that more than 94% of respondents viewed the tool as generally dependable in terms of accuracy. In contrast, only a small portion of participants, 2.94% each, found the tool "Sometimes accurate" or "Rarely accurate," indicating that only a minority had concerns about the tool's reliability.

Most participants found the AI tool to be consistently accurate in solving tasks, with very few expressing doubts about its precision. This shows the tool's general effectiveness in providing correct solutions for the majority of users. The majority of participants found the AI tool to be dependable for providing accurate information when learning new material. Specifically, 52.94% indicated the tool was "Mostly reliable," while 26.47% found it "Often reliable," and 11.76% described it as "Always reliable." This suggests that more than 90% of respondents viewed the AI tool as generally trustworthy for learning purposes. A smaller portion of participants, 5.88%, found the tool only "Sometimes reliable," and 2.94% viewed it as "Rarely reliable," indicating that a minority encountered issues with its accuracy when learning new material. Most participants considered the AI tool to be a reliable source for accurate information, with only a small fraction expressing concerns about its dependability for learning.

The comments provided by participants offer a diverse range of perspectives on the use of AI tools in education. Many participants highlighted the positive aspects of AI, its ability to quickly provide information, save time, and clarify previously explained concepts. For instance, several respondents noted that AI tools are particularly helpful for reviewing material and getting quick answers, eliminating the need for extensive searches across various sources. However, there were also reservations. Some participants expressed concerns about the potential for over-reliance on AI, which could diminish student effort, lead to laziness, or result in academic dishonesty, such as copying and cheating. This sentiment reflects a worry that AI tools may offer too much convenience, undermining the deeper learning process. Many participants acknowledged the value of AI as a supplement to traditional teaching rather than a replacement. Several comments suggested that AI tools should be used alongside teacher guidance, with lectures and human interaction remaining essential for a full understanding of the material. There was a general consensus that while AI can assist in learning, teacher explanations are often clearer and more effective in mastering new content. Some users also pointed out the need for further improvements in AI tools, particularly in translation and user-friendliness, with Gemini AI receiving specific criticism compared to ChatGPT. Additionally, a few respondents mentioned the mixed emotions they experience when using AI tools, feeling guilty about taking an "easier" route that requires less effort.

These comments reflect a balanced view of AI in education, it's seen as a valuable tool for efficiency and clarification, but there are concerns about dependency, the potential for academic dishonesty, and the ongoing importance of human teachers in the learning process. The comments are divided into 3 categories, positive, negative, and neutral (Table 2).

Table 2. Participants comments related to the use of AI tools in teaching

Positive Comments	Negative Comments	Neutral Comments
It's excellent for recalling concepts that have been explained before; if a part of the material is unclear, AI is the quickest way to explain it. I mostly use it to save time from searching for the same data on websites.	Honestly, I don't support the use of AI tools for many reasons and believe it would be better not to implement them in teaching.	I think AI was helpful, but lectures (teacher explanations) would help more in better understanding the material. Perhaps the best option would be to hold a lecture first, and only after that, give assignments where AI can be used if something isn't clear.
I recommend using it with appropriate guidance from the teacher. First work with the teacher, then use AI for assignments.	It's quick and simple to get answers, but it can lead to copying and cheating in class.	A new and interesting way of learning, but the highest quality explanations and guidance for mastering new content still come from teacher lectures.
I think it's a really good learning aid because we can quickly access necessary information without spending time searching and reading through various sources.	Useful, but I wouldn't recommend introducing it fully.	I think introducing AI to help with material is a good idea, but personally, I still need additional help from teachers.

continued on following page

Table 2. Continued

Positive Comments	Negative Comments	Neutral Comments
Quick and accurate answers, so you don't have to Google and search for information.	I still feel some guilt when using it because I know I'm using an easier way, putting in less effort, and it makes me feel lazy and somewhat less intelligent.	I believe it was useful, but teacher explanations clarify the material much better.
I think it can greatly contribute during learning as it saves students a lot of time.	Gemini AI was made with good intentions, but there's still a lot to improve.	
It makes learning easier and quicker to find answers.		
Fast and simple.		

Based on the comments from respondents, the key challenges with AI tools in educational settings can be summarized into 6 categories, over-reliance on AI and reduced effort (1), lack of human interaction (2), inaccuracies of information (3), risk of cheating and academic dishonesty (4), challenges with AI in local contexts (5), and complexity and usability issues (6).

Over-Reliance on AI and Reduced Effort (1)

Some respondents expressed concerns that AI tools make it too easy to find information, potentially leading to a decrease in personal effort, learning motivation, and critical thinking skills. One respondent mentioned feeling guilty about relying on AI, as it made them "lazy" and less involved in the learning process.

Lack of Human Interaction (2)

Several comments indicated that AI tools, while helpful, cannot fully replace teacher explanations. Respondents often mentioned that the most effective learning still comes from teacher-led lectures and personalized guidance, with AI serving as a supplementary tool rather than a primary resource.

Inaccuracies of information (3)

Some users noted that AI occasionally provides incorrect or unclear answers, prompting them to seek additional sources like Google. This can lead to confusion and reliance on other resources to clarify AI-generated content.

Risk of Cheating and Academic Dishonesty (4)

A few respondents highlighted the potential for AI tools to be misused for copying and cheating, particularly in educational settings. The concern is that ease of access to answers could undermine students' learning integrity.

Challenges With AI in Local Contexts (5)

Specific issues with AI tools translating poorly into the Croatian language (for example, Gemini AI) were mentioned. These respondents felt that such tools are not fully developed or optimized for their linguistic and educational needs.

Complexity and Usability Issues (6)

While many found AI tools quick and easy to use, others preferred certain tools (like ChatGPT) over others due to usability differences. One respondent explicitly mentioned that Gemini AI has room for improvement compared to other tools.

These challenges highlight the need for careful integration of AI tools in education, ensuring that they complement human teaching rather than fully replacing it, and addressing concerns about accuracy, usability, and ethical use.

In addition, respondents' comments highlights also the benefits of AI tools in education which cover several elements, time-saving, access to information, support, ease of use revision of materials, accessibility, personalization, reduced dependence on search engines, and new learning methods and approaches.

Time-Saving

Many respondents highlighted how AI tools help save time by quickly providing answers or explanations, which reduces the need to search through multiple sources like books or websites. This efficiency allows students to focus on understanding the material rather than spending time gathering it.

Quick Access to Information

AI tools are praised for their ability to provide fast responses to questions and clarify difficult concepts. Respondents appreciated the instant access to relevant information, which aids in learning without delays.

Support in Understanding Complex Topics

AI tools were noted to help students grasp complex or previously unclear topics, especially when they need quick clarification outside of class. This makes AI a valuable resource for reinforcing or revisiting concepts taught by teachers.

Ease of Use

Many students found AI tools easy and intuitive to use. The simplicity of accessing information without complicated processes was a key factor that made AI tools appealing in educational contexts.

Revision

Some respondents used AI tools to refresh their memory on previously covered material. This function of AI as a supplementary learning aid helped them recall terms and concepts efficiently.

Accessibility

AI tools provide a flexible learning option, allowing students to use them anytime and anywhere. This is especially useful for self-study or when additional help is not immediately available from teachers.

Personalization

AI tools allow students to tailor their learning experience to their own needs, adapting the level of detail or type of information they require. This can lead to more personalized and effective study sessions.

Reduced Dependence on Search Engines

Instead of manually searching for information across multiple websites, AI tools compile relevant information in one place. This reduces the need to rely on search engines like Google and makes the learning process more focused and streamlined.

New Learning Approaches

Some respondents saw AI as a novel and interesting approach to learning. The innovation that AI brings to education makes learning more engaging and encourages students to explore new ways of interacting with educational content.

AI tools are appreciated for their ability to save time, provide quick and clear information, help with revision, and offer a flexible and personalized learning experience.

RESEARCH ANALYSIS

This section presents a detailed analysis of the responses gathered from students regarding the use of AI tools in an educational setting. The primary focus of the analysis is on how students perceive the effectiveness, reliability, and usability of AI tools for solving tasks and learning new materials. The results were obtained from a survey designed to capture their experiences and attitudes toward AI's role in their learning process. The interpretation of the results is divided into 7 categories, perceptions of AI for learning new materials (1), perceptions of AI for solving tasks (2), reliability of AI in providing accurate information (3), ease of use of AI tools (4), students' overall preferences (5), challenges and concerns with AI tools (6) and benefits of AI tools in education (7).

Perceptions of AI for Learning New Materials (1)

One of the aspects of the survey involved assessing how effective students believe AI tools are in helping them learn new materials. When asked whether AI helped them better understand new content, 44.12% of students agreed, and 20.59% strongly agreed, indicating that a significant portion of the student body sees value in AI for learning new material. However, a considerable number of students (23.53%) were neutral, neither agreeing nor disagreeing with the statement. This neutrality suggests that while many students find AI helpful in understanding new concepts, a large group remains undecided, indicating that AI's role in this domain is not yet fully established in their learning process. On the other end, 8.82% strongly disagreed and 2.94% disagreed with the statement, indicating that a minority of students do not perceive AI as a beneficial tool for learning new materials. This group may find AI lacking in depth, clarity, or adaptability to their specific learning needs, highlighting a potential area for improvement in AI tools aimed at educational content delivery.

Perceptions of AI for Solving Tasks (2)

When it comes to solving tasks, the data suggests that students perceive AI as more effective in this area than in learning new materials. 44.12% of students agreed that AI helped them solve tasks more easily, while 32.35% strongly agreed. This higher rate of strong agreement compared to learning new material indicates a stronger preference for AI when it comes to task-oriented activities. The relatively lower percentage of neutral responses (17.65%) further supports the view that students are more decisive about AI's utility in this domain. Moreover, only 5.88% of participants strongly disagreed with the statement, suggesting that most students find AI useful in completing their assignments. The positive response reflects AI's potential to support students in practical problem-solving and immediate task execution, areas where it excels due to its efficiency in generating solutions and saving time.

Reliability of AI in Providing Accurate Information (3)

Reliability is a one of the factors in determining the effectiveness of AI tools in education. When asked if AI provided reliable information for learning new material, the majority of students responded positively, with 52.94% agreeing that AI was mostly reliable, and 26.47% feeling it was often reliable. This suggests that nearly 80% of participants believe AI tools can generally be trusted to provide accurate information for learning purposes. However, only 11.76% of students strongly agreed that AI was always reliable, reflecting some hesitation to fully trust AI-generated content without question. On the other hand, 5.88% of respondents felt that AI was only sometimes reliable, and 2.94% rated it as rarely reliable. These responses highlight a smaller group of students who may have encountered inaccuracies or inconsistencies when using AI tools. This underscores the importance of continuous improvements in AI algorithms, particularly in ensuring content accuracy and clarity, especially for subjects that require deep conceptual understanding and human intervention with fact checking.

Ease of Use of AI Tools (4)

Ease of use is a one of the advantages of AI tools in education, and this was reflected in the survey results. 52.94% of students found the AI tool very easy to use, and 41.18% rated it as easy to use, indicating a strong preference for AI tools based on their user-friendliness. Only 5.88% of students felt neutral about the ease of use, with no negative responses recorded in this category. This positive reception suggests that AI tools are accessible and intuitive, enabling students to focus more on learning and task completion rather than struggling with complex interfaces or workflows.

Students' Overall Preferences (5)

The comparative analysis of students' responses reveals that AI tools are more favored for task-solving than for learning new material. When asked whether AI helped them solve tasks, 32.35% of students strongly agreed, compared to 20.59% who strongly agreed that AI helped them learn new content. Similarly, fewer students remained neutral or disagreed about AI's effectiveness for task-solving than for learning. This indicates a clear preference for using AI tools in more practical, exercise-based learning environments, where quick, accurate solutions are needed. In contrast, students were more cautious about AI's role in helping them understand new materials, possibly due to the more abstract and complex nature of such content.

Challenges With AI Tools (6)

While the majority of students responded positively about AI's role in their learning, several challenges were noted. Some students expressed concerns about the accuracy of AI tools, particularly when dealing with more conceptual or theoretical content. A small group of students felt that AI occasionally provided unclear or incorrect answers, which could linger their learning process rather than support it. Additionally, concerns about over-reliance on AI, leading to a reduction in personal effort and critical thinking, were mentioned in the comments. Another concern raised by students was the risk of academic dishonesty, with some feeling that AI tools made it too easy to copy answers rather than engage with the material fully. This highlights a need for teachers and educators to create guidelines on how AI should be used ethically within the learning environment.

Benefits of AI Tools (7)

Despite the challenges, students clearly see significant benefits in using AI tools, particularly in terms of efficiency and time-saving. Many respondents appreciated the speed with which AI could provide answers or explanations, reducing the need to search for information across multiple sources. The ability to use AI tools for revision or as a supportive resource along with traditional teaching methods, e.g. presentation, textbook, etc. was also an advantage noted by students.

Students' Perception of AI Tools for Learning New Materials and Solving Exercises

Based on the analysis of the survey responses, it is evident that students perceive AI tools as being slightly more effective for solving exercises than for learning new materials.

When asked if AI helped them solve tasks more easily, 32.35% of participants strongly agreed, and 44.12% agreed, showing that a significant portion of students found AI highly useful for this purpose. In comparison, only 20.59% strongly agreed that AI helped them better understand new material, while 44.12% agreed. This suggests that a majority of students recognize the value of AI in learning new content, the enthusiasm for its use in task-solving is notably higher.

Neutral responses were more common when it came to learning new material, with 23.53% of students remaining neutral on AI's effectiveness in this area, compared to 17.65% neutrality for task-solving. This indicates that a larger group of students may still be undecided about how beneficial AI is for understanding new concepts compared to using it for exercises.

Additionally, there was more disagreement regarding the role of AI in learning new materials (8.82% strongly disagreed and 2.94% disagreed) than in solving tasks (5.88% strongly disagreed).

Students generally find AI tools useful for both purposes, the data suggests that AI is perceived as more effective for solving tasks than for learning new materials, with a higher proportion of strong agreement for exercises and fewer disagreements overall. This indicates that students might see AI as a valuable tool for practical applications and problem-solving rather than for acquiring new theoretical knowledge. This suggests that AI tools are currently perceived as better suited to helping with specific, task-oriented learning rather than more complex, conceptual education.

Students' Perceptions of the Reliability of AI Tools

Based on the survey data, students' perceptions of the reliability of AI tools in providing accurate information for learning new material reveal a generally positive outlook, though with some variation in confidence levels. The majority of respondents (52.94%) agreed that the AI tool was mostly reliable in providing accurate information, and an additional 26.47% felt that it was often reliable. This suggests that approximately 79.41% of students believe that AI tools can generally be trusted to deliver accurate information, indicating strong overall confidence in AI reliability. However, a smaller portion of respondents were more cautious or critical. Only 11.76% of students strongly agreed that AI was always reliable, reflecting some hesitancy about complete trust in AI for accuracy. Additionally, 5.88% of respondents felt that AI was only sometimes reliable, while 2.94% rated it as rarely reliable.

Students feel that AI tools are dependable, there is still a notable group who remain uncertain or skeptical about the consistent accuracy of AI in learning contexts. This suggests that while AI tools are broadly seen as reliable, further improvements in accuracy or clearer guidance on when to trust AI-generated content may be needed to build stronger confidence among all students.

Comparison of Responses for AI Tool's Opportunities

Comparison of the results for the areas, the AI tool's impact on confidence in knowledge, understanding of tasks, development of problem-solving skills, and adaptability of the learning method provide insights into how users perceive the utility and effectiveness of the AI tool in various aspects of learning. Figure 5 shows the comparison results.

Figure 5. Comparison of responses for AI tool's effectiveness

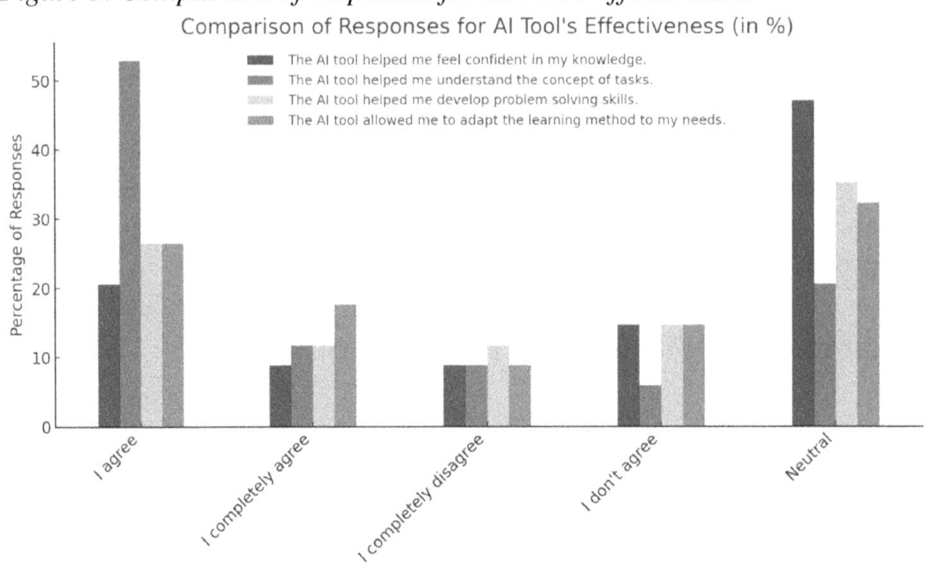

The results show that while a major part of students responded positively, the distribution indicates that confidence-building through the AI tool is somewhat lower compared to other metrics. A moderate percentage of respondents agreed that the tool helped them feel confident, but it's evident that the sentiment wasn't overwhelmingly strong. This suggests that while the AI tool may assist in knowledge acquisition, it does not consistently provide users with the assurance or certainty they seek in mastering material. The ability of the AI tool to induce confidence appears to be behind other strengths, indicating that users may need additional enhancement or validation of learning results.

In contrast to confidence in knowledge, the AI tool's ability to help users understand tasks was the strongest area, with the highest percentage of positive responses. The Figure 20 indicates that a large proportion of users found the AI tool highly effective in breaking down and clarifying task-related concepts. This aspect of the AI tool is particularly notable as it shows that it excels in task-related guidance, likely providing clear instructions and examples. Compared to the other areas, the percentage of strong agreement is significantly higher, suggesting that this is where the AI tool provides the most immediate and tangible value to users.

The AI tool's effectiveness in developing problem-solving skills presents a more balanced set of responses. While a number of participants acknowledged that the tool aided in this area, the distribution was more evenly spread, with fewer participants expressing strong agreement compared to task understanding. This suggests that while the AI tool does offer some support in enhancing problem-solving abilities, it is not perceived as a primary strength. The percentage of positive responses in this category is lower than for understanding tasks, implying that users may not feel the tool fully prepares them to approach complex problems independently or adaptively.

The AI tool's ability to allow users to tailor the learning method to their individual needs is another area where responses were mostly positive, though not as concentrated as for task comprehension. A solid percentage of users agreed that the tool offers some level of customization or adaptability, but the spread of responses indicates that there may be limitations in how flexibly the AI tool can adjust to diverse learning styles. The lower percentage of strong agreement, when compared to task understanding, suggests that while the tool has some capacity for adaptation, it may not fully meet the unique requirements of all users. This indicates a potential area for improvement in making the tool more responsive to individual learning preferences. In comparing the four areas, it is clear that task understanding is the strongest metric, with the highest percentage of users reporting positive experiences. The AI tool is particularly effective at helping users navigate and comprehend tasks, which might be due to the clarity of its instructions and examples. On the other hand, confidence in knowledge is where the AI tool appears to have the least impact, with a relatively lower percentage of users expressing strong confidence in their knowledge after using the tool. This suggests that while the AI helps users understand concepts, it may not reinforce them enough to build lasting confidence. Problem-solving skills and adaptability to learning methods fall in between these two extremes. The AI tool provides moderate support in enhancing problem-solving abilities, but it is not as highly regarded as its capacity for explaining tasks. Similarly, while the tool offers some level of adaptability, the percentage of strong agreement in this category is lower, indicating room for improvement in personalization features. According to data the AI tool's strongest suit is in helping users understand tasks, but it could improve in providing confidence and better supporting personalized learning and problem-solving skill development. The percentage distribution across these four metrics shows that an AI tool is effective in instructional clarity but could benefit from enhancements in its adaptive learning capabilities and confidence-building mechanisms.

CONCLUSION

This research provides into the 4 research questions. For research question (1) to what extent do AI tools improve the understanding of new concepts compared to traditional learning methods, results revealed that AI tools offer certain advantages, particularly in efficiency and ease of access to information, their ability to improve the understanding of new concepts is somewhat limited compared to traditional learning methods. A significant portion of students (64.71%) found AI tools helpful for understanding new material, with 20.59% strongly agreeing that AI tools helped their understanding. However, there remained a considerable group (23.53%) who were neutral, suggesting uncertainty about AI's effectiveness for deeper learning and understanding. Students often found AI tools more effective in task-solving and practical exercises, but when it came to learning complex, theoretical concepts, many still preferred traditional teacher-led instruction. Students thought that teacher explanations were more comprehensive, and they felt that AI tools sometimes lacked the depth required for full understanding of new lessons. This points to a gap in how AI tools support conceptual understanding compared to the traditional methods. AI tools can supplement traditional learning by providing quick answers and reinforcing previously taught material, they are not yet viewed as a sufficient replacement for traditional methods when it comes to fully understanding new and complex learning concepts. The integration of AI tools should be complementary, supporting but not replacing the role of teachers in learning.

For research question (2) refereeing to the benefits, challenges, and limitations students experience when using AI tools independently for learning, students reported that AI tools provided significant benefits in terms of efficiency, accessibility, and ease of use. A large proportion of students appreciated quick access to information and the ability to solve tasks faster, reducing the time spent searching for content across multiple web sources. Students thought that AI tools were flexible, allowing them to learn at their own pace and revisit unclear concepts outside of the classroom setting. Many found the tools useful for reinforcing previously taught material, enabling a more personalized learning experience. However, the research also highlighted several challenges regarding the use of generative AI tools. One of the main issues students faced was the lack of clarity and depth in AI-generated responses, particularly when learning new concepts. While AI was effective for practical tasks and exercises, sometimes did not provide students with comprehensive explanations what lead to confusion. Many students expressed a need for additional teacher support when using AI tools, indicating that AI alone was insufficient for independent learning of more abstract topics. Additionally, some students raised concerns about the risk of over-reliance on AI, which could reduce personal effort, critical thinking, and engagement with the material. There were also ethical concerns, as AI made it easier to copy answers without fully engaging in the learning process and understand the content provided. Language and localization challenges, such as poor translations in non-English environment, also impacted the learning experience for some students. In this research AI tools offer benefits in terms of efficiency and task-solving, their limitations in clarity, depth, and reliability, particularly for independent learning. This suggest that they are best used as complementary to traditional teaching methods. These tools can support learning but are not yet capable of fully replacing the need for human guidance in education.

The research question (3) regarding how AI tools impact students' confidence and self-efficacy in learning the results of the research demonstrates that the use of AI tools has a mixed impact on students' confidence and self-efficacy in learning. AI tools are considered useful for solving tasks and strengthening the understanding of learning materials, but their impact on students' confidence in the learning of new concepts is less evident. A significant portion of students (47.06%) remained neutral when asked whether AI tools improved their confidence in their knowledge, indicating that AI helped them complete tasks, it did not consistently boost their sense of mastery over the material. About 29.41% of students felt that using AI tools did increase their confidence, with 20.59% agreeing and 8.82% strongly agreeing. However, 23.53% reported that AI tools did not contribute to their confidence, with some students expressing concerns over the accuracy and depth of the AI-generated content. Students think that the AI provided them with support in task-solving because it often make clear to them certain aspects of their assignments which allow them to complete tasks more easily. However, when it came to more complex learning or understanding new material in depth, students were less likely to feel confident relying solely on AI, often seeking additional help from teachers. AI tools can enhance students' confidence in completing practical tasks and solving problems, their impact on broader learning self-efficacy is limited. For long-term confidence and mastery of complex subjects, students still prefer the guidance by teachers that suggests that AI should be used as a supportive tool rather than a primary resource for building self-efficacy in learning.

The research question (4) examined can AI tools effectively supplement traditional learning models. In this research the focus was put on technical subjects like computer science. The results of the research indicate that AI tools can effectively supplement traditional learning models in technical subjects like computer science, but it is best used as a complementary resource than a replacement for traditional methods. AI tools proved to be highly beneficial in task-oriented activities such as solving problems, applying concepts, and reinforcing learning through practical examples. Students found AI tools useful for quickly accessing information and completing exercises. AI tools were helpful for reinforcing what teachers had already taught students but were not perceived as sufficient on their own to teach students new concepts.

The research highlighted the need for a balanced integration of AI tools into traditional learning models.

Chapter 6
Case Study of Using AI Tools in Vocational School

ABSTRACT

This chapter presents an examination of a case study conducted in a vocational school environment, where the teacher used specific AI tools to develop customized learning materials, exercises, and assignments for their students. Through an analysis of this case study, the research explores both the teacher's perspective on integrating AI tools into classroom practices and the resulting impact on student engagement and motivation. By capturing insights from the teacher, the study offers observations and reflections on the potential use of AI tools in secondary education settings.

OVERVIEW OF THE RESEARCH

The research explores the integration of AI tools in a vocational school in Croatia where focus is on how educators use these tools to customize learning materials, assignments, and teaching strategies for students. The research was conducted through a case study involving interviews and classroom activities, and the aim was to analyze teacher's experience with AI tools and their impact on student engagement and learning outcomes. This case study focuses on a Computer Science teacher from a vocational school in Zagreb, Croatia, during the 2023/2024 school year. Teacher A has participated in this research with the class that consists of 24 students. During the research,

DOI: 10.4018/979-8-3693-3474-4.ch006

Teacher A decided to integrate personalized learning strategies, particularly aimed at students struggling with data interpretation and analysis in program Excel. This case study explores how Teacher A used AI tools, such as ChatGPT, to create personalized lesson plan and exercises that simplify complex tasks, breaking them down into manageable parts. The goal of this study was to research how and if generative AI tools could support students in developing their analytical skills by using more accessible tasks, visual aids, and step-by-step learning methods. Through this process, Teacher A goal was to improve student comprehension and engagement with data analysis topics, focusing on practical, individualized support for learners who face difficulties in this area.

This chapter addresses the following research questions:

1. How can AI tools support the personalization of learning materials for students with learning difficulties in vocational schools?
2. How does AI tool integration impact student engagement and motivation in vocational education?
3. How do AI tools assist teachers in preparing lessons and adapting teaching strategies to suit diverse student abilities?

METHODOLOGY AND RESEARCH STRUCTURE

The goal of the research was to examine teachers' perspective about using AI tools in classrooms in secondary schools. The research is structured around a series of interviews and teaching activities that explore the integration of AI tools in the classroom. It consists of the 3 stages that include pre interview with Teacher A, interview during the preparation stage and pos interview that is conducted after the implementation and use of AI tools for preparation of personalized teaching unit. The structure of this research will give the overview of the process, which include teachers' background knowledge and skills related to AI tools, motivation, experience and thoughts about use of technology and AI tools in classrooms and for creating teaching materials, process of preparation and use of AI tools, adapting the teaching materials with AI tools, experience working with these tools and observation of students motivation and engagement during the class. The research is structured as follows:

1. Initial interview on teaching structure and knowledge of AI tools.
   a. The first interview focuses on the teacher's current teaching structure and their familiarity working with AI tools.
   b. Adapting learning lesson
      i. During this phase, the teacher prepared a teaching unit with the help of AI tools.
   c. Development of exercises for the teaching unit
      i. The teacher develops exercises that accompany the teaching unit, using AI tools.
   d. Development of homework for students
      i. The teacher prepares homework assignments for students, using AI tools to generate tasks.
2. Second interview on the teaching preparation process
   a. A follow-up interview with the teacher took place, focusing on their experience and the process of preparing the lesson using AI tools.
   b. Teaching implementation with AI tools
      i. The teacher conducts a lesson in which students use AI tools individually. The AI tools were used to help students acquire new knowledge and solve exercises during the lesson.
   c. Independent use of AI tools for homework:
      i. Students independently used AI tools to complete their homework assignments, applying the skills they learned during the lesson.
3. Third interview on AI use and student outcomes
   a. The third interview examined the teacher's experience with using AI tools in direct classroom with students.

The aim of this research methodology structure is to examine the integration of AI tools, both in the preparation and direct teaching, and their impact on student learning, engagement and motivation based on teacher perspective and experience. The example of interview questions can be found in section Appendix under Appendix B.

TEACHING UNIT

Teacher A has decided to use generative AI, ChatGPT to modify the teaching materials for students that have difficulties with learning and comprehension of learning materials regarding the data analysis and interpretation. During the research Teacher A used ChatGPT to modify and adjust teaching materials about data analysis and interpretation in Excel. Figures 1, 2 and 3 show Teacher A correspondence with ChatGPT regarding the adjustment and development of learning materials and tasks for students. The correspondence with ChatGPT is in Croatian language but interpretation of this correspondence is explained further below. The teaching materials of Teacher A can be found in section Appendix under the Appendix C.

Figure 1. Teacher A correspondence with ChatGPT

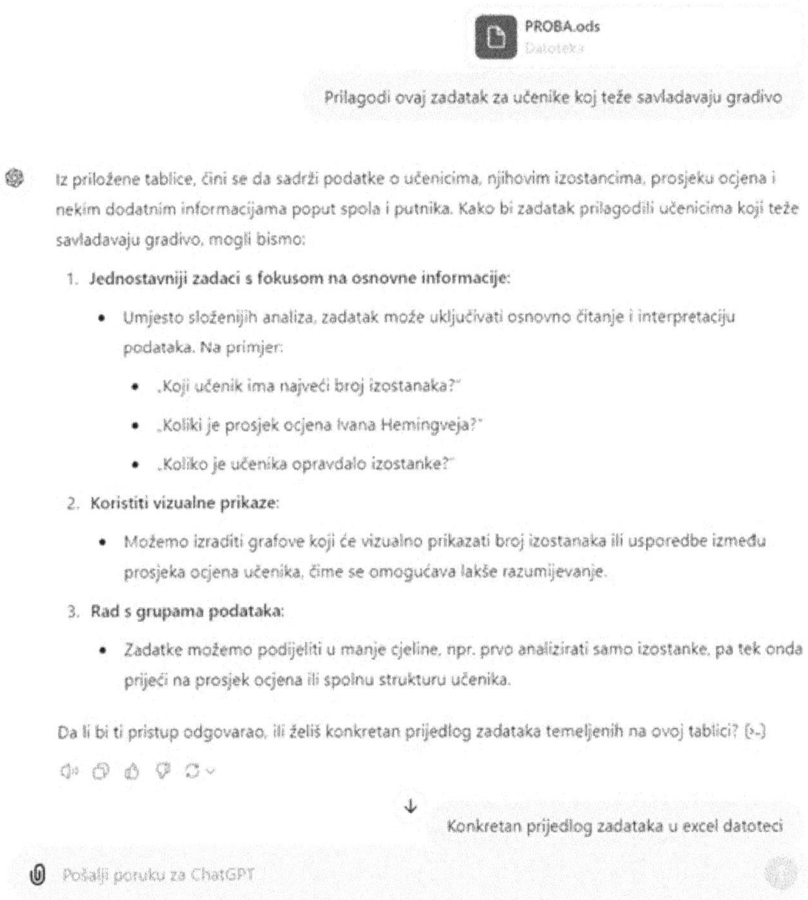

Teacher A has developed teaching materials that are specifically adapted to support students who struggle with learning. Based on the provided materials, Teacher A has simplified the tasks to make them more accessible. Rather than requiring complex analyses, the tasks focus on basic data interpretation. For example, students are asked to identify which student has the highest number of absences, calculate the average grade for a specific student, or determine how many students have justified absences. Teacher A has a breakdown task into three categories:

1. Simplified tasks focused on basic information

a. Instead of complex analyses, the task includes basic reading and interpretation of data, such as:
   i. “Which student has the highest number of absences?”
   ii. “What is the average grade of Ivan Hemingway?”
   iii. “How many students have justified absences?”

These tasks are straightforward and allow students to work with direct information.

2. Use of visual representations
   a. The teacher suggests creating graphs to visually present data such as the number of absences or comparisons between students' average grades. Visual aids help students better understand the material through easier interpretation of information.
3. Data grouping
   a. The task can be broken into smaller parts, for instance:
      i. Analyzing absences first.
      ii. Then moving on to examining average grades or gender structure.

Teacher A has structured the material in a way that but emphasis on clarity, visual aids, and gradual exploration of the data. This allows students who find learning challenging to engage with the material more comfortably and progressively. This step-by-step approach helps students focus on one aspect at a time, making the learning process less overwhelming and more structured. Through these adjustments, Teacher A created a learning environment that is supportive and adapted to the needs of students who may find it challenging to keep up with the curriculum.

Figure 2. Teacher A correspondence with ChatGPT for visual aids

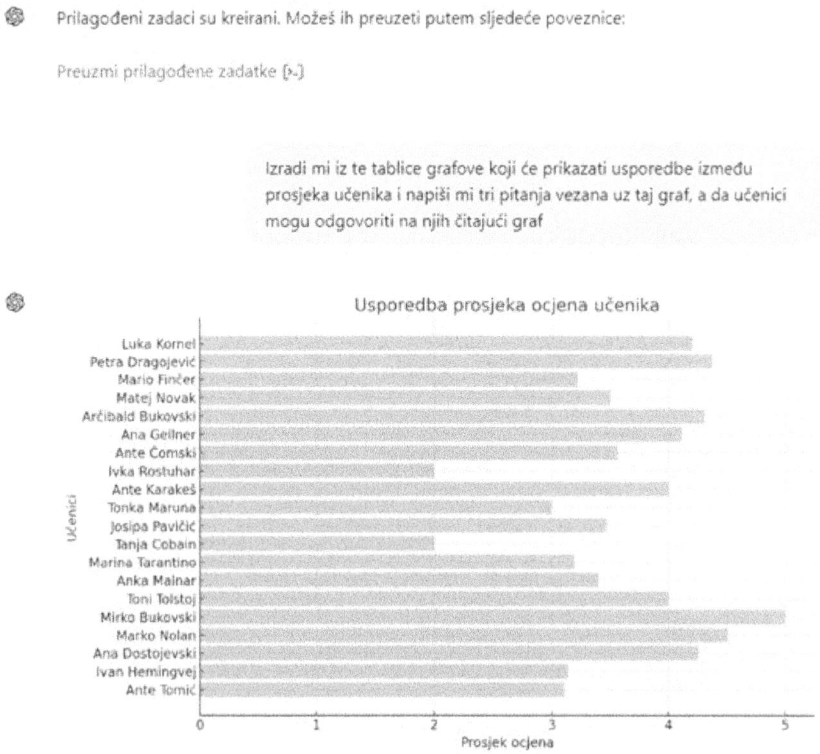

Figure 2 shows that Teacher A has created teaching materials that include a visual representation in the form of a bar graph comparing the average grades of different students. The graph provides a visual aid that allows students to compare the performance of their peers. Additionally, Teacher A has designed three questions related to the graph that students can answer by interpreting the data.

This approach can help students engage with the material by interpret the graph and extract relevant information. By asking specific, data-related questions, Teacher A encouraged students to practice their data analysis skills in a manageable and visually supported way. The combination of a graph and targeted questions can be a effective method for guiding students in understanding and working with comparative data.

Figure 3. Teacher A correspondence with ChatGPT regarding the data comparison

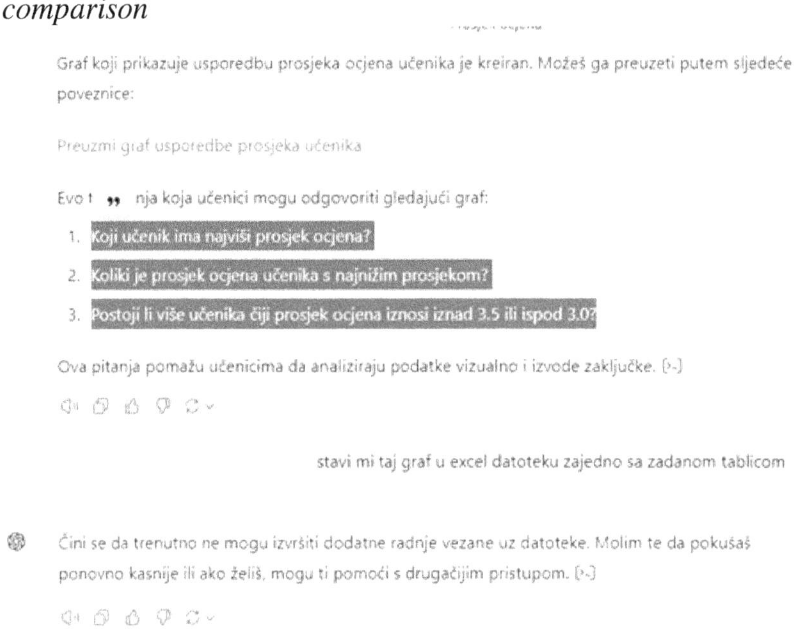

Figure 3 shows how Teacher A has designed a task that includes a graph comparing the average grades of students. The graph is accompanied by three specific questions that encourage students to interpret the data directly from the visual representation. These questions are:

1. Which student has the highest average grade?
2. What is the average grade of the student with the lowest average?
3. Are there multiple students with an average above 3.5 or below 3.0?

These questions are created to guide students in analyzing the graph and extracting relevant information. The focus is on helping students visually interpret the data and draw conclusions from it. Teacher A states that these questions can help students in developing skills to analyze data and make informed observations based on the visual information presented in the graph.

Teacher A has stated that further assistance and intervention by teacher side was needed. Based on Teacher A comment, it appears that ChatGPT provided useful assistance, but Teacher A still had to make some adjustments and organize the material manually. The Teacher A mentions she/he created a file named *prilagodjenizadaci_AI*.xlsx (adjusted tasks) where she/he added a table with the adapted tasks and a graph. The graph also includes corresponding questions related to the data. However, Teacher A acknowledges that although ChatGPT provided some initial content (e.g., tasks, graph suggestions, and questions), she/he had to further modify, adapt, and organize the material themselves. This comment suggests that ChatGPT was helpful in generating ideas, content, and visualizations, which Teacher A could then build upon. ChatGPT saved Teacher A time by offering a base to work from, but it wasn't a complete solution. Teacher A still needed to customize the final materials to better fit specific requirements and instructional style.

ChatGPT was useful as a tool for generating initial content, such as the graph and questions, but Teacher A had to take an active role in refining and structuring the material to align with teaching objectives. This can be seen as the collaborative nature of AI in education, where AI provides a starting point, and teachers adapt the output to meet classroom and student's needs.

THE STRUCTURE OF TEACHING AND KNOWLEDGE OF WORKING WITH AI TOOLS

In examining the role of technology and AI in education, it's important to understand how teachers integrate these tools into their teaching practices. The following analysis delves into an interview with a secondary school teacher who has spent 10 years teaching Computer Science to students aged 15 to 17 in vocational school in Zagreb, Croatia. This teacher's use of digital and AI tools, with the approach to personalized learning, provides insights into educational strategies. By exploring methods of lesson preparation, direct instruction, and adaptation of teaching materials, this interpretation aims to highlight the effectiveness of technology in enhancing educational outcomes and addressing student needs. The interview provides an overview of a secondary school Teacher A experience, particularly in the context of using digital and AI tools.

In this research participated Teacher A who works in vocational school in Zagreb, Croatia for 10 years and teaches Computer Science. Teacher A has master's degree in computer science and is familiar with the use and implementation of technology in the education system. In this research Teacher A has worked with one class that consists of 24 students.

Because of the long experience as a teacher of Computer Science, the Teacher A has a solid foundation in education and classroom management. Managing six classes of 24 students each, Teacher A is familiar with handling a sizable group, which includes a majority of female students. The average grade in the class is 3.4 out of 5, suggesting a moderate level of academic performance.

Teacher A frequently uses AI tools, both for personal purposes and for lesson preparation, almost daily. This frequent engagement indicates a strong comfort level with and reliance on AI tools to enhance their teaching practice. Teacher A uses a range of AI tools, including ChatGPT, Bard, Eduaide.ai, and Diffit, which serve various functions from natural language processing to educational support. This indicates a broad application of AI across different educational tasks.

In terms of lesson planning and direct instruction, Teacher A integrates digital tools extensively. Teacher A uses these tools for every lesson, demonstrating a significant commitment to incorporating technology into teaching methodology. The tools used include Microsoft Office Suite, Google Drive, and Canva, highlighting Teacher A ability to leverage diverse platforms to support different aspects of teaching.

Personalized learning is a key focus for Teacher A, who defines it as creating individualized programs tailored to each student's needs. This approach is evident in Teacher A practice of adapting materials and learning processes to better fit individual students' requirements. Teacher A proactive efforts to personalize education reflect a strong student-centered approach. Teacher A explains the difference between personalized teaching materials from other materials:

> *"When creating materials using AI tools, I can input queries that take into account the students' age and abilities. This is done through the GRADE option—regardless of the students' actual grade level, this option allows me to select a lower grade or higher, for more advanced students, which is beneficial for students who struggle to grasp the material or have lower abilities)." (Teacher A, 2024)*

However, Teacher A identifies problem-solving tasks as particularly challenging for students, which may suggest a need for additional support or revised strategies in this area. On the other hand, students adopt new concepts relatively quickly, indicating that the introduction of new material is generally effective.

One area that could benefit from further exploration is the professional development opportunities available for effectively using AI tools in teaching. The absence of specific details on this topic suggests a potential gap that might be addressed to improve the teacher's ability to utilize AI tools more effectively in the classroom.

Teacher A integration of digital and AI tools into teaching practice is robust and reflects a high level of comfort and adaptability. The focus on personalized learning and consistent use of technology highlights a forward-thinking approach to education, while identifying challenges and potential areas for professional growth could further enhance teaching effectiveness.

Teacher A stated:

"AI tools enable me to create assignments tailored to each student's abilities. For example, I can design more complex tasks for advanced students, while for those struggling with the material, I create tasks, scenarios, and resources that help them better grasp the content. I used to do all of this on my own, but now AI tools save me time." (Teacher A, 2024)

THE PROCESS OF LESSON PREPARATION USING AI TOOLS

In the second interview, Teacher A provided information about experience with using AI tools to enhance lesson preparation and personalization. This analysis explores the impact, advantages, and challenges associated with AI tools from Teacher A perspective.

Teacher A experience with AI tools, particularly Eduaide.ai, ChatGPT, Bard, and Padlet, highlights a significant shift in approach to lesson preparation. AI tools have improved Teacher A ability to create personalized materials, tailored to the diverse abilities of students. This has allowed Teacher A to develop more complex tasks for advanced learners and simpler tasks for those who struggle with the material. The process involves inputting key topics and student age into Eduaide.ai, which then suggests materials that are reviewed and adjusted as necessary. This method has save time and inspire new ideas for lesson planning for Teacher A which is evident form the comment:

"AI tools saves time in creating the teaching materials themselves, and the suggested answers often inspire new ideas as well." (Teacher A, 2024)

One of the primary benefits of AI tools, as described by Teacher A, is the time saved in creating educational content. AI tools help reduce the time spent on technical aspects such as writing questions and scenarios, thus allowing for more efficient preparation. However, Teacher A also notes that the use of AI tools can sometimes be counterproductive. Instances where AI generate either too challenging or too simplistic tasks necessitate additional modifications, which can offset some of the time savings.

Despite these challenges, the positive side of AI tool usage is evident. The ability to quickly generate ideas and the ease of creating customized content stand out as advantages. For instance, the AI's functionality to adapt materials based on student age and ability has made it easier to cover individual learning needs of students. Teacher A also faced challenges such as encountering inaccurate information or content that does not always align with educational goals. This often requires using multiple tools or manually adjusting the material, which can lead to additional time being spent.

Teacher A about advantages and disadvantages of AI tools for lesson preparation states:

> *"The advantages are time savings and the ability to create personalized content, but a drawback is that sometimes the generated content isn't applicable, requiring the use of multiple tools, which in turn consumes more time, or the teacher needs to modify the tasks themselves." (Teacher A, 2024)*

Teacher A choice of Eduaide.ai is attributed to its user-friendly interface and the flexibility it offers for content customization. AI's ability to generate materials suited to various student levels is particularly valuable. While Teacher A does not currently have foreign students, Teacher A states that AI could be beneficial for creating personalized lessons for non-native speakers, based on positive experiences shared by colleagues.

AI tools have significantly changed the Teacher A approach to lesson planning. The automation of content creation has allowed for the rapid development of creative and engaging tasks. However, the effectiveness of these tools can vary depending on the type of material. For theoretical content, AI tools offer substantial time savings and personalization, while for more technical tasks, such as mathematical problems, traditional methods may still be preferable.

Teacher A has successfully personalized materials using AI, though this sometimes requires further adjustment. AI-generated examples have been more engaging for students in some cases, enhancing their learning experience. Teacher A plans to continue using AI tools and aims to integrate them into student learning processes, teaching students how to effectively use and evaluate AI-generated content.

Teacher A sees AI tools as a valuable asset in education, contributing to their professional development and enhancing their teaching practices. To optimize the use of AI in education, Teacher A recommends ongoing self-directed learning and sharing of best practices among teacher communities. Teacher A thinks that AI tools should be integrated into curricula in a way that promotes students' ability to create and evaluate content, thereby supporting diverse learning styles and needs.

Teacher A experience shows the potential of AI tools for developing lesson preparation and personalization while also highlighting the need for careful management of the tools' limitations and integration into existing educational frameworks and curriculums.

THE TEACHER EXPERIENCE OF USING AI TOOLS IN DIRECT TEACHING WITH STUDENTS AND THE RESULTS OF STUDENTS' INDEPENDENT USE OF AI TOOLS FOR SOLVE EXERCISES AND TASKS

The third interview shows Teacher A experience with AI tools in direct teaching and their impact on students' independent use of these tools for solving exercises and tasks. Teacher A selected AI tools primarily for their ability to save time and create personalized content. While these tools offer some advantages, such as efficient lesson preparation and customization, they also have some challenges. One major issue is that AI tools sometimes produce content that is not fully applicable, which requires additional time for the teacher to adjust or supplement the materials. This can somewhat diminish the time-saving benefits.

The reactions of students to the integration of AI tools in direct teaching varied widely. For some students, the use of AI tools was exciting and engaging, adding a fun element to the learning process. Others found the experience boring or unremarkable, and a portion of the students struggled with the tasks even when assisted by AI tools. For some students, the integration of AI tools made little difference compared to traditional classroom methods.

Teacher A experience of the integrating AI tools changed the teacher's role from actively engaging students with questions to being more of a facilitator or guide. This change meant that the Teacher A role became more focused on supporting students as they navigated tasks rather than directly interacting through questions. Teacher A observed that more time was required for students to complete tasks using AI tools, which presented a challenge, especially given the constraints of classroom time of 45 minutes.

Based on the experience of Teacher A, AI tools were useful in preparing personalized lessons and adapting materials for individual students. They allowed Teacher A to create additional tasks for more advanced learners and adjust content for those needing more support. However, Teacher A also noted some limitations of AI tools, e.g. tasks often required further modification to suit individual learning needs effectively. Although the tools were beneficial, they were not entirely sufficient on their own.

Regarding age appropriateness, Teacher A did not specify if AI tools were suitable for all age groups but implied that they were beneficial in their current teaching context. Teacher A also mentioned that they did not use AI tools to overcome language barriers, so they could not comment on their effectiveness in that field.

Teacher A comment regarding the possibilities for customizing and adjusting AI tool responses to better suit the specific needs of students is as follows:

> *"So far, I haven't seen options that take into account various student difficulties (cognitive, physical, and psychological-emotional). This is an area that could use further development." (Teacher A, 2024)*

According to Teacher A, students encountered several technical difficulties while using AI tools, such as receiving incorrect or incomplete answers, which presented challenges in ensuring the accuracy of their work. Teacher A invested approximately 45 minutes teaching students how to use the AI tools, highlighting the need for initial training to make the tools effective in the classroom with direct interaction.

When Teacher A compared in class use versus homework tasks, students generally showed better performance and engagement with AI tools when using them for homework. However, Teacher A stated that there were instances where students simply copied answers rather than using tools to deepen their understanding.

Teacher A states that AI tools have increased engagement for some students and simplified personalized lesson planning. In addition, challenges such as the need for additional time to address technical issues and varying student reactions suggest areas for improvement. Teacher A plans to continue using AI tools in the classroom with students but refining AI integration into classroom practices and further addressing the limitations encountered in the process of preparation of personalized learning materials.

RESEARCH ANALYSIS

Based on the case study from secondary school in Croatia the research analysis focuses on the impact and effectiveness of integrating AI tools into a vocational school environment. The study reflects both the teacher's perspective and student outcomes, offering an overview of role of AI in school settings.

The research is structured around multiple stages, including pre-interviews, lesson preparation, teaching unit creation, and post-interviews with the teacher, all aimed at examining the teacher's experience and students' engagement. The teacher used AI tools such as ChatGPT, Eduaide.ai, Bard, and others to prepare personalized learning materials depending on different student abilities.

Teacher A found that AI tools significantly improve the process of preparing lessons, exercises, and homework. AI tools saved time by generating lesson ideas and materials that could be further customized for individual student needs. Teacher A noted that AI-generated content was not always accurate or fully aligned with educational goals, which required manual adjustments. While the AI tools were useful, they were not a complete solution, and Teacher A intervention was needed to fine tune the materials to meet specific instructional objectives.

According to the Teacher A experience, the students responded differently to the use of AI tools. Some found the experience engaging, as the integration of AI added an element of innovation and fun to the learning process. Others found it less impactful, expressing indifference toward AI-assisted tasks. For some students, the use of AI tools improved performance, especially for homework, where they showed more engagement compared to in-class activities. However, there were instances where students misused the tools by copying and pasting answers without fully understanding the presented material.

AI tools allowed Teacher A to create differentiated tasks for various student abilities. For example, simpler tasks were generated for students with learning difficulties, while more complex exercises were designed for advanced learners. The ability to quickly adjust materials based on student needs helped create a more inclusive and supportive learning environment. In addition, Teacher A found that further customization was often necessary to ensure that the materials were effective and appropriate for all students.

While AI tools were beneficial in lesson preparation and personalization, several challenges emerged based on Teacher A experience. Students encountered technical difficulties with the tools, such as receiving incomplete or incorrect answers. Teacher A also observed that using AI tools during class required additional time, which was a challenge given the limited time of 45 minutes available during lessons. The effectiveness of AI tools varied based on the type of content, e.g. for theoretical subjects, AI tools were more useful, but for technical or problem-solving tasks, traditional methods were often more reliable according to Teacher A.

Teacher A role was changed, teacher was more as adviser or informer that led student during the use of AI tools. As students used AI tools to complete tasks, the teacher provided support and guidance rather than actively leading the lesson. This change allowed Teacher A to focus more on helping students navigate and understand the material, but it also introduced challenges related to time management and ensuring that students fully understood the content and lesson. The integration of AI tools into the vocational school classroom offered both opportunities and challenges. According to Teacher A, AI tools helped improve lesson preparation and enabled Teacher A to personalize learning experiences for students. However, the tools were not without limitations, and Teacher A had to make significant adjustments to ensure that the AI-generated materials were suitable and effective for students. While some students benefited from the use of AI tools, others found them less engaging or struggled with technical issues and writing prompts.

The research based on Teacher A perspective gives insight to the potential of AI in education as a supportive tool for both teachers and students. However, it also emphasizes the importance of human oversight in refining and adapting AI-generated content to meet educational standards and student needs. The study suggests that ongoing professional development and training for teachers are essential to maximize the benefits of AI tools in the classroom and the integration of mastering the use of AI tool for students is also one of the facts that needs to be considered when using AI tools for educational purposes. The tools allowed for a more dynamic approach to lesson preparation and gave teachers the flexibility to develop differentiated tasks to meet individual student needs. In addition, the research suggests that these tools should be considered as collaborative assistants rather than complete educational solutions.

Regarding the guidelines or resources for teachers who want to better understand and more effectively use AI tools in their practice, Teacher A states:

> *"It requires self-directed effort to research and educate oneself on using AI tools, as well as keeping up with available training. Sharing examples of best practices and personal experiences, whether within the school or outside of it, is far more beneficial than attending various courses." (Teacher A, 2024)*

In addition, Teacher A states that for better and easier use of AI tools for integration of the personalized learning into existing curriculum and educational programs the following needs to be addressed:

> *"AI tools can be integrated through topics and activities where students use the tools themselves, gaining skills and knowledge in crafting accurate queries, distinguishing correct from incorrect information, and using the tools to better understand concepts that may not be entirely clear to them." (Teacher A)*

CONCLUSION

The analysis of this case study regarding the research question (1) about the support of the AI tools for the personalization of learning materials for students with learning difficulties in vocational schools shows that AI tools, e.g. ChatGPT support the personalization of learning materials. The AI tool allowed Teacher A to simplify complex tasks and create step-by-step learning activities, that enable students to engage with materials at their own pace. In this case study, the AI tools helped break down data analysis tasks in Excel, providing visual aids, simplified exercises, and gradual exploration of topics. In addition, this research revealed that AI-generated content often required further customization by Teacher A to ensure it fully met the specific needs of students, highlighting the collaborative role of AI and human expertise in the learning process.

The second research question (2) regarding the integrating AI tools into vocational education had mixed effects on student engagement and motivation. Based on the Teacher A perspective for some students, the use of AI tools added an element of excitement and entertainment, making the learning process more engaging, especially when visual aids were introduced. Some students found the use of AI tools to be less impactful, expressing indifference or struggling with tasks even when AI assistance was provided. Teacher A observed that students tended to perform better when using AI tools for homework rather than in-class activities, suggesting that the self-paced nature of AI-based assignments might contribute positively to engagement and motivation.

Regarding the third research question (3) results show that AI tools played a supportive role in helping Teacher A prepare and adapt lessons to suit diverse student abilities. AI tool provided initial content ideas, customized materials based on student abilities, and helped Teacher A to develop tasks for both advanced learners and those with learning difficulties. For Teacher A AI tools saved time in creating initial drafts of exercises and lesson plans, Teacher A still needed to refine and adapt the generated materials to meet specific educational goals. This can results shows the importance of teacher intervention to ensure accuracy and alignment with educational objectives. These findings reveled that AI tools could be useful in supporting personalized education and improving efficiency, are not standalone educational solutions. Teacher active involvement is crucial to customize AI-generated materials to effectively meet the unique needs of students.

Chapter 7
Case Study of Using AI Tools in Primary School

ABSTRACT

This chapter presents a detailed examination of a case study conducted in a primary school environment, wherein educators used specific AI tools to develop customized learning materials, exercises, and assignments for their students. Through an analysis of this case study, the research explores both the teacher's perspective on integrating AI tools into classroom practices and the resulting impact on student engagement and motivation. By capturing insights from both educators and students, the study offers valuable observations and reflections on the potential of AI tools in primary education settings.

OVERVIEW OF THE RESEARCH

The case study analyzes how AI tools, e.g. ChatGPT, was used by a teacher in primary school in Poreč, Croatia, to support a student who is a non-native Croatian speaker during the school year 2023/2024. The study focuses on the use of AI tools to guide teachers to prepare and teach lessons and explore how they can address language barriers and tailor learning. During this process, AI tools were used to adapt complex topics such as the life cycle of flowering plants to simplified languages, allowing students with limited Croatian abilities to gain access and understanding of the learning materials. Teacher B used ChatGPT to simplify vocabulary, provide visual aids, and suggest practical activities, enabling the student to engage more fully with the lesson. The study highlights the benefits and limitations of the use of AI

DOI: 10.4018/979-8-3693-3474-4.ch007

tools in primary education. Although artificial intelligence has contributed to adapting the content of the lessons, Teacher B still must make adjustments to adapt the materials to the needs and cultural context of the students.

This chapter explores the following research questions:

1. How can AI tools be used to support non-native speakers in primary school education, in adapting learning materials to meet their language needs?
2. What are the challenges and benefits of integrating AI tools into primary education for teachers and students?
3. What role do AI tools play in helping teachers adapt their teaching strategies to address the specific educational needs of students?

METHODOLOGY

The goal of the research was to examine Teacher B perspective about using AI tools for lesson preparation in primary school. The research is structured around a series of interviews and teaching activities that explore the integration of AI tools for adaptation, adjustments and personalization of teaching units. It consists of the 2 stages that include pre interview with teacher, interview during the preparation stage and pos interview that is conducted after the implementation and use of AI tools for preparation of personalized teaching units. The structure of this research will give the overview of the lesson preparation process, which include teachers' background knowledge and skills related to AI tools, motivation, experience and thoughts about use of technology and AI tools in classrooms and for creating teaching materials, process of preparation and use of AI tools, adapting the teaching units with AI tools, experience working with these tools and observation of students motivation and engagement during the classes. The research is structured as follows:

- Initial interview on teaching structure and knowledge of AI tools.

    a. The first interview focuses on the teacher's current teaching structure and their familiarity working with AI tools.
    b. Lesson preparation using AI tools

i. In this stage, the teacher prepares a teaching unit with the help of AI tools, using AI to plan and structure the lesson.

c. Creation of exercises for the teaching unit

i. The teacher develops exercises that accompany the teaching unit, using AI tools to enhance and tailor the materials.

- Second interview on the teaching preparation process

a. A follow-up interview with the teacher takes place, focusing on their experience and the process of preparing the lesson using AI tools.

This structure aims to examine the integration of AI tools in both lesson preparation, as well as their impact on student learning and engagement. The example of questions for the interview with Teacher B can be found in section Appendix under the Appendix B.

TEACHING UNIT

Teacher B teaching unit focuses on the concept of the life cycle of flowering plants, helping students understand and explore the growth, reproduction and development of plants. The unit is designed to include specific learning outcomes, inter-curricular connections and various teaching and evaluation methods aimed at engaging students in theoretical and practical learning experiences.

The lesson starts with an introduction phase designed to attract the interest of the students and prepare them for the new content. Teacher B starts by announcing the viewing of a video that presents the life cycle of a plant, accessible via a digital link. This video serves as a visual and conceptual entry point, allowing students to see the different stages of plant development. The video encourages students to briefly reflect on what they have learned, stimulate active recall, and reinforce key points. This introduction is enhanced by the textbook's motivational question, which asks students to think about the concept of a cycle. By solving the exercise in the textbook, students understand that cycles are the cycle of repeated events. This initial engagement with the concept of cycles laid the foundation for the main content of the lessons, which revolves around the life cycle of flowering plants.

The main part of the lesson introduces new teaching materials. Students read texts from textbooks that provide detailed information on plant life cycles. Teacher B guides them in reading, explaining unfamiliar terms, and answers any questions they have. This helps to ensure that all students understand the material, regardless of their previous knowledge. Students also see the images of the textbook, visually representing various stages of plant growth and reproduction, adding a layer of understanding. In this section, students are assigned to explain the life cycle of common flowering plants dandelion, allowing them to apply their new knowledge to concrete examples. This activity encourages critical thinking and strengthens their understanding of the cyclical nature of plant life.

To further improve their learning, students copy a structured plan from the board, which outlines the key stages of the plant life cycle. They then create drawings to represent these stages, allowing them to express their understanding through visual and creative means. This helps students internalize the information but also contributes to different learning styles by combining written, verbal, and artistic methods. This part of the lesson is essential to help students synthesize materials and establish connections between real examples of plant life cycles and texts. In the final phase of the lesson, Teacher B uses the worksheets and cards as a form of assessment to assess students' understanding of the material. These tools give students an opportunity to demonstrate what they have learned by answering questions or completing activities related to flowering plant life cycles. In addition, students make self-evaluations to examine whether they can describe the life cycles of flowering plants. This self-reflection encourages students to take responsibility for learning and helps identify areas that may need more clarification or practice. The entire unit focuses on interoperability, especially language and art. For example, students learn language skills by describing plant growth and reproductive phases and improve their ability to clearly communicate scientific concepts. In addition, the artistic components of the lesson, in which students show the life cycle of plants, enable them to engage in content at a creative level. The integration of this subject helps to enhance the learning experience and makes teaching more dynamic and stimulating for students.

The evaluation of this unit has several aspects. In addition to the above-mentioned forms and self-assessment, Teacher B regularly monitor the progress of students by observing their participation in discussions, the accuracy of answers to questions, and the quality of work on tasks such as the establishment of life cycles. The use of formal evaluation during a lesson helps Teacher B provide immediate feedback to students, which is crucial to guide learning and ensure that they achieve the desired results. This lesson also includes additional activities for advanced students and those who complete tasks early. For example, students are encouraged to study the plant life cycle in forests and pastures and then illustrate and explain the stages of plant development. This task encourages independent learning and enables students to expand their knowledge beyond the basic lesson content. Furthermore, a long-term project is introduced to establish a greenhouse that requires students to collect and maintain plant specimens to strengthen their understanding of plant diversity and life cycle. This may include tasks simplified, additional explanations provided, or alternative resources provided. By making these adjustments, teachers ensure that all students can participate in the lessons and achieve the learning results.

This unit of teaching about the life cycle of flowering plants is designed to engage students through visual, verbal and hands-on learning activities. Integrated teaching methods that introduce new concepts, guidelines, creative expressions, and various forms of evaluation not only help students understand the stages of plant life, but also link this knowledge to broader biological principles and examples of the real world. Cross-curricular integration, continuous evaluation and adaptability ensure that it meets the different needs of students and offers effective and comprehensive educational experiences. The whole teaching unit of Teacher B can be found in section Appendix under the Appendix D.

TEACHERS' PREPARATION PROCESS

The case study revolves around a fourth-grade student who is learning Croatian as a second language. Prior to attending regular lessons, student underwent a 70-hour preparatory course to help her acquire basic proficiency in Croatian. By the time of the lesson preparation, student had made noticeable progress, particularly in communication. However, the language skills of student was still at a moderate level compared to native-speaking peers, with specific issues related to limited vocabulary, simplified sentence structures, and deviations in pronunciation. Despite these challenges, student was highly motivated and eager to continue learning the language.

Given these circumstances, Teacher B recognized the need to adapt the curriculum to student linguistic abilities, ensuring that student could participate fully in class while continuing to develop language skills. Teacher B decided to use ChatGPT to help prepare a lesson on the topic of the "Life Cycle of Flowering Plants", a part of the fourth-grade curriculum for the subject *Nature and Society*.

During the preparation process and use of ChatGPT Teacher B used prompts shown in Table 6.

Table 1. List of teacher's prompts for ChatGPT

	Prompt
1.	What are the exact scientific facts and recommendations for working with children who are non-native speakers with a limited vocabulary and poor pronunciation during schoolwork in lower grades of elementary school?
2.	How can a lesson, such as "The Life Cycle of Flowering Plants" in the fourth grade of elementary school (in Croatian, 4th grade, subject: nature and society), be adapted for a non-native speaker with a limited vocabulary?
3.	Can you recommend an adjustment for the introductory part of the lesson?
4.	Can the choice of font help?
5.	How would you adapt the key vocabulary words from the lesson plan on the board?
6.	How can you help a non-native speaker with pronunciation or accent issues during the lesson?

Each prompt has a specific educational focus that Teacher B has addressed during the research.

Prompt 1. *What are the exact scientific facts and recommendations for working with children who are non-native speakers with a limited vocabulary and poor pronunciation during schoolwork in lower grades of elementary school?*

This prompt emphasizes the need for evidence-based methods and recommendations for supporting young non-native speakers in elementary school. It seeks scientific studies or expert-backed strategies that address the specific issues of limited vocabulary and poor pronunciation. The prompt suggests looking into specialized interventions like phonological awareness, bilingual education strategies, or the role of speech therapy.

Prompt 2. *How can a lesson, such as "The Life Cycle of Flowering Plants" in the fourth grade of elementary school (in Croatian, 4th grade, subject: nature and society), be adapted for a non-native speaker with a limited vocabulary?*

The main aim of this prompt is curriculum adaptation for non-native speakers. It calls for a reworking of a specific lesson that is content-heavy and likely filled with complex, subject-specific vocabulary. The lesson needs to be adapted to make the content comprehensible to students who may struggle with language barriers. Strategies could include using simplified language, visual aids, bilingual glossaries, or hands-on learning activities to make the concept of plant life cycles accessible.

Prompt 3. *Can you recommend an adjustment for the introductory part of the lesson?*

This prompt focuses on lesson design, particularly how to introduce a new topic in a way that engages and is understandable to non-native speakers. The introduction is critical for setting the stage for the entire lesson. This could involve using more visual cues, providing pre-teaching of key vocabulary, starting with familiar concepts, or incorporating multimedia elements to reduce language demands while piquing interest.

Prompt 4. *Can the choice of font help?*

This is a more specific and somewhat technical question that touches on whether font choice can assist in learning, particularly for children with language difficulties.

Prompt 5. *How would you adapt the key vocabulary words from the lesson plan on the board?*

This prompt specifically addresses the adaptation of vocabulary instruction, highlighting the importance of making key terms accessible to non-native speakers. Strategies could include using visuals, breaking down complex words, providing synonyms, or using real-world examples to contextualize vocabulary. Another effective approach could be using graphic organizers like word maps or interactive word walls.

Prompt 6. *How can you help a non-native speaker with pronunciation or accent issues during the lesson?*

This prompt is concerned with oral language development, particularly how to support non-native speakers in improving their pronunciation and dealing with accent differences during lessons.

The general themes generated by these prompts focus on how Teacher B can effectively create a comprehensive and supportive learning environment for non-native speakers. One of the themes is differentiation and adaptation, and most of the motivations emphasize the need to modify the teaching and learning strategies to address the unique challenges facing non-native speakers. This suggests a necessity for differentiated instruction and careful lesson design that accommodates language barriers while maintaining educational standards.

Another key theme is language and content integration. Several prompts focus on teaching complex subject matter, such as science, alongside language development. This requires a delicate balance, as educators must ensure that students undestand both the content and the language. The use of content-based language training and simplified materials is important for this process.

Multimodal learning also highlights the importance of using various learning methods, visual, auditory and kinesthetic to help non-native speakers understand vocabulary, pronunciation and key concepts. This not only helps understand, but also accommodates different learning styles and makes content more accessible.

Inclusive practice is a recurring theme in prompts focusing on creating a classroom environment that supports non-native speakers. The aim is to solve language challenges while ensuring that students are fully involved and succeed without being overwhelmed by language barriers. Teacher B approach reflects support for both language acquisition and content understanding for non-native speakers in an inclusive and adaptable learning environment.

The key challenge for the Teacher B was how to effectively present the scientific content of the life cycle of plants in a way that student, with limited knowledge of Croatian, could understand and engage with. The original lesson plan included detailed scientific vocabulary, descriptions, and activities that might overwhelm a student still developing basic language proficiency. Teacher B needed a way to simplify the language while preserving the educational integrity of the lesson.

Another challenge was how to provide visual and hands-on elements to reinforce learning. While the existing lesson plan already included images and activities, these needed to be adapted to ensure student could relate the content to her existing knowledge and follow along with the class.

To address these challenges, Teacher B used ChatGPT to modify the lesson content. Teacher B modification and adjustment can be divided into several categories:

1. Simplifying Vocabulary and Language Structure

The original lesson on the life cycle of flowering plants involved complex terminology such as "germination," "pollination," "dispersal," and "fertilization." ChatGPT suggested to Teacher B more simple terms in order to make unite more accessible to student. For instance, the AI tool recommended using simple phrases like:

- "The seed starts to grow" (instead of "germination").
- "Bees help the flowers" (instead of "pollination").
- "The fruit has seeds inside" (instead of "fertilization and seed development").

This simplification allowed the teacher to maintain the scientific accuracy of the lesson while ensuring that student could follow along. The AI tool also suggested using short, clear sentences, such as "The plant grows," and "The seed becomes a plant," which were easier for student to understand and repeat.

2. Incorporating Visual Aids and Practical Activities

During the research and use of ChatGPT, the tool recommended to Teacher B the use of visual aids to complement the lesson. The AI tool advised Teacher B to use images that clearly show each stage of the plant life cycle. These included illustrations showing the seed, sprout, flower, and fruit, allowing student to visually connect the stages to the corresponding vocabulary.

In addition, ChatGPT suggested hands-on activities to improve the learning process. For example, the AI proposed a seed-planting activity where student and classmates would plant seeds and observe their growth over time. This approach of AI tool was aimed to connect theory and real-world experience, and to provide student a concrete, sensory-based way of understanding the plant life cycle. The AI tool also recommended that Teacher B ask student to draw each stage of the life cycle, thus implementing art skills as a learning tool that will improve student's understanding of the learning materials.

3. Using Repetition and Contextual Learning

One of the educational strategies proposed by ChatGPT was the use of repetition and contextual learning to improve student understanding of the content. The AI advised Teacher B to repeat key words and phrases throughout the lesson. For example, during each stage of the life cycle, the tool suggested to Teacher B continuously using the word "seed" and relate it to familiar objects or experiences, such as "A seed is like the beginning of a new plant, just like an egg is the beginning of a chick." This contextual approach could help students to use a new vocabulary to understand concepts that are easier to understand.

Additionally, ChatGPT recommended the use of context-based questioning, such as:

- "What happens when we water the seed?"
- "What do you see when the plant grows?"

These questions could help student to practice lesson using the new vocabulary in a meaningful, context-based way.

4. Addressing Pronunciation and Language Skills

Student also struggled with pronunciation, particularly of certain Croatian sounds and word so Teacher B used ChatGPT to create pronunciation models for the student to use during the lesson. By repeating the correct pronunciation slowly and clearly, Teacher B was able to model the sounds for student, who then practiced them in class.

ChatGPT also suggested to Teacher B to create small-group activities where student could practice speaking with other classmates in a less formal, low-pressure environment. This activity could allow student to receive peer feedback and practice pronunciation in a supportive environment.

5. Monitoring Progress and Outcomes

Regarding the monitoring progress, ChatGPT had recommended to Teacher B to use formative assessment techniques, such as "exit tickets" (short written responses at the end of the lesson) or simple worksheets, to check student understanding. These tools could provide Teacher B with immediate feedback on student comprehension of the life cycle topic, allowing Teacher B to adjust future lessons accordingly.

At the end of the lesson, the teacher reported that student was able to explain the basic stages of the plant life cycle using simplified vocabulary. While her pronunciation and sentence structure still needed work.

Teacher's Reflections and Future Implications

Teacher B reflected positively on the use of ChatGPT in preparing the lesson. By simplifying the language, offering practical activities, and incorporating visual aids, the AI tool provided technical support in overcoming language barriers. One of the conclusions from this case study was the realization that AI tools like ChatGPT can serve as additional tool in inclusive education, particularly for students who are non-native speakers.

However, Teacher B also noted some limitations in the use. ChatGPT's suggestions were primarily based on English-language models, which occasionally required further adaptation for the Croatian language. Additionally, the AI tool was unable to generate culturally specific examples or illustrations tailored to Croatian learners, meaning Teacher B had to supplement the AI's output with additional resources.

In addition, Teacher B plans to continue using ChatGPT for lesson preparation, especially for language learners. However, Teacher B will use AI tool in combination with other teaching strategies and materials to ensure a more relevant approach.

This case study shows how AI tools like ChatGPT can effectively support primary school teachers in preparing lessons for students with language barriers. By simplifying language, providing visual aids, and suggesting interactive learning activities, ChatGPT made the complex scientific topic of the plant life cycle accessible to student, a non-native Croatian speaker.

RESEARCH ANALYSIS

Teacher B comments reflect both the benefits and challenges of using ChatGPT for lesson adaptation, particularly when working with children who have specific educational needs. Based on this experience, Teacher B suggests that the tool has great potential for assisting in lesson customization, especially when used with precise questions and follow-up inquiries. This indicates that ChatGPT can be an additional and accessible resource for teachers, allowing them to adjust and adopt different learning materials to meet diverse learning requirements for students. However, the effectiveness of the tool largely depends on the quality and precision of the input. It performs well somewhat clear when, structured questions and prompts are composed, but can make mistakes if the prompts are vague or too general. This insight points to the need for teachers to use tools in a systematic and specialized manner to achieve optimal results.

One of the major benefits the teacher notes is the usefulness of the AI image generator, which is great for English-language instruction where teacher stated:

> *"The ChatGPT application can be very helpful in adapting lessons for children with specific needs, it requires precise questioning and mandatory follow-up questions when there are doubts about the accuracy of suggestions, along with asking for sources. The AI image generator, included in the paid version, is useful and ideal for teaching English, but for Croatian language lessons, it can be used depending on the situation. The image generator predominantly uses English text and makes errors when switching to Croatian, and often, after a command, it cannot remove the text from the illustration. Generating appropriate images needs to be requested specifically, and the program does not automatically place them in appropriate parts of its response." (Teacher B, 2024)*

However, when applied to Croatian language instruction, the AI generator has significant limitations. It struggles to switch between English and Croatian, often producing errors in the transition, especially when dealing with text in illustrations. This highlights a clear gap in the tool's multilingual support. Teacher B also notes technical difficulties, such as the ChatGPT inability to automatically integrate images into appropriate parts of its responses, this part requires manual intervention of human. These challenges suggest that while the visual generator can be a beneficial, it is not yet fully optimized for full use, particularly in non-English contexts.

Figure 1 shows the image generated by ChatGPT based on the Teacher B prompt. The image shows language distortion and how AI tool did not provide correctly written terms of the seasons of the year in Croatian. In image it is evident that the text is half in English and half in Croatian language.

Figure 1. Example of image generated by ChatGPT

Teacher also highlighted following:

"It cannot adapt the entire lesson plan, it needs to be asked very precise questions for each phase where the teacher thinks it can help." (Teacher B, 2024)

This comment shows that ChatGPT is more effective when teachers ask targeted, specific questions related to individual lesson parts. This demonstrates that the AI tool cannot be used as a standalone educational tool, but it can provide assistance for development or adjustment of specific elements in lesson design. Consequently, teachers must use ChatGPT in a way to ask exact questions in order to extract the most useful information at each stage of the lesson. This also indicates that AI tools such as ChatGPT may need to be further developed to handle more comprehensive educational tasks.

Additionally, Teacher B notes that ChatGPT sometimes makes errors when recommending applications suitable for use with the Croatian language:

"It makes mistakes when suggesting applications suitable for the Croatian language. It often responds more accurately if the question is posed in English first and then a translation is requested." (Teacher B, 2024)

This remark points to a potential knowledge gap in the AI's understanding of local educational tools, which might limit its practical use for teachers who need localized, language-specific recommendations. There is also a broader implication about the AI's optimization for global classrooms. Teacher B finds that ChatGPT often provides more accurate responses when the initial question is asked in English, followed by a request for translation into Croatian. This suggests that the tool is more robust in processing English-language queries, highlighting a potential disparity in the AI's effectiveness based on the language used.

These comments show both the opportunities and constraints of using AI in the classroom. According to Teacher B, ChatGPT shows benefits and positive characteristics in helping teachers customize teaching lessons and generate supplementary materials, particularly in an English-language context. However, its limitations in adapting to non-English languages, handling complete lesson plans, and integrating visuals reflect a need for further adjustment and improvement. Developers in collaboration with researchers and teachers could explore further how AI models like ChatGPT can be improved to support more diverse linguistic and educational contexts, with an emphasis on making them more adaptable and accessible for global use. The feedback from Teacher B also suggests that future AI tools could benefit from enhanced capabilities in handling complex, multilevel educational tasks, reducing the need for highly structured input from teachers, and better integration of visual materials so the AI tools could be used more easily for learning across different subjects and languages.

CONCLUSION

The results for the research question (1) regarding the how AI tools can be used to support non-native speakers in primary school education, in adapting learning materials to meet their language needs, showed that AI tools, such as ChatGPT, can support non-native speakers by simplifying complex vocabulary, adapting materials, and suggesting visual and hands-on learning activities. In this case study, ChatGPT helped adapt learning materials for a non-native Croatian speaker by providing simplified vocabulary, thereby making complex topics more accessible. Nevertheless, challenges emerged due to the AI's reliance on predominantly English-language models, requiring additional customization by the teacher to adjust materials for the cultural and linguistic needs of the students. This emphasizes the need for further refinement of AI tools to effectively address diverse linguistic contexts.

The research question (2) regarding the challenges and benefits of integrating AI tools into primary school education revealed that this process has its positive and negative aspects. Benefits include personalized support for students, engagement through visual learning, and simplification of content. The results show that AI tools can help reduce teacher workload by offering quick suggestions for content adaptation. Challenges include the limitations of AI tools in supporting non-English languages effectively, the need for teacher oversight to ensure cultural relevance, and the necessity for precise prompts to achieve useful outputs. This means that teachers still play a main role in customizing AI-generated content to meet specific educational needs, ensuring the relevance and accuracy of adapted materials.

The third research question (3) about the role of AI tools in adapting teaching strategies reveled that AI tools serve as supplementary resources to help teachers adapt their teaching strategies to meet specific student needs. In this study, ChatGPT provided lesson with certain adaptations, such as simplifying language for a student with limited proficiency in Croatian. The AI tool recommended activities for varied learning styles, such as visual and kinesthetic learning, and supported language development through context-based learning strategies. The results show that for the effective use of AI tools teachers need to provide precise and structured prompts what can help in process of personalization of learning materials, but teachers are essential in guiding AI tools to optimize its impact on student learning.

Chapter 8
Framework for Implementing AI Tools in Personalized Teaching and Learning

ABSTRACT

This chapter will provide an overview of existing European and international frameworks for using and implementing generative AI tools in education. Based on the analysis of frameworks, research results from three case studies, and use of generative AI tools, this chapter will provide a framework for use of generative AI tools in the educational environment for personalized learning. The framework can be used for all levels of education, from primary to higher education. The goal of this chapter is to provide teachers with basic guidance for implementing AI tools in their teaching process and classrooms for addressing the specific needs of their students.

OVERVIEW OF THE EXISTING FRAMEWORKS FOR USE OF AI IN EDUCATION

The increasing presence of artificial intelligence (AI) in education has sparked global efforts to establish frameworks that guide its responsible and effective use. AI has the potential to improve educational practices by personalizing learning, enhancing administrative efficiency, and supporting teachers in their instructional roles. However, these advancements come with

DOI: 10.4018/979-8-3693-3474-4.ch008

challenges such as ethical concerns, data privacy, and the risk of exacerbating educational inequalities. As a result, several institutions and organizations have developed comprehensive frameworks to address these challenges while promoting AI literacy among educators, students, and educational leaders.

This chapter provides an overview of existing frameworks that outline how AI can be integrated into educational environments. These frameworks offer guidelines for fostering AI literacy, ensuring equitable access to AI technologies, and promoting ethical usage. For instance, Barnard College's *Framework for AI Literacy* emphasizes the importance of advancing AI understanding among faculty, students, and staff through four levels of proficiency. Similarly, the National Center on Education and the Economy's *Framework for AI-Powered Learning Environments* focuses on the short- and long-term strategies for incorporating AI into classrooms, while addressing its ethical implications and impact on leadership roles. Other notable contributions, such as the *Beijing Consensus on AI and Education* and the OECD's guidelines, underscore the necessity of balancing AI's benefits with careful attention to ethical standards, inclusivity, and the ongoing development of teacher competences.

This section will explore frameworks in greater detail, examining their goals, strategies, and recommendations for integrating AI into educational systems. This overview aims to highlight the diverse approaches taken by educational institutions worldwide to harness AI's potential while safeguarding the values of equity, transparency, and human-centered learning.

Barnard College AI Literacy Framework

Barnard College developed *A Framework for AI Literacy* which goal is to advance AI education within higher education. It emphasizes the need for AI literacy, advocating that understanding AI will help faculty, students, and staff make informed decisions about AI use. The framework outlines four levels of proficiency aimed at advancing AI literacy within educational institutions, particularly focusing on students, faculty, and staff.

Four Levels of AI Literacy

- Understand AI

This foundational level introduces basic AI concepts and terminology. Users at this level become familiar with key definitions, such as "artificial intelligence," "machine learning," and "neural networks." They are equipped to recognize the benefits and limitations of AI and can differentiate between types of AI, such as artificial narrow intelligence (ANI) and artificial general intelligence (AGI). The focus is on grasping how AI works, what it can and cannot do, and understanding technical concepts, such as the differences between open-source and closed AI models.

- Use and Apply AI

At this stage, users progress from understanding AI to practically engaging with it. They can apply AI tools like ChatGPT to achieve specific outcomes. This includes mastering prompt engineering techniques, experimenting with various prompts, and refining them to improve AI-generated responses. Critical here is the ability to recognize and address issues such as AI "hallucinations" (false outputs) and biases. Users also learn about important ethical concerns, such as privacy and intellectual property rights when working with AI technologies.

- Analyze and Evaluate AI

The third level requires a critical examination of AI beyond its immediate outputs. Users engage in deeper analyses of how AI impacts society, ethics, and disciplines such as environmental sustainability, labor, and privacy. They assess AI systems for biases and ethical implications, evaluating AI through lenses like race, gender, and misinformation. This level is about questioning and critiquing AI's broader societal effects, which calls for knowledge of AI as well as critical thinking skills to argue for or against its applications in various contexts.

- Create AI

At the highest level of proficiency, users are empowered to create and conceptualize new AI technologies. This includes building AI models, developing software that leverages AI, or proposing new theories about AI's future applications. Users at this level synthesize their knowledge to innovate, designing AI solutions that go beyond existing technologies. They consider how human creativity and AI can be combined, focusing on what is uniquely human versus what AI can replicate or enhance. This level nurtures the ability to shape the future of AI development actively.

As AI continues to advance and permeate various aspects of higher education, Barnard's focus on iterative learning and adaptive programming will be crucial. The immediate next steps involve expanding educational efforts beyond the basics, fostering deeper engagement with AI's ethical and practical implications, and addressing the diverse needs and perceptions of the academic community. Ultimately, this initiative not only seeks to enhance technical proficiency but also to ensure that AI usage is aligned with ethical considerations and human values, paving the way for a more informed and reflective approach to integrating AI into educational practices.

Framework for AI-Powered Learning Environments from National Center on Education and the Economy

The National Center on Education and the Economy developed F*ramework for AI-Powered Learning Environments* that is a strategic guide aimed at helping education leaders integrate artificial intelligence into their education systems. Document outlines best practices for the adoption of AI within classrooms and broader education systems. The framework focuses on both short-term (18–20 months) and long-term (2–6 years) goals, providing a roadmap for safely and effectively implementing AI in schools. The short-term goals aim to introduce AI into current education systems, aligning it with the science of learning and ethical usage. Schools are encouraged to use AI across all learning areas, including core academics and career-technical programs. The long-term goals aim to fully integrate AI into education systems, transforming how students learn, collaborate, and acquire knowledge. The framework envisions a future where AI enhances leadership roles, supports adaptive instruction, and reshapes education for a rapidly changing world.

AI-powered tools are acting as co-pilots for teachers, enabling them to optimize their time for collaboration, action research, and planning. This allows educators to focus on personalized teaching, resulting in environments similar to top-performing global education systems. For students, AI helps structure learning experiences that emphasize critical thinking and creativity, making education more authentic and relevant. AI is being used to transform leadership responsibilities by supporting strategic thinking, innovative problem-solving, and operational management. AI tools help school leaders streamline administrative tasks like resource allocation, scheduling, and decision-making. This integration creates a more efficient school management system, akin to the operational improvements seen in other industries. Advanced AI models, such as adaptive learning systems, use machine learning to provide personalized educational content for students. This customization is expanding in countries like Singapore and South Korea, where AI enhances equitable access to education through personalized tutoring and digital textbooks. Document is providing examples of implementation of AI in education, e. g. in Estonia, the ProgeTiger platform, has introduced programming and robotics to students for the past decade, added new modules in 2023. These modules cover AI's role in various sectors and ethical considerations, guiding students in effectively using AI tools. In the United States, Florida's Department of Education developed the "Artificial Intelligence Foundations" program in collaboration with the University of Florida, aiming to boost AI literacy and prepare students for AI-related careers. Singapore launched NAIS 2.0, a national AI strategy focused on empowering individuals to confidently use AI, supported by the LearnAI platform for students and professionals.

The framework prioritizes ensuring that all students, especially those from underserved communities, have access to AI-powered tools. It stresses the importance of addressing equity issues in the integration of AI into education. The document emphasizes the importance of AI literacy for all stakeholders, including students, teachers, and parents. AI literacy involves understanding how AI works and how to use it effectively. This foundation is crucial to support the integration of AI into learning environments, ensuring its usefulness and accessibility.

The document on AI-powered learning environments discusses the ethical and safe use of AI. It highlights the need for a culture of ethical decision-making when using AI tools, including ensuring responsible usage. This involves addressing privacy, data security, and the appropriateness of AI content, particularly with the advent of generative AI. Safe AI use involves maintaining the privacy and security of data, making sure that AI models do not compromise the users' personal information. The document underscores the importance of equitable access to AI technologies, stressing that every student should benefit from AI advancements, particularly those from underserved communities. This aligns with the broader ethical responsibility of the education system to ensure fairness and inclusivity. It also draws attention to the environmental impact of AI technologies, urging schools and companies to consider sustainability in AI development and usage. This includes accountability for carbon footprints and other ecological effects linked to AI infrastructure.

The Framework of Using Artificial Intelligence Tools in Teaching, Student Work, and Research at the University of Zagreb Faculty of Organization and Informatics

University of Zagreb Faculty of Organization and Informatics (FOI) developed the document called *The framework of using artificial intelligence tools in teaching, student work, and research at the Univeristy of Zagreb Faculty of Organization and Informatics that o*utlines a comprehensive approach to integrating AI into teaching, student work, and research. This framework emphasizes the role of AI in enhancing academic activities while ensuring its application adheres to ethical, legal, and educational standards.

Through the framework FOI supports the development of AI competencies among students, faculty, and researchers. The framework is divided to 3 categories, guidelines for using AI in student works, guidelines for using AI in teaching and guidelines for using AI in scientific research and professional work.

Guidelines for using AI in student works states that students are permitted to use AI tools as part of their academic work, provided they adhere to specific guidelines to ensure ethical and transparent practices. AI tools can be employed in a manner similar to using references, images, or texts sourced from scientific papers or online research. When incorporating AI tools into their assignments, students must detail their usage in the methodology section of their work. This includes specifying the name and version of the AI tool used, the queries inputted, and any relevant session details. It is crucial that students do not submit AI-generated content without acknowledging its origin. They must clearly indicate which parts of their work were generated by AI and provide appropriate citations for the tools used.

Additionally, students are responsible for critically evaluating the AI-generated content, addressing any potential biases, and correcting inaccuracies. They must avoid using sensitive or private data when interacting with AI tools unless it complies with relevant privacy laws and guidelines. If students have any uncertainties about how to properly use AI tools, they should seek guidance from their teachers or mentors. AI tools often include features to export or share conversation history, which can help in documenting and verifying the process of AI use. This functionality supports transparency and allows students to provide evidence of their interactions with the AI tool.

Guidelines for using AI in teaching encourage teachers to use AI tools to aid in lesson planning and material creation. However, they must remain aware of potential limitations and challenges, such as issues of accuracy, bias, and ethical concerns. It is crucial to critically evaluate and selectively apply these tools to avoid introducing inaccuracies or biases into educational materials. The data and models used by these tools may be outdated or biased, as they rely on large but time-limited databases. Therefore, AI-generated content should be meticulously reviewed to ensure it aligns with course objectives and learning outcomes. Teachers must also disclose when and how AI has contributed to the creation of educational materials, especially if the contribution is significant, all while adhering to copyright and ethical standards.

AI should support rather than replace the fundamental academic efforts required in content preparation. Teachers have the discretion to set limits on the use of AI tools for specific tasks to ensure course objectives are met. If a teacher chooses to restrict or allow AI use, they must provide clear instructions, grading criteria, and deadlines to students. Students must follow academic writing practices and, if requested by the teacher, explain their use of AI in their work. Furthermore, teachers should design courses in a way that does not disadvantage students, such as by requiring them to purchase AI tools. AI tools should not be the sole means of verifying the authenticity of student work. All AI applications in teaching must comply with relevant legal frameworks, including data protection and privacy regulations, particularly concerning student data. Guidelines for using AI in scientific research and professional work is guided by a commitment to uphold the integrity of academic work while fostering innovation. FOI emphasizes that AI should be used to enhance, not replace, the skills and judgment of researchers. This entails a critical approach where researchers must effectively integrate AI tools into their research, ensuring that these tools complement their work rather than undermine it. Researchers are advised to be aware that while AI tools can produce content, they do not inherently constitute plagiarism, though there is a risk that AI might generate plagiarized material. It is crucial for researchers to assess and address any potential biases in the AI-generated content and to be cautious of incorrect data outputs, known as "hallucinations" in AI terminology.

In addition, FOI mandates that any work involving AI must clearly attribute responsibility to the human authors since AI tools cannot be recognized as authors due to their inability to assume responsibility for content. Researchers are required to transparently disclose all AI tools used in their work, including details about how these tools were applied in their research methodologies and acknowledgments. This approach ensures that the use of AI in research remains academically, ethically, and legally sound, aligning with the standards set by leading scientific publishers and contributing to responsible and innovative research practices. Document mentions training on the ethical and effective use of AI tools, with a focus on understanding both their potential and limitations. AI usage must comply with ethical norms and legal regulations, respecting privacy and intellectual property. AI tools cannot be credited as authors of academic work, and users must verify the accuracy and address biases in AI-generated content. Academic activities involving AI should be transparent. Users must disclose how AI tools were used, including in methodology, data analysis, and acknowledgments. Misrepresenting AI-generated content as solely one's own work is considered unethical. Students can use AI tools in their work but must cite and describe the AI's involvement. They must critically evaluate AI results, correct biases, and avoid using sensitive personal data improperly. Teachers can set specific guidelines regarding AI tool use in assignments and exams. AI tools should enhance the quality of education, foster digital competencies, and encourage innovative teaching methods. However, teachers must be aware of the limitations and potential biases of AI tools and should clearly communicate their use to students. AI should not replace thorough academic preparation but can support the creation of teaching materials. In research, AI tools must complement human skills and intuition. Researchers should be aware of AI's potential biases and inaccuracies, and clearly identify all AI tools used in their research. AI tools cannot be listed as authors, and any use of AI must be transparently documented. Researchers should also adhere to copyright laws and ethical standards, particularly when using AI-generated images or multimedia. FOI is committed to regularly updating its regulations and guidelines to align with technological advancements and European regulations. AI tools classified as high-risk by current standards will not be used for tasks such as monitoring exams.

FOI's AI framework promotes the responsible and ethical use of AI in academia by setting clear guidelines for its application in teaching, student work, and research. The framework emphasizes the importance of transparency, ethical compliance, and the proper attribution of AI contributions. It supports the development of AI competencies while ensuring that AI usage does not compromise academic integrity or legal standards. The guidelines aim to foster innovation and enhance educational practices while respecting intellectual property and ethical norms.

Beijing Consensus on Artificial Intelligence and Education

The Beijing Consensus on Artificial Intelligence (AI) and Education, which emerged from an international conference held in Beijing in May 2019. The consensus represents a collective agreement on how AI should be integrated into educational systems globally to achieve sustainable development goals, particularly Sustainable Development Goal 4 (SDG 4), which focuses on ensuring inclusive and equitable quality education and promoting lifelong learning opportunities for all. Although, in 2019 generative AI like ChatGPT, Gemini and other were not available this document is important for the understanding of AI use in education environments. The consensus highlights the necessity of systematically incorporating AI into education, teaching, and learning processes to foster innovation within educational systems. It advocates for leveraging AI to create open and flexible educational environments that provide equitable learning opportunities across diverse contexts. Central to the consensus is the emphasis on developing AI technologies that are human-controlled and centered on enhancing human capacities. The consensus stresses that AI should be deployed ethically, without discrimination, in an equitable, transparent, and auditable manner. A significant aspect of the consensus is the role of AI in facilitating lifelong learning. It supports the use of AI to create personalized learning pathways, ensuring that learning opportunities are accessible anytime, anywhere, and to everyone, thus promoting a lifelong approach to education. The consensus also addresses the role of teachers, emphasizing that while AI can support educators in their roles, human interaction between teachers and students must remain at the core of education. It advocates for ongoing teacher training to equip educators with the necessary skills to thrive in AI-enhanced educational settings.

Inclusivity and equity are central themes in the Beijing Consensus. It reaffirms the commitment to using AI to improve access to quality education for all, ensuring that AI does not exacerbate existing inequalities. The consensus specifically highlights the importance of supporting vulnerable groups, including those with disabilities and those in remote areas, through the application of AI in education. Gender equality is also a focal point, with a strong commitment to developing AI applications in education that are free from gender biases and actively promote equality. Lastly, the consensus calls for continuous research and evaluation of AI's impact on education. This ongoing assessment is deemed essential to guide future policy-making, ensuring that AI contributes positively to educational outcomes and broader societal goals. The Beijing Consensus provides a comprehensive framework for governments, international organizations, and stakeholders to align their educational policies and practices with the advancements in AI, ensuring that these technologies contribute effectively to global educational and social progress. The document emphasizes the importance of gender equity in the development and application of AI, particularly within educational contexts. It highlights that the existing gender gap in digital skills contributes to the underrepresentation of women in AI-related professions, which, in turn, exacerbates existing gender inequalities. To address this, the Beijing Consensus underscores the commitment to developing AI applications in education that are free from gender bias. It stresses that the data used in AI development should be sensitive to gender considerations, ensuring that AI tools promote gender equality. In addition, the document advocates for the promotion of gender equality in the development of AI tools. It calls for empowering girls and women with the skills needed to engage with AI, which is seen as essential for promoting gender equality within the AI workforce and among AI employers. By equipping women and girls with AI-related competencies, the goal is to reduce the gender gap and ensure that women can fully participate in and benefit from the opportunities that AI presents, thereby advancing gender equality across all sectors influenced by AI.

OECD: Opportunities, Guidelines and Guardrails for Effective and Equitable Use of AI in Education

The document discusses the opportunities, guidelines, and guardrails for the effective and equitable use of AI in education, developed by the OECD Secretariat and Education International in 2023. It highlights the increased role of digital technology in education, particularly after the COVID-19 pandemic, and the rapid advancements in AI, such as generative AI tools, which are beginning to impact traditional educational models. The document identifies several opportunities that AI and digital technology offer in education, such as enhancing personalized learning, supporting inclusive education, and reducing teachers' administrative burdens. It suggests that AI-powered tools can provide real-time feedback, help in managing classrooms, and support learners with disabilities or those at risk of dropping out. Additionally, AI has the potential to foster collaboration among educators and students and enhance the overall quality of education. However, the document also outlines significant risks associated with the use of AI and digital technologies in education. These include exacerbating existing inequalities due to unequal access to technology, potential biases in AI algorithms, data privacy concerns, and the risk of reducing human skills through over-reliance on technology. The document stresses the importance of maintaining a balance between digital and non-digital activities to protect the mental health and well-being of students and teachers. To mitigate these risks, the document proposes several guidelines, including ensuring equitable access to digital resources, promoting teacher agency in the use of AI tools, safeguarding data privacy, and involving educators and students in the co-creation of AI-enabled tools. It also emphasizes the need for research and evidence-based innovation in the application of AI in education, ensuring transparency and explainability of AI systems, and maintaining human support and alternatives in education processes. The overall aim of these guidelines is to harness the potential benefits of AI in education while addressing its risks, ensuring that the technology supports educational goals of equity, quality, and efficiency. The document concludes by advocating for collaborative efforts among governments, educators, and stakeholders to develop and implement these guidelines effectively.

The document presents nine key guidelines for the effective and equitable use of AI in education:

1. Equitable Access to Connectivity

Governments should ensure that all students and educators have access to affordable, high-quality internet connectivity and digital infrastructure. This is crucial for enabling the widespread use of advanced technology in education and for preparing for any future shifts to remote learning.

2. Equitable Access to Digital Learning Resources

Educational jurisdictions should provide quality digital learning resources that are accessible to all students and teachers both in and outside of school. Teachers should have the autonomy to use these resources within the context of school policies, ensuring that all learners can develop their digital skills.

3. Teacher Agency and Professional Learning

The use of digital tools should be an integral part of teachers' professional competencies, supported by ongoing professional development. Teachers should be empowered to critically engage with digital resources and have the autonomy to make pedagogical choices in their classrooms.

4. Student and Teacher Wellbeing

The development and use of AI-enabled technology should prioritize the wellbeing and mental health of both students and teachers. A balanced approach between digital and non-digital activities is essential to maintaining the relational and social aspects of education.

5. Co-Creation of AI-Enabled Tools

Teachers, students, and other end users should be involved in the design and development of AI-enabled educational tools. This co-creation process ensures that the tools are pedagogically sound, culturally relevant, and meet the actual needs of the educational community.

6. Research and Evidence-Based Innovation

Jurisdictions should support research on the effective use of digital tools in education, including practice-engaged research projects that involve teachers in the innovation process. This research should focus on the impact of technology on learning outcomes and equity.

7. Ethics, Safety, and Data Protection

Strong data protection policies are essential to safeguard the privacy and security of students and teachers. Jurisdictions should ensure that AI tools are tested for bias, safety, and opportunities before being introduced into education systems, and that ethical guidelines are established for their use.

8. Transparency and Explainability

When using AI-enabled tools in education, particularly those with high stakes, jurisdictions should be transparent about how these tools work and the objectives behind their use. The functioning of AI systems should be explained to educators, students, and parents, ensuring that these tools are used in a trustworthy manner.

9. Human Support and Alternatives

While AI tools can automate parts of the educational process, it is crucial that human support remains available. Jurisdictions should ensure that when issues arise, learners and educators can access timely human assistance. Additionally, human alternatives should be provided when appropriate, particularly in high-stakes scenarios like assessments.

AI Report by the European Digital Education Hub's Squad

The European Digital Education Hub's Squad AI provided report on artificial intelligence in education called AI Report by the European Digital Education Hub's Squad on Artificial Intelligence in Education in 2023. The European Digital Education Hub (EDEH) is an initiative of the European Commission, funded by the Erasmus+ program (2021-2027) and operated by a consortium of 13 organizations under a service contract with the European Education and Culture Executive Agency (EACEA). It emphasizes the need for teachers to develop new competences to effectively teach in an AI-driven environment. These competences are categorized into teaching *for* AI, teaching *with* AI, and teaching *about* AI, each requiring specific skills and knowledge. The document outlines that teaching *for* AI involves developing competences that enable both teachers and students to engage confidently, critically, and safely with AI systems. The focus is on equipping all citizens, including educators and learners, with the necessary knowledge, skills, and attitudes to live and work in a world increasingly shaped by AI. This approach emphasizes understanding AI as a pervasive technology that influences various aspects of daily life and society.

Teachers are expected to foster digital literacy, critical thinking, and ethical awareness in students, helping them navigate the complexities of AI systems. The competences needed for teaching *for* AI are not solely technical but also involve a broader understanding of how AI affects society, ethics, and individual rights. The goal is to prepare students to interact with AI applications in a way that is informed, critical, and aligned with democratic values.

The document also notes that teaching *for* AI can be integrated into various subjects across the curriculum, not just in technical courses. This means embedding AI-related topics in areas like language, history, natural sciences, and the arts, to ensure that all students, regardless of their academic focus, develop a foundational understanding of AI and its societal implications. In summary, teaching *for* AI is about preparing students to be informed and responsible users of AI technologies, equipping them with the competences to critically assess and interact with AI in various aspects of their lives. The document emphasizes that *teaching with AI* focuses on how educators can effectively integrate AI tools into their teaching practices to enhance educational outcomes. This approach involves using AI systems to support various aspects of teaching and learning, including personalized learning experiences, real-time feedback, and the automation of routine tasks, allowing teachers to focus more on student engagement and higher-order thinking skills. Competences for teaching *with* AI require teachers to have a solid understanding of AI technologies, including how they function, their potential benefits, and their limitations. Educators need to develop the ability to critically assess AI tools, understanding when and how to use them appropriately to support their pedagogical goals. This includes knowledge of the underlying algorithms, data governance, and the ethical implications of using AI in education. Teachers should be able to select and apply AI-based tools that align with their curriculum and educational objectives while considering the efficacy, ease of use, and privacy issues associated with these tools. They are also expected to understand the impact of AI on student learning, such as how AI systems might affect student autonomy, the development of critical thinking skills, and the potential for algorithmic bias.

In addition, the document highlights the importance of continuous professional development for teachers in the context of AI. Educators need to stay updated on the latest AI advancements and be prepared to adapt their teaching strategies accordingly. This involves not only learning how to use AI tools effectively but also understanding the broader implications of AI in education, such as the need for transparency, accountability, and fairness in AI-driven decisions. In essence, teaching *with* AI requires educators to be knowledgeable about AI technologies and their applications in education, enabling them to use these tools to enhance teaching and learning processes while being mindful of their ethical and practical implications.

The document outlines that teaching *about* AI involves educating students on the technical and foundational aspects of artificial intelligence, preparing them to understand and potentially contribute to the development of AI technologies. This approach is more specialized and technical compared to teaching *for* or *with* AI, and it focuses on imparting knowledge about how AI systems work, their underlying principles, and the broader implications of AI. Competences for teaching *about* AI require educators to have a deep understanding of AI concepts, including machine learning, data analysis, algorithms, and the ethical and societal impacts of AI. Teachers need to be able to explain the fundamentals of AI, such as perception, representation and reasoning, learning, and the impact of AI on society. This includes differentiating between AI and related concepts like machine learning, as well as providing students with a clear understanding of AI systems as autonomous agents that interact with their environments. The curriculum for teaching *about* AI should cover topics like supervised and unsupervised learning, data collection and processing, computer vision, natural language processing (NLP), and robotics. Educators are encouraged to provide hands-on experiences where students can develop simple AI-based solutions, such as programming tasks or projects that involve AI applications. In addition, teaching *about* AI also involves discussing the ethical implications of AI, including issues of bias, privacy, and the societal consequences of AI technologies. Students should be made aware of the potential risks and benefits of

AI, and how AI systems can influence decision-making and policy. Teaching *about* AI is aimed at providing students with a comprehensive understanding of AI technologies, preparing them not only to use AI but also to critically analyze and contribute to the field. This requires teachers to be well-versed in both the technical aspects of AI and the broader ethical and societal issues that arise from its use.

The report highlights the importance of supporting teachers through professional development, helping them understand the technology, its applications, and its ethical implications. The document also provides practical examples and scenarios for integrating AI into different levels of education. These examples range from teaching AI ethics and computational thinking to more technical topics like machine learning. The report underlines the necessity of educating students about the fundamentals of AI, its history, applications, and societal impact, ensuring they are prepared for future careers involving AI.

In terms of governance, the report advocates for a risk-based approach to AI in education, stressing the importance of protecting students' data and ensuring fairness. Ethical considerations are central to the report, urging educators to be aware of AI's potential biases and its impact on human rights. The report states that effective integration of AI into education requires a multifaceted approach that includes developing teacher competences, supporting educational institutions, and ensuring ethical governance. In addition, AI should be used as a tool to enhance educational outcomes, but it is essential to be aware of its limitations and potential risks, particularly concerning data privacy and algorithmic bias. One of the main points is ongoing support, training, and policy development that are necessary to ensure that AI contributes positively to education, empowering both teachers and students in a rapidly changing digital landscape.

Personalization

The document discusses the role of AI in personalizing education, emphasizing that AI has the potential to tailor learning experiences to individual students' needs, abilities, and learning styles. Personalization through AI is seen as a significant advantage in education because it allows for more targeted and effective teaching, especially in large classes where it is difficult for teachers to provide individualized attention. AI can personalize learning by analyzing large amounts of data about a student's performance, behavior, and preferences. This data-driven approach enables AI systems to offer customized feedback, suggest appropriate learning materials, and adapt the pace and content of lessons to suit each student's unique needs. The document highlights that personalization is particularly beneficial in identifying and addressing the strengths and weaknesses of students, thereby helping them achieve better educational outcomes. In addition, the document also notes the importance of teachers being aware of the limitations and potential risks associated with AI-driven personalization. For instance, there is a concern that AI systems may reinforce biases if they rely on biased data or algorithms. Therefore, teachers must be equipped with the knowledge to critically assess AI tools and ensure that the personalization provided by these systems is fair, ethical, and aligned with educational goals.

The document suggests that AI can support not only the personalization of student learning but also the professional development of teachers by recommending relevant training materials and helping them improve their teaching strategies based on data-driven insights. The document acknowledges the potential of AI to revolutionize personalization in education, offering significant benefits in tailoring learning experiences. However, it also underscores the need for careful consideration of the ethical implications and the importance of teacher involvement in ensuring that AI-driven personalization is used effectively and responsibly.

Recommendations

The report provides several recommendations which are aimed at enhancing the integration of AI into educational systems and ensuring that both educators and students can benefit from its potential while mitigating its risks. Chapter about teacher competence emphasis the need to develop specific competences for teaching *for*, *with*, and *about* AI. This includes understanding the impact of AI on education, being able to critically assess AI tools, and knowing how to integrate AI into various teaching contexts. There is a need for differentiated competences based on whether teachers are using AI as a support tool or teaching the technical aspects of AI. All teachers should understand AI's impact on society and be equipped to teach students about these implications. The chapter about teachers support for teachers using AI states that educational institutions should provide continuous professional development opportunities for teachers to learn about AI, its applications, and its ethical implications. Schools should ensure that AI tools come with adequate training materials and support for teachers to integrate them effectively into their teaching practices. Regarding the institutional and national support, schools and educational institutions should allocate time and resources for teachers to develop their AI-related skills and integrate AI into their daily practice. This could include providing access to AI-based class management tools and creating learning groups based on student abilities rather than age. At the national level, there should be guidance on teacher competences for AI, and AI should be integrated into initial teacher education and professional development catalogues. The report covers also curriculum and teaching strategies and highlights that AI, coding, and statistics should be included in the curriculum for initial teacher education. Educational leaders should start planning for how AI will affect teaching roles and how teachers can use AI to enhance learning outcomes. Integrated learning scenarios that use AI as a tool to create more transdisciplinary approaches should be encouraged. AI can also help generate overviews of content taught in different classes, aiding in the creation of integrated teaching strategies. Institutions should organize discussions and reflections on the legal and ethical questions surrounding AI use in education. This includes considerations of data privacy, algorithmic bias, and the broader societal impact of AI technologies. Schools and educators should be involved in planning the deployment of AI in education to ensure it aligns with ethical standards and educational goals. There should be policies and incentives at both national and European levels to encourage the use of AI in education, supported by guidelines such as the Ethical Guidelines on the Use of Artificial Intelligence (AI) and Data in Teaching and Learning. AI-related education should focus on building both technological and human dimensions of AI understanding in students, ensuring they are prepared for the future labor market regardless of their career paths.

UNESCO AI Competency Frameworks for Teachers and Students

The Framework AI Competency Framework for Teachers

The framework *AI Competency Framework for Teachers* (AI CFT) developed by UNESCO as part of their Education 2030 Agenda outlines a comprehensive framework aimed at helping teachers develop competencies in the age of artificial intelligence. The framework seeks to guide educators in navigating the growing role of AI in education, enabling them to use AI tools effectively while maintaining human-centered teaching and learning approaches.

AI is acknowledged for its potential to process vast amounts of information, generate content, and provide insights that can enhance education management and decision-making. However, the framework also stresses the risks of AI, including issues related to data privacy, inequality, and the potential to devalue the roles of teachers.

The AI Competency Framework addresses these challenges by identifying the essential knowledge, skills, and values that educators need in this new AI-driven environment. The framework is divided into five key dimensions of competency:

1. Human-centered mindset
    a. This emphasizes the importance of safeguarding human agency, rights, and interaction in the use of AI within educational environments.
2. Ethics of AI
    a. This dimension focuses on ensuring that teachers understand and can apply ethical principles related to AI, including privacy, data security, and fairness.
3. AI foundations and applications
    a. Teachers are expected to gain an understanding of how AI works, how AI models are trained, and how to select appropriate AI tools for teaching.
4. AI pedagogy
    a. This involves integrating AI into teaching strategies to enhance learning experiences, assessment, and student support.
5. AI for professional development
    a. This aspect emphasizes the use of AI to support teachers' ongoing professional growth, helping them personalize their learning and collaborate more effectively.

Each of these dimensions is further divided into three levels of progression—Acquire, Deepen, and Create—that reflect the gradual mastery of AI-related competencies, from basic understanding to advanced, innovative use of AI in education.

Acquire Level

At the Acquire stage, the goal is to provide teachers with fundamental AI knowledge and skills. This level is designed for teachers who have little or no prior exposure to AI. The focus is on establishing AI literacy by helping educators understand what AI is, how it functions, and the basic ethical issues involved. Teachers are expected to gain a critical understanding that AI is a human-led technology with significant impacts on human agency, rights, and social justice.

The Acquire level involves:

- Understanding human-led AI

Teachers learn that AI tools are created and controlled by people, which means the consequences of AI's use, including both benefits and risks, are determined by human decisions.

- Ethical awareness

Teachers are introduced to the fundamental ethical issues surrounding AI, such as data privacy, inclusion, and sustainability, and how these can affect their students.

- Basic technical knowledge

Teachers are taught basic concepts of AI, such as how AI models are trained, and the different types of AI tools. They also learn how to select and use appropriate AI tools for education.

- Integration into professional development

Teachers explore how AI tools can enhance their own professional growth by identifying learning needs and personalizing their professional development pathways.

Deepen Level

At the Deepen level, teachers move beyond basic knowledge to a more proficient and in-depth understanding of AI and its application in the classroom. This stage targets teachers who have some experience using AI in their teaching and are ready to integrate it more deeply into their practices.

The Deepen level involves:

- Human accountability

Teachers become responsible for ensuring the safe and ethical use of AI in educational settings. They learn how to critically assess AI tools for their ethical implications, ensuring that they are used in a manner that is inclusive and respects students' rights to privacy and safety.

- Advanced AI application

Teachers develop the ability to select, evaluate, and implement AI tools that enhance teaching and learning. They are expected to be more adept at using AI to design pedagogical strategies that align with human-centered teaching methods.

- Professional collaboration

Teachers at this level are encouraged to use AI to foster collaborative professional development, using AI tools to enhance peer learning within their institutions.

Create Level

At the Create level, teachers are expected to master AI in such a way that they can innovate and lead the use of AI in educational environments. This level is intended for expert teachers who have already gained significant experience and understanding of AI and are ready to explore creative applications of AI to transform teaching and learning.

The Create level involves:

- Innovative AI integration

Teachers at this stage develop new, creative ways to use AI in education. They are expected to explore advanced AI tools and systems to design transformative educational practices, reshaping how AI is used to improve learning outcomes.

- Co-creating ethical rules

Teachers are involved in the co-creation of ethical guidelines and policies for AI in education, contributing to the broader conversation about AI's role in education and society.

- AI leadership in professional transformation

Teachers lead the use of AI to support broader professional transformations, not only in their own teaching practice but also in shaping organizational learning and school-wide AI initiatives.

A human-centered approach is at the heart of the framework, which means that AI should always be used to enhance human capacities rather than replace them. The guidelines encourage educators to critically assess AI tools, ensuring their safe and ethical application in classrooms.

The framework also highlights key principles that underpin this approach, such as the protection of teachers' rights, promoting sustainable AI practices, and ensuring inclusive access to AI technologies for all educators, regardless of their prior experience with digital tools.

Overall, the AI Competency Framework aims to equip teachers with the tools they need to harness the benefits of AI while mitigating its risks, ensuring that technology complements and enhances their teaching rather than undermining it. The framework serves as a global reference for developing national AI competency programs, providing educators with strategies for continuous learning and professional development in an evolving digital landscape.

AI Competency Framework for Students

This framework is designed to prepare students to engage with AI technology as informed users, creators, and responsible citizens. The core goal of the framework is to integrate AI literacy into global education systems, fostering a human-centered, ethical, and sustainable approach to AI.

The framework emphasizes that AI is becoming an essential part of our lives, and students must be equipped with the values, knowledge, and skills necessary to understand and contribute to AI's development. It identifies four key aspects of AI competencies, Human-centered mindset, Ethics of AI, AI techniques and applications, and AI system design. These competencies are developed across three progression levels: Understand, Apply, and Create, reflecting different stages of mastery.

Human-Centered Mindset

This aspect focuses on the values, beliefs, and critical thinking skills that students must develop to engage meaningfully with AI. A human-centered mindset emphasizes AI's role in serving human needs and promoting sustainable development. It encourages students to critically assess AI tools to ensure they are appropriate for specific purposes, consider their ethical and societal implications, and recognize the importance of human agency and accountability.

Key competencies within the human-centered mindset include:

- Human agency

Students learn that AI is human-led, and they understand the importance of human control over AI systems, recognizing the consequences when human agency is compromised.

- Human accountability

Students develop awareness that humans are accountable for the design and use of AI, especially in high-stakes decision-making. This competency ensures students understand legal and ethical responsibilities.

- Citizenship in the AI era

Students gain an understanding of how AI impacts society and develop a sense of responsibility to promote inclusive and sustainable AI practices. This competency also encourages lifelong learning and engagement with AI.

Ethics of AI

The ethics of AI focuses on the moral and social considerations of using AI technologies. This aspect emphasizes students' ability to navigate ethical dilemmas, comply with AI regulations, and internalize key ethical principles. As AI becomes more pervasive, it is crucial that students develop a strong ethical foundation.

Key competencies in the ethics of AI include:

- Embodied ethics

Students are expected to understand core ethical debates around AI, such as its impact on human rights, social justice, inclusion, and climate change. This includes understanding concepts like "do no harm," proportionality, non-discrimination, sustainability, and transparency.

- Safe and responsible use

Students are taught to use AI tools responsibly, ensuring their data privacy is protected, and they understand the risks involved in AI systems.

- Ethics by design

Students learn to adopt ethical principles from the outset in the design and implementation of AI systems, ensuring AI aligns with ethical standards throughout its life cycle.

AI Techniques and Applications

This aspect covers the technical knowledge and practical skills required to engage with AI tools. It emphasizes an understanding of AI's foundations, from algorithms to data models, and encourages students to apply these concepts in real-world tasks.

Key competencies in this aspect include:

- AI foundations

Students develop a basic understanding of AI concepts, including data, algorithms, and the processes behind AI tools.

- Application skills

Students are expected to apply AI knowledge in practical settings, adapting AI tools to specific tasks and real-world challenges.

- Creating AI tools

Advanced students are encouraged to go beyond using AI tools and actively participate in creating and improving AI systems, focusing on designing solutions that address real-world problems.

AI System Design

AI system design focuses on the comprehensive set of skills needed to design, develop, and optimize AI systems. This aspect encourages students to engage in problem-solving and creative exploration of AI, applying engineering principles to AI system development.

Key competencies include:

- Problem scoping

Students are taught how to define and scope problems that AI systems can address, a fundamental skill in AI development.

- Architecture design

Students learn to design AI system architectures, including how to choose and configure the right models, data sources, and algorithms.

- Iteration and feedback loops
- This competency teaches students to refine AI systems through iterative processes, testing, and optimization, ensuring systems are effective, ethical, and suitable for real-world deployment.

These four key aspects together provide a holistic approach to AI education, balancing technical knowledge with ethical considerations and human-centered design, preparing students to be responsible, skilled participants in AI-driven societies.

The framework also describes three progression levels, Understand, Apply, and Create which describe increasing levels of mastery over AI competencies for students. These levels guide the development of AI knowledge, skills, and ethical considerations as students move from basic understanding to advanced creation of AI solutions.

Understand

At this level, all students are expected to develop a foundational understanding of AI. It is considered essential for everyone, as AI is becoming a ubiquitous part of daily life. The focus is on ensuring that students gain a basic awareness of what AI is, its ethical implications, and how it impacts society.

- Goal

To provide all students with the knowledge and values to safely and responsibly interact with AI in their personal and social lives.

- Content

Students are introduced to AI concepts, ethical principles, and human-centered perspectives. They should be able to explain basic AI processes, relate them to real-world examples, and grasp the ethical and social issues AI presents.

- Outcome

This level lays the groundwork for further study of AI and does not expect students to specialize in AI-related fields. It provides an essential knowledge base, including understanding the values behind AI design and its broader societal impacts.

Apply

This level goes beyond understanding and focuses on practical engagement with AI. Students are expected to actively use AI tools and apply their knowledge in real-world contexts. The "Apply" level is relevant for all students, regardless of whether they intend to specialize in AI, as AI is integrated across many sectors and industries.

- Goal

To enable students to become responsible and effective users of AI in various contexts, from education to future work environments.

- Content

Students are expected to use AI tools and techniques to solve practical problems, demonstrating their ability to apply theoretical knowledge in more complex situations. This includes adapting AI tools for specific purposes, as well as critically assessing the technical methods behind them.

- Outcome

At this level, students will develop transferable AI-related knowledge and skills, and be able to use AI in diverse applications. Some students may conclude their AI education at this level, while others may progress to the next stage.

Create

At the "Create" level, students are encouraged to take on an active role as AI co-creators, developing new AI tools and solutions. This level requires a deep understanding of AI, including the ability to innovate, design, and improve AI systems. Students at this level are expected to take a leadership role in AI design, focusing on human-centered and ethical AI solutions that address real-world challenges.

- Goal

To prepare students to become AI innovators and leaders, capable of designing new AI systems that positively impact society.

- Content

Students engage in designing, implementing, and testing AI tools, integrating ethical considerations throughout the process. They are also expected to understand the broader social, ethical, and regulatory implications of AI.

- Outcome

Students at this level will gain the skills to create AI tools that address real-world challenges. They will also reinforce their role as ethical co-creators of AI, capable of personalizing AI for societal benefit, and they may pursue further specialized study or careers in AI.

These three progression levels serve as a structured pathway for students to develop their AI competencies. The framework ensures that all students, regardless of their future career plans, acquire fundamental AI knowledge and ethical awareness, with the option to specialize in AI design and creation at the highest level.

One of the main highlights is the human-centered approach, which advocates for AI that prioritizes human dignity, agency, and justice. It stresses the importance of students critically assessing AI's social, ethical, and environmental impacts. The ethical aspect encourages responsible AI use, emphasizing transparency, privacy protection, non-discrimination, and sustainability. This focus ensures students become conscious decision-makers about when AI should be used and how it should be designed.

The framework also promotes inclusivity, ensuring that AI education is accessible to all students, regardless of their backgrounds or abilities. It underlines the need for lifelong learning, with AI competencies that are adaptable to new technologies and contexts.

The document provides guidelines for curriculum development, highlighting the importance of progressive, age-appropriate learning sequences. It aims to prepare students not just to adapt to AI but to actively participate in shaping AI-driven societies. This framework serves as a global reference point to help nations build AI-related educational programs that align with ethical, social, and environmental objectives.

Digital Competence Framework (DCF)

Developing digital competencies through the use of generative AI can provide students with valuable skills that are increasingly important in today's world. Digital Competence Framework (DCF) for the European schools was developed in 2020 based on the 5 competence areas and the 21 sub-competences' of the European Digital Competence Framework for Citizens (DigComp), which provides a common language and structure for digital competence. It defines the skills necessary for individuals to use digital technologies confidently, critically, and responsibly. The DigiComp framework (European Framework for the Digital Competence of Educators) outlines the digital competencies required for educators to effectively integrate digital technologies into teaching and learning. AI tools can support the achievement of these competencies across the various areas defined by DigiComp. Document Digital Competence Framework for the European Schools outlines a structured approach to developing digital competence in students across European schools. It provides a comprehensive guide for educators to integrate digital skills into the curriculum, ensuring that every student acquires essential digital knowledge, skills, and attitudes necessary for education, work, and civic life in a rapidly evolving technological landscape. The framework is designed for educators and students in the European schools system, spanning from nursery to upper secondary education. It provides proficiency levels that align with different educational stages and helps teachers tailor digital competence development to the needs and capacities of students across all age groups. The framework promotes the integration of digital skills across various subjects and levels, rather than treating it as a standalone subject. This allows students to apply digital skills in multiple contexts, helping them develop holistically over time. To aid implementation, the document includes examples of pedagogical activities that educators can adapt to foster digital skills in their classrooms. This framework is intended to support the mission of European schools to equip students with the digital skills necessary for lifelong learning and active participation in society. The document offers several practical examples of pedagogical activities that educators can use to develop digital skills in their classrooms. For instance, in the area of Information and data literacy, teachers can engage younger students in an online scavenger hunt where they search for specific images using simple keywords. As students progress, older groups can take on more challenging tasks, such as finding detailed information or exploring current events through online newspapers. Another related activity encourages students to experiment with different search engines, comparing the opportunities of various search terms to develop a deeper understanding of how online information is organized and accessed. When it comes to fostering Digital content creation, one suggested activity involves having students create their own multimedia books. These digital books can incorporate text, drawings, audio, and even video, offering students a way to practice integrating different types of content while developing technical skills. Similarly, educators can guide students in creating stop-motion movies, an activity that nurtures both creativity and an understanding of digital media production. In the domain of Digital identity management, teachers can introduce activities that help students reflect on their online presence. For example, students might create digital avatars or manage profiles that represent their personal or academic identities. This activity not only helps students grasp the importance of protecting their data but also gives them a practical understanding of how to manage digital identities ethically and responsibly. These activities are designed to integrate digital skills into various subjects, allowing students to develop competencies such as creativity, collaboration, and critical thinking while engaging with technology in meaningful ways. In Table 1 can be seen all categories and subcategories of European Framework for the Digital Competence of Educators.

Table 1. European framework for the digital competence of educators

1	**Information and data literacy**	
	To articulate information needs, to locate and retrieve digital data, information and content. To judge the relevance of the source and its content. To store, manage, and organize digital data, information and content.	1.1 Browsing, searching and filtering data, information and digital content
		1.2 Evaluating data, information and digital content
		1.3 Managing data, information and digital content
2	**Communication and collaboration**	
	To interact, communicate and collaborate through digital technologies while being aware of cultural and generational diversity. To participate in society through public and private digital services and participatory citizenship. To manage one's digital identity and reputation.	2.1 Interacting through digital technologies
		2.2 Sharing through digital technologies
		2.3 Engaging in citizenship through digital technologies
		2.4 Collaborating through digital technologies
		2.5 Netiquette
		2.6 Managing digital identity
3	**Digital content creation**	
	To create and edit digital content. To improve and integrate information and content into an existing body of knowledge while understanding how copyright and licences are to be applied. To know how to give understandable instructions for a computer system.	3.1 Developing digital content
		3.2 Integrating and re-elaborating digital content
		3.3 Copyright and licences
		3.4 Programming
4	**Safety**	
	To protect devices, content, personal data and privacy in digital environments. To protect physical and psychological health, and to be aware of digital technologies for social well-being and social inclusion. To be aware of the environmental impact of digital technologies and their use.	4.1 Protecting devices
		4.2 Protecting personal data and privacy

continued on following page

Table 1. Continued

1	Information and data literacy	
		4.3 Protecting health and well-being
		4.4 Protecting the environment
5	**Problem solving**	
	To identify needs and problems, and to resolve conceptual problems and problem situations in digital environments. To use digital tools to innovate processes and products. To keep up-to-date with the digital evolution.	5.1 Solving technical problems
		5.2 Identifying needs and technological responses
		5.3 Creatively using digital technologies
		5.4 Identifying digital competence gaps

FRAMEWORK FOR USING AI TOOLS FOR CONDUCTING PERSONALIZED TEACHING

Creating a framework for the use of generative AI in education involves considering how these technologies can improve learning while addressing potential challenges. According to the AI report (The European Digital Education Hub's Squad, 2023) recommendations for development of AI competency frameworks should be guided by frameworks that include AI literacy, AI and pedagogy, and ethics of AI. These frameworks should help educators understand AI tools, the influence of AI on education, and the ethical considerations involved in its use. Azukas (2019, pp. 281–282) and Pane et al. (2015) acknowledged the significant variation in the instructional models of the schools they studied. However, they identified five key strategies that characterized personalized learning environments, which were based on a framework developed by the Bill and Melinda Gates Foundation. Each of these strategies included a range of tools or features within the personalized learning environment, some of which were fundamental to the approach, while others served as enablers to support its implementation.

The personalization framework has five components. First, learner profiles (1) are used to record individual student strengths, needs, motivations, progress, and goals, which are collaboratively developed by teachers and students. These profiles are informed by data gathered from various sources, such as projects, tests, presentations, quizzes, and software, and are regularly reviewed in discussions between students and teachers to tailor learning strategies. Second, personal learning paths (2) are established, allowing students to meet performance standards through multiple pathways. This model grants students the autonomy to make choices about the content and structure of their learning. Schools use diverse instructional strategies and curriculum materials to accommodate the varied needs of all learners. In addition, one-on-one academic support is integrated into the school day, with opportunities for students to engage in learning experiences outside of the classroom. Competency-based progression (3) is another essential component, where student progress is assessed against clearly defined learning goals. Assessments are administered when students are ready to demonstrate their competency, allowing them to progress at their own pace and earn credit upon mastery. The framework also emphasizes the importance of flexible learning environments (4). Schools adapt the physical aspects of the learning space, such as size, classroom organization, and furniture, to support personalized learning. Staff and time are utilized flexibly to meet the needs of students, with data-driven decisions guiding learning time and grouping strategies. Technology plays a significant role in this approach and is made available to all students. Finally, the framework focuses on promoting college and career readiness (5). Curricula, activities, and programs are designed to foster academic and non-academic skills, such as through college visits, college-level courses, internships, and career surveys.

This framework is based on the *A comprehensive AI policy education framework for university teaching and learning* by Chan (2023), *The potential impact of artificial intelligence on equity and inclusion in education OECD Education Working Paper No. 320* by OECD (2024) and analysis of three case studies conducted in primary and secondary schools and higher education which are presented in the chapters *Case Study of using AI tools in primary school, Case Study of using AI tools in vocational school* and *Case Study of using AI tools in higher education.* The main purpose of the framework is to provide guidance to teachers and educators for developing personalized learning materials for different types of students and their needs with generative AI tools. In addition, the stakeholders and principals can use the framework for implementing the use of generative AI tools into their schools, curriculum and institutions. The framework consists of 5 categories and 22 subcategories.

In addition to the framework, this chapter provides learning scenarios that teachers can use and adapt to their needs and subjects they are teaching. The learning scenarios are developed based on the proposed framework and its elements. They are divided into 5 categories and were developed with the help of ChatGPT. This is important because it shows how generative AI tools can help in building and developing personalized learning materials and activities for students.

The proposed framework for the use of generative AI tools in personalized learning is designed to integrate AI into educational practices, enhancing traditional methods while focusing on individual student needs. The framework emphasizes AI literacy for educators, ensuring they have a basic knowledge of AI fundamentals, its potential applications, and limitations. This knowledge enables them to make informed decisions about incorporating AI tools into their teaching strategies. The framework aims to integrate generative AI with existing teaching methods, ensuring that these tools complement rather than replace traditional practices. It supports personalized learning by using AI tools to develop customized content, learning pathways, and assessments for each student's needs. The use of generative AI tools also aims to boost student engagement and motivation by providing interactive and dynamic learning experiences.

The proposed framework can be seen in Table 2 and it offers an approach to integrating generative AI tools in personalized learning, ensuring that AI strengthen education by being inclusive and aligned with individual student needs.

Table 2. Framework for implementing generative AI tools in personalized teaching and learning

1. AI LITERACY AND TRAINING				
AI Literacy is essential for teachers to understand how AI works, its potential applications in education, and its limitations, enabling informed use of AI tools.				
1.1. Understanding AI Fundamentals	**1.2. Generative AI Tools**	**1.3. Critical AI Evaluation**	**1.4. Facilitation and Customization**	**1.5. Continuous Professional Development**
2. PEDAGOGY				

continued on following page

Table 2. Continued

<table>
<tr><td colspan="7">1. AI LITERACY AND TRAINING</td></tr>
<tr><td colspan="7">Pedagogy involves integrating AI tools into teaching methods in a way that complements traditional educational practices, focusing on personalized learning.</td></tr>
<tr><td>2.1. Integration with Teaching Strategies</td><td>2.2. Curriculum Alignment</td><td>2.3. Guidelines for Personalized Content Creation</td><td>2.4. Resource Recommendations</td><td>2.5. Cross-Subject Integration</td><td>2.6. Student Engagement and Motivation</td><td>2.7. Collaboration and Peer Learning</td></tr>
<tr><td colspan="7">3. LANGUAGE AND ACCESSIBILITY</td></tr>
<tr><td colspan="7">Accessibility ensures that AI tools help make education more inclusive, providing support for diverse learning needs of students.</td></tr>
<tr><td colspan="3">3.1. Accessibility</td><td colspan="2">3.2. Language and Cultural Inclusivity</td><td colspan="2">3.3. Age-Specific Guidelines</td></tr>
<tr><td colspan="7">4. EVALUATION</td></tr>
<tr><td colspan="7">Evaluation means that teachers need to continuously evaluate AI tools and how they influence on students’ performance.</td></tr>
<tr><td colspan="3">4.1. AI evaluation</td><td colspan="2">4.2. Students feedback</td><td colspan="2">4.3. Transparency and Accountability</td></tr>
<tr><td colspan="7">5. ENGAGEMENT STRATEGIES</td></tr>
<tr><td colspan="7">Engagement strategies ensure that AI tools are used for development of personalized leaning materials.</td></tr>
<tr><td colspan="2">5.1. Multimodal Learning</td><td colspan="2">5.2. Interactive Learning</td><td colspan="2">5.3. Contextual and Repetitive</td><td>5.4. Customized Task Difficulty</td></tr>
</table>

Category 1 AI Literacy and Training

AI literacy and training enable teachers to understand and exploit the power of artificial intelligence in education and allow accurate and responsible integration of artificial intelligence in teaching. Training ensures that teachers can critically evaluate AI tools and adapt their content to specific educational contexts. The subcategories of AI Literacy and training are shown below in Table 3. Teachers and students must develop digital literacy skills to interact effectively with AI tools which includes understanding how AI systems function, evaluating their outputs critically, and recognizing potential biases thus AI literacy can empower students to navigate AI-driven learning environments confidently and responsibly (Keengwe, 2023).

Table 3. Subcategories of Category 1 AI Literacy and training

Subcategory	Description
1.1. Understanding AI Fundamentals	Teachers learn the basics of AI, including machine learning, natural language processing, and AI limitations.
1.2. Generative AI Tools	Training on how to use AI tools like ChatGPT, image generators, and other generative AI technologies for content creation.
1.3. Critical AI Evaluation	Teachers develop the ability to critically assess AI outputs, identifying bias, errors, and inaccuracies in AI-generated content.
1.4. Facilitation and Customization	Teachers learn to adjust AI tools to fit curriculum goals, customizing AI-generated materials to meet student needs and educational standards.
1.5. Continuous Professional Development	Ongoing AI education for teachers, focusing on emerging AI tools, ethical AI usage, and best practices for classroom integration.

1.1. Understanding AI Fundamentals

Understanding the basics of artificial intelligence is essential for integrating artificial intelligence effectively into classrooms. This subcategory focuses on the establishment of basic knowledge about AI, including its principles, functions, and potential application in education. Teachers need to learn the basics of AI, such as machine learning, natural language processing, and data-driven algorithms. This knowledge enables teachers to recognize the advantages of artificial intelligence tools, such as personalized learning experiences, automatic assessment and simplified complex tasks. In addition, understanding of the fundamentals of AI equips teachers with the ability to identify the limitations and challenges of AI, such as algorithmic biases, data privacy concerns and human supervision. This subcategory aims to teach the teachers to make informed decisions about the use of artificial intelligence in their teaching practices and to ensure that artificial intelligence serves as a supportive tool, not as an alternative to traditional teaching methods. Teachers need to be able to evaluate AI tools critically to ensure that they are ethically and effectively used to improve student learning outcomes. This knowledge allows teachers to create personalized materials using artificial intelligence tools such as generative AI (e.g. ChatGPT), while having in mind the effects and responsibilities associated with their use.

1.2. Generative AI Tools

Generation AI tools are advanced AI technologies that generate content based on user inputs, such as text, images, and multimedia. In educational contexts, these tools can help teachers produce personalized learning materials, simplify concepts and improve students' engagement through interactive content creation. Tools such as ChatGPT, Gemini, Copilot and image generators can be used to design exercises, quizzes, learning plans, and visual aids adapted to the specific needs of individual students as shown in chapters 5 to 7. For example, as found in the research, teachers use generative AI to simplify scientific terms and concepts for students with language barriers or learning difficulties. Generative AI also supports the creation of multimodal content, providing visual, auditory and text resources for students to take into account different learning styles. This adaptability enables teachers to offer personalized and specialized content to students with different levels of ability. In addition, generative AI tools can be used to automate the creation of training, tasks and even feedback, saving teachers time and focusing on the quality and relevance of educational content. The aim of this subcategory is to empower teachers with the required practical knowledge and skills to use generative AI tools in the educational environment.

1.3. Critical AI Evaluation

Critical AI assessments involve assessing the accuracy, reliability, and adequacy of content generated by AI in an educational context. This subcategory focuses on the importance of teachers having the knowledge to examine and evaluate the results of AI tools and ensure that they are compatible with curriculum objectives, culturally relevant, and free of errors or biases. Research has shown that although AI tools such as ChatGPT can be useful in generating personalized content, they are not foolproof. Teachers must identify cases where AI-generated materials contain inaccuracies such as incorrect interpretation of concepts, inappropriate cultural references or incorrect translations. For example, the research reveals that AI-generated content may require further adaptation of local languages and contexts, especially in situations where the AI tool is trying to change between different languages. Teachers must ask critical questions about the quality and relevance of the content. This includes verifying scientific or factual information, ensuring that data are potentially biased and ensuring that materials are appropriate for students and their abilities. Through critical assessment of AI, teachers can ensure that AI is effectively used as a tool to enhance learning and maintain high standards of accuracy and suitability.

1.4. Facilitation and Customization

Subcategory Facilitation and customization refer to the role of teachers in adapting content generated by AI to specific educational contexts and specific needs of students. Although artificial intelligence tools (e.g. ChatGPT) can efficiently produce learning materials, exercises and educational help, teachers play an important role in the customization of learning content to ensure that it complies with curriculum objectives, student learning objectives and classroom dynamics. In this study, it was found that teachers often use artificial intelligence to generate initial content such as simplified explanations, personalized tasks, or visual aids but the opportunities of these outputs depends on the teacher's ability to adapt them to their unique classroom environment. For example, AI-generated tasks may require further adjustments to accommodate students with learning difficulties or language barriers. Teachers must intervene by simplifying complex tasks, or integrating culturally relevant examples, to support student understanding. In cases presented in the research, teachers were using artificial intelligence to divide complex topics into manageable steps, but they need to organize these steps logically, modify examples and ensure that the artificial intelligence output is in line with the educational content. This is particularly important when it comes to non-native speakers or students with special educational needs, where AI proposals often require additional cultural or linguistic adaptations. The aim of this subcategory is the active participation of teachers in the development, adaptation and personalization of the content generated by artificial intelligence, to meet the various learning needs of their students. This process needs to ensure that the AI tools are used effectively as part of a teacher-educational approach.

1.5. Continuous Professional Development

The subcategory Continuous professional development focuses on the ongoing education and training of teachers, that needs to ensure that they are informed of the latest advances in artificial intelligence tools and their applications in education. As AI technologies evolve, teachers must actively engage in lifelong learning to effectively integrate these tools into teaching practices, maintaining ethical and effective use. Research indicates that AI tools such as ChatGPT offer opportunities for personalized learning, but that all of these opportunities can only be realized if teachers receive appropriate technical and educational training. This includes understanding how to select appropriate AI tools, adapt them to different educational environments, and navigate the limitations and challenges of these technologies. The teachers in this research noted that while AI tools can save time and improve classroom planning, they still need to understand how AI outputs are adjusted to meet the curriculum objectives and student's unique needs. This subcategory is about educating teachers about emerging trends, best practices and ethical considerations related to artificial intelligence. This is especially important because new tools and updates are often introduced, and teachers need to stay informed about changes in AI capabilities, potential biases in AI output, and the importance of protecting student data. The research indicates that AI-generated content requires teachers to adapt the results in non-English contexts, and states that professional development should also cover the use of local and culturally responsive AI. The aim of this subcategory is to ensure that teachers have the necessary skills and knowledge to make effective and responsible use of artificial intelligence in classrooms. This subcategory needs to encourage continuous learning, collaboration and adaptation that will enable teachers to use AI tools as part of their education toolkits, maintaining competence and confidence.

Category 2 Pedagogy

Category Pedagogy is about the integration of AI tools into teaching methodologies to support and enhance traditional education, with a focus on personalized learning. The subcategories of category Pedagogy are shown below in Table 4.

Table 4. Subcategories of category 2 Pedagogy

Subcategory	Description
2.1. Integration with teaching strategies	AI is embedded in existing teaching practices, complementing traditional methods to enhance learning outcomes.
2.2. Curriculum alignment	AI-generated content and tools are aligned with the existing curriculum, ensuring that AI supports rather than disrupts the learning process.
2.3. Guidelines for personalized content creation	AI tools are used to create individualized lesson plans and materials that address students' unique learning needs and abilities.
2.4. Resource recommendations	AI suggests additional learning resources, reading materials, and exercises tailored to student progress and curriculum standards.
2.5. Cross-subject integration	AI helps in connecting concepts across subjects (e.g., science and language arts) to create a more interdisciplinary and engaging learning experience.
2.6. Student engagement and motivation	AI tools offer interactive and adaptive content to boost student engagement, motivation, and participation in the learning process.
2.7. Collaboration and peer learning	AI supports collaboration among students by generating tasks for group work, promoting peer learning through shared AI-assisted projects.

2.1. Integration with Teaching Strategies

The subcategory Integration with teaching strategies focuses on integration of artificial intelligence tools into existing teaching frameworks to improve learning outcomes and complement traditional teaching methods. Instead of replacing conventional strategies, AI needs to be used to increase learning opportunities, instruction and improve engagement. The research indicates that teachers use AI tools such as ChatGPT to support and simplify complex topics, especially for students facing learning challenges. For example, the teachers of the study used artificial intelligence to create personalized lessons plans that divided the difficult content into smaller and more manageable tasks, allowing students to progress at their own pace. This example has shown differentiated teaching, where AI-generated content is adapted to the specific needs of students, thus improving individual learning. The integration of AI-generated resources can help strengthen the key concepts through multi-modal learning approaches, covering various learning styles such as visual, auditory and kinesthetic. In particular, AI can be used to align lessons with a curriculum, while providing feedback in real time, allowing teachers to maintain the continuity of education. Effective integration requires teachers to strategically align the AI output with their school and classroom objectives. Teachers need to assess when and where AI tools can provide the benefits, in order to ensure that they improve the learning experience rather than complicate it. For example, artificial intelligence can be used to provide additional practice materials or generate visual representations of data in technical subjects as research has shown, giving students more options to interact with the content. Integration with teaching strategies emphasizes the careful use of artificial intelligence to support and improve traditional educational approaches.

2.2. Curriculum Alignment

The subcategory Curriculum alignment refers to the process of ensuring that the output of AI tools and the curriculum are consistent with established educational curriculum, learning objectives, and standards. The use of artificial intelligence in education should support and improve the objectives of the curriculum, rather than divert it, providing teachers with innovative and relevant content that matches academic requirements. Research has shown that artificial intelligence tools such as ChatGPT have been successfully used to create teaching plans, exercises and personalized learning materials adapted to specific courses. For example, teachers use AI to simplify complex subjects such as plant life cycles, while maintaining the integrity of the curriculum. This allows non-native speakers and students with learning disabilities to access the same curriculum content as their peers, but in a more suitable format for their needs. AI tools also help identify relevant resources and create exercises that complement the curriculum, ensuring students continue to understand the key concepts while achieving their learning objectives. However, the research notes that AI can produce useful content, but teachers must review and adjust materials to ensure that they are appropriate for curriculum standards. This includes modifying AI output to better suit local contexts, language requirements, or specific learning outcomes. Furthermore, the alignment of the curriculum with AI tools helps teachers ensure that their classes are coherent. Using artificial intelligence to generate materials that are directly related to the curriculum, teachers can provide students with a structured learning experience that builds on previous knowledge and guides them to achieve long-term goals. The aim of subcategory Curriculum alignment is on effective integration of AI tools to support existing educational goals and standards. It aims to ensure that content generated by AI is relevant, accurate and appropriate to the curriculum, allowing teachers to deliver lessons that meet educational requirements while benefiting from the personalized and opportunities provided by AI.

2.3. Guidelines for Personalized Content Creation

The subcategory for personalized content creation guidelines focuses on using AI tools to develop personalized learning materials that meet the individual needs, learning styles and abilities of students. This subcategory emphasizes the importance of using artificial intelligence to create a different content to ensure that each student receives instruction suited to his or her unique learning profile. This research shows how teachers can modify and adapt curriculum content to meet the needs of various learners using AI tools such as ChatGPT. For example, AI has been used to simplify complex vocabulary and topics such as scientific terms for non-Native speakers and students with learning difficulties. These AI-generated materials have helped make topics more accessible. In addition, AI provided suggestions for visual aids and practical activities that could further support the comprehension of students, especially for learners benefiting from visual and practical experiences. Personalized content creation also includes the development of exercises, quizzes and assignments that are adapted to each student's progress and difficulty areas. The research shows how AI tools have been used to create different levels of tasks, simpler for students who are struggling with concepts, and more advanced exercises for students who are ready to tackle more challenging material allowing personalized learning experience. In addition, the AI tool supports real-time customization, with teachers using AI to quickly generate or adapt content onsite and respond to individual student needs in the course.

2.4. Resource Recommendations

The resource recommendation aims to use AI tools to recommend additional materials, activities and resources that are consistent with curriculum and improve student learning. The subcategory focuses on how AI can assist teachers in identifying and providing additional content tailored to students' individual needs and supporting their understanding of topics. Research has shown that AI tools such as ChatGPT can generate a variety of educational resources, such as simplified explanations, visual aids, interactive exercises, and reading materials. These recommendations are often customized to specific student characteristics and address different levels of competence, learning challenges or linguistic barriers. For example, the research describes how artificial intelligence was used to recommend simplified vocabulary to non-native speakers and visual aids to students struggling with scientific concepts, making all learners more accessible to their lessons. AI tools also play an important role in suggesting resources to promote multi-modal learning and offer students various ways to interact with materials, e.g. videos, articles, quizzes or practical exercises. The teachers found that AI-generated resource recommendations are particularly useful for creating personalized learning paths that allow students to explore topics at their own pace and in formats adapted to their learning preferences. However, the research also noted the importance of teachers' supervision in selecting and improving these AI-recommended resources. Teachers must critically assess proposed materials and see if they meet the specific needs of their classrooms. This subcategory focuses on how artificial intelligence can help teachers identify and integrate a wide range of educational materials to meet different learning needs. Through artificial intelligence, teachers can ensure that students have access to personalized resources to improve their understanding and engagement with learning materials.

2.5. Cross-Subject Integration

Cross-subject integration subcategory refers to the ability of artificial intelligence tools to help teachers combine content from different disciplines and subjects and promote integrated learning. This approach can help students see connections between different fields of study, improving critical thinking and problem solving skills. Using AI to link concepts across subjects, teachers can create more engaging lessons. The research shows that artificial intelligence tools, such as ChatGPT, have been used to create learning materials that incorporate elements from multiple subjects. For example, when teaching about the life cycle of flowering plants in primary school classes, artificial intelligence generated materials that helped students develop language skills by simplifying scientific terms and prompting descriptive tasks. This integration of science and language learning enables students to better understand both subjects simultaneously. In addition, AI tools can help to create interdisciplinary projects that apply knowledge from one subject to another. For example, in vocational education, artificial intelligence is used to create exercises that combine data analysis (from mathematics) with technology applications in the real world (Excel task). This not only strengthened the students' understanding of topics, but also made learning more relevant by linking them to the practical contexts of the real world. Teachers benefit from AI's ability to propose resources and activities that connect different subject areas, facilitating a smooth integration of interdisciplinary content. However, the research also points out that teachers must review and adapt the materials generated by artificial intelligence to ensure that they are consistent with curriculum standards and relevant to each subject. This subcategory is focused on how AI tools promote the development of interdisciplinary learning experiences. By connecting different topics, AI can help teachers design lessons that encourage students to think broader and apply their knowledge in different fields, making learning more interdependent and meaningful.

2.6. Student Engagement and Motivation

The subcategory Student engagement and motivation focuses on how AI tools can be used to increase students' participation in learning processes and increase their motivation. Artificial intelligence-driven learning materials and interactive activities can provide dynamic and personalized educational experiences, adapted to individual preferences and learning styles, which contributes to increased enthusiasm and commitment to learning. The research points out that AI tools such as ChatGPT have contributed to a personalized learning experience that responds to the needs of individual students, especially those who struggle with complex topics or language barriers. By simplifying the materials of learning and providing interactive tasks, AI tools help to motivate and engage students. For example, during the research, teachers use artificial intelligence to create step-by-step guides, visual aids and hands-on activities that divide difficult concepts into more accessible parts and encourage students to participate more actively in courses. AI also contributes to motivation by providing immediate feedback to help students see their progress in real time. This research highlights how AI-assisted tasks such as quizzes and practice exercises can provide instant validation that strengthens students' confidence and encourages them to continue to engage in learning. The ability to customize tasks' difficulty based on student levels ensures that learners are not bored or frustrated and maintains optimal challenge levels that motivate them. In addition, the use of artificial intelligence to create interactive and gamified learning experiences such as AI-created games or simulations adds fun and creativity to the educational process and significantly increases student participation. The research found that incorporating these elements into the curriculum helps students to remain motivated and interested, especially when they deal with traditionally difficult topics such as data analysis in vocational education. The focus of this subcategory is on how artificial intelligence can personalize learning experiences, provide instant feedback, and introduce interactive elements that maintain student engagement and motivation.

2.7. Collaboration and Peer Learning

Subcategory Collaboration and peer learning is about the use of artificial intelligence tools to facilitate group work and enhance collaborative learning environments where students share knowledge and learn from each other. This subcategory emphasizes the role of AI in creating collaborative tasks, providing personalized guidance, and supporting communication between students who work together on common projects. Research shows that AI tools such as ChatGPT have been used to develop groups and projects to promote peer learning. Teachers use artificial intelligence to create collaborative exercises where students can work together, share ideas and solve problems together. For example, AI-generated data analysis tasks in vocational education allow students to work in teams to interpret complex data sets using Excel, while promoting teamwork and enhancing their individual knowledge of the subject. AI tools can also personalize collaborative activities by assigning roles or tasks to each student based on their strengths and learning needs to ensure that everyone contributes meaningfully to the group. This approach can promote peer support, and students can help those who need more help and improve the overall learning experience of all participants. AI-driven platforms and tools can improve communication between students outside classrooms, enabling them to collaborate remotely on projects and assignments. This supports the development of social and teamwork skills that are essential in collaborative working environment. This subcategory highlights how artificial intelligence tools support group learning, enabling student interaction, customizing group tasks, and improve communication.

Category 3 Language and Accessibility

AI tools ensure education is accessible to all learners, regardless of language or physical abilities. They remove barriers by providing tailored support for diverse student populations. The subcategories of Language and Accessibility are presented in Table 5.

Table 5. Subcategory of category 3 language and accessibility

Subcategory	Description
3.1. Accessibility	AI provides accessibility features such as speech-to-text, text-to-speech, and visual aids to support students with disabilities.
3.2. Language and Cultural Inclusivity	AI adapts content for students from diverse cultural and linguistic backgrounds, offering translation services and culturally relevant materials.
3.3. Age-Specific Guidelines	AI content is tailored to be age-appropriate, ensuring that lessons and tasks are suited to the cognitive and emotional development of students.

3.1. Accessibility

Accessibility focuses on the role of AI tools to make education more inclusive by supporting students with different learning needs, including students with physical, cognitive or linguistic disabilities. Artificial intelligence enables teachers to create more accessible learning environments by adapting content, providing assistance technology, and removing obstacles that can prevent students from fully engaging in educational materials. Research shows that artificial intelligence tools such as ChatGPT can be used to simplify complex content for students with learning disabilities and language barriers. For example, teachers use AI to break scientific concepts into simpler languages and provide visual aids, making it easier for non-Croatian speakers to understand them. This method ensures that all students can access and understand the curriculum, regardless of their language skills or learning challenges. Artificial intelligence tools also improve accessibility through use of technologies, such as text-to-speech, text-to-text, and visual representation functions. These tools can support disabled students by providing alternative ways to interact with educational content (CAST, n.d.). For example, students with reading disabilities may benefit from having AI read texts loudly, while students with visual impairments may use AI to convert texts into audio or Braille (World Economic Forum, 2021). The research also focuses on the ways in which AI-generated resources can be adjusted to meet specific accessibility requirements in order to ensure that the learning materials are inclusive and support all learners. AI helps teachers to create a more equitable and accessible learning environment by providing customized support to students who need additional help. This subcategory emphasizes how AI tools can improve the integration of education by adapting content to meet student needs. With the help of simplified content and personalized learning methods, AI can ensure that all students have equal access to quality education, regardless of their abilities, challenges and finances.

3.2. Language and Cultural Inclusivity

Subcategory Language and cultural inclusion refer to the use of artificial intelligence tools to adapt educational content to the diverse linguistic and cultural backgrounds of students, ensuring that all learners can access and participate in the material in a way that matches their linguistic abilities and cultural context. This subcategory emphasizes the importance of using AI to bridge language gaps, adapt to different cultural perspectives and create an inclusive learning environment for students of various backgrounds. The research has shown that artificial intelligence tools such as ChatGPT have been used to simplify educational content and convert complex subjects into more accessible languages for non-native speakers. For example, in primary school, AI was used to adapt scientific vocabulary to a simpler vocabulary, allowing students with limited vocabulary skills to understand plants' life cycle. This adaptation ensures that all students, regardless of their language skills, can participate in the lessons. AI can also support cultural inclusion by offering appropriate contextual content that reflects the cultural background of students. The research shows that the content generated by AI sometimes requires more localization to ensure its cultural relevance for students, especially when AI is confronted with language transitions or provides examples that are not consistent with the cultural context of students. Teachers have played a key role in tailoring AI outputs to better suit the cultural and linguistic diversity of their classrooms, ensuring that students better understand the materials. In addition, AI tools provide translation and multilingual support, providing access to learning materials in the language of students' and teachers choice. This ensures that language barriers do not prevent students from learning and comprehending the curriculum which is leading to a more inclusive learning environment for students of different linguistic backgrounds.

3.3. Age-Specific Guidelines

Age-specific guidelines subcategory focuses on adapting educational content generated by AI to the stages of development, cognitive abilities and emotional maturity of students at different age levels. This subcategory emphasizes the importance of adapting learning materials and activities to the specific needs of students of various ages, to ensure that the content generated by AI is appropriate. Research has shown that artificial intelligence tools such as ChatGPT, Gemini and Copilot can produce content that is highly adaptable to all age groups, from early primary school to secondary and higher education. For example, AI can simplify language and concepts for young students and provide more complex and challenging materials for older students. In primary education, the materials generated by AI could focus on interactive, game-based activities and explain core concepts using simple words. In contrast, secondary and higher education students benefit from the ability of artificial intelligence to generate deeper, detailed content and complex problem-solving tasks that promote critical thinking and analysis. Teachers should guide AI to provide appropriate levels of support to ensure that activities are not too difficult or too simplistic for the age of students. In addition, the research suggests that AI tools are useful in creating personalized content that adapts to individual student progress, allowing teachers to follow age-specific guidelines while at the same time adapting to the learning path of each student. The goal of this subcategory is to ensure that AI-generated content is appropriate to students' developmental stages and offers age-appropriate learning activities that support personalized learning.

Category 4 Evaluation

Category Evaluation is essential to measure the opportunities of AI tools in education. This process ensures that AI is positively impacting student outcomes and is being used ethically and transparently. The subcategories of Evaluation are shown below in Table 6.

Table 6. Subcategories of category 4 evaluation

Subcategory	Description
4.1. AI Evaluation	Teachers regularly assess the accuracy, opportunities, and educational value of AI-generated content and tools.
4.2. Student Feedback	Student feedback is collected to measure engagement and the opportunities of AI in meeting learning objectives.
4.3. Transparency and Accountability	AI usage is transparent, with clear guidelines on how AI decisions are made, ensuring accountability for AI outputs and student impact.

4.1. AI Evaluation

Subcategory AI assessment refers to the process of evaluating the opportunities, accuracy, and educational impact of artificial intelligence tools used in classrooms and by teachers. This subcategory focuses on monitoring and evaluating how AI-generated content and tools contribute to learning outcomes and ensures that AI improves student progress. Research shows that AI tools such as ChatGPT are very effective in creating personalized content and simplifying complex topics, but that their output is not always perfect. Teachers found that AI-generated materials sometimes contained inaccuracies, cultural inconsistencies or oversimplifications that required further adjustments. As a result, it is essential for teachers to regularly evaluate the quality of AI outputs, verify the accuracy, adequacy, and consistency of the curriculum. Evaluation of artificial intelligence tools and its content can include the evaluation of the impact of artificial intelligence on the performance and engagement of students. The research emphasizes that teachers should monitor how AI tools influence students' understanding of subjects, motivation and ability to retain information. For example, AI can help certain students to solve complex problems, but if AI suggestions are not assessed and adjusted, they may not fully meet the educational needs of students. By constantly assessing the opportunities of AI, teachers can make informed decisions on how to integrate AI tools best into their teaching strategy. These limitations, such as language inconsistencies or biases in content recommendations, require teachers to critically assess AI outputs to avoid inadvertently reinforcing misconceptions or presenting inappropriate material. This subcategory involves the ongoing assessment of AI tools to ensure their opportunities, accuracy, and alignment with educational goals. By critically evaluating AI-generated content and its impact on student learning, teachers can make necessary adjustments and ensure that AI is used responsibly and effectively in the classroom.

4.2. Students Feedback

Subcategory Students feedback is the practice of collecting and analyzing student responses to the use of artificial intelligence tools in learning processes. This subcategory focuses on understanding how students perceive the opportunities, engagement and relevance of content produced by AI to continuously improve the integration of AI in education. The research emphasizes that the process of collecting student feedback can help in assessing the support of AI tools. Students' insight can provide information on whether AI-generated materials are readable, engaging and beneficial for their learning goals. For example, this research allowed students to provide feedback on tasks and lessons generated by AI, indicating a variety of degrees of satisfaction and challenges, such as the need to clarify or improve AI-generated content. Some students find AI tools attractive and useful for personal learning, while others find AI outputs without clarity or cultural relevance confusing or dissatisfied. Students' feedback can also show how AI tools match different learning styles and needs. By actively involving students in the assessment process, teachers can better understand how to adapt AI-generated content to individual preferences, thereby improving the overall learning experience. Feedback helps identify areas in which AI tools may lack, such as content oversimplification or tasks that are too complicated or irrelevant and enables teachers to make necessary changes. Student feedback can inform teachers about the motivational effects of AI tools. The research found that AI's ability to provide instant feedback and personalized learning materials often increased the engagement of students. However, without continuous input from students, teachers cannot fully understand how AI tools affect their motivation and whether it actually improves their learning experience. Student feedback is essential to assessing the opportunities and impact of AI tools in education. Through the collection and analysis of student feedback, teachers can adjust the content generated by AI to better meet student needs and ensure that AI promotes both engagement and learning results. This feedback cycle helps ensure that AI tools remain relevant, accessible and beneficial for all learners.

4.3. Transparency and Accountability

Subcategory Transparency and accountability is about the importance of open communication about the use of AI in education, ensuring that teachers and students understand the processes and implications of the content generated by AI. This subcategory emphasizes the need for clear guidelines and responsible use of AI in classrooms to promote trust, ensure ethical practices and maintain responsibility for the results generated by AI systems. Research shows that AI tools such as ChatGPT provide assistance in generating personalized learning materials, but it is important for teachers to be transparent about how these tools work and their limitations. Teachers must clearly communicate to students how AI systems create content, their dependence on data, and potential biases and inaccuracies. This helps students assess the information provided by AI critically, promotes digital literacy, and monitoring of the output generated by AI. Responsibility is another aspect of reviewing and adapting the materials produced by AI before being used in classrooms. Teachers must ensure that the content generated by AI complies with the curriculum standards and is free of errors and prejudices that could have a negative impact on students' learning (UNESCO, 2021; World Economic Forum, 2021). This includes maintaining control over AI-driven evaluations to ensure that automated evaluation and feedback systems do not introduce unfair or inaccurate results. Teachers and institutions must ensure that AI tools comply with data privacy regulations and ethical guidelines to protect students' data. This subcategory focuses on the responsible and ethical use of artificial intelligence in education. By clearly communicating how AI works, maintaining control over the content generated by AI and protecting student data, educators can promote trust in AI technologies and ensure that they are used in fair, accurate and corresponding ways to educational goals.

Category 5 Engagement Strategies

AI tools can be leveraged to improve student engagement through personalized and interactive learning materials that apply to individual learning styles and needs. The subcategories of Engagement strategies are presented in Table 7.

Table 7. Subcategories of category 5 engagement strategies

Subcategories	Description
5.1. Multimodal Learning	AI integrates various learning modes (visual, auditory, tactile) to address different learning preferences, making education more engaging.
5.2. Interactive Learning	AI-driven tasks and activities (e.g., simulations, quizzes, games) that actively involve students in their learning process.
5.3. Contextual and Repetitive Learning	AI tools reinforce learning through context-based tasks and repetition to help students retain and apply knowledge.
5.4. Customized Task Difficulty	AI adjusts the difficulty of tasks based on individual student progress, offering personalized challenges and support as needed.
5.5. Supporting diverse learning styles	Using AI to recognize and cater to different learning preferences, ensuring inclusive education.

5.1. Multimodal Learning

Subcategory Multimodal learning refers to the use of artificial intelligence tools to provide various forms of content delivery to complement different learning styles by combining visual, auditory, textual and kinesthetic elements (Guo et al., 2014; Moreno & Mayer, 2007). This subcategory is dedicated to process how AI tools can improve engagement and understanding, allowing students to interact in different ways, responding to their specific preferences and needs. The research points out that artificial intelligence tools such as ChatGPT have generated personalized multi-modal content that adapts to different student learning styles. For example, AI has created various resources, including text explanations, visual aids, interactive exercises, to help students understand material in a variety of ways. This approach is especially beneficial to students struggling with traditional learning and offers an alternative way of understanding and processing information. Ability of AI tools to generate and adapt content quickly allows teachers to provide multimodal learning experiences without wasting long-term preparation time. For example, in vocational education, AI was used to create Excel data interpretation tasks that supported visual representations such as graphics and graphs and helped students better understand abstract concepts. By providing content in multiple formats, AI tools can ensure that auditory, visual, and kinetic learners have access to resources that meet their learning preferences (Luckin et al., 2016). In addition, the research mentions that multimodal learning through artificial intelligence promotes deeper understanding and retention, as students can approach the same material from different angles. AI-generated tasks create a more engaging and comprehensive learning experience by combining visual diagrams with text-based instructions or combining audio explanations with exercises. Multimodal learning in this framework uses artificial intelligence to provide content in different formats (visual, auditory, text and interactive) adapted to the students' different learning preferences (NCAI, 2021).

5.2. Interactive Learning

Subcategory Interactive learning refers to using artificial intelligence tools to create dynamic and participatory learning experiences where students actively participate in an educational environment. This subcategory emphasizes the importance of interactive tasks, quizzes, simulations and real-time feedback, all of which are supported by AI tools to promote a active participation in the learning process. The research highlights the use of AI tools such as ChatGPT and other educational platforms to create interactive activities that enable students to explore concepts in a practical way. For example, AI is used to create personalized quizzes and interactive exercises that adapt to students' progress, offering more challenging and simplified questions depending on their performance. This adaptability allowed students to engage in the learning process because the content was continuously adjusted to the pace and needs of their learning. When students complete tasks or questions generated by AI, they can get immediate responses, and correct mistakes. This continuous interaction and feedback cycle encourages active learning and motivates students to make progress. AI tools can create simulations and virtual environments in which students can engage in real-world scenarios and apply theoretical knowledge to practical situations. This is especially evident in vocational education, where AI-generated tasks enable students to practice data analysis in Excel or interact with virtual models imitating real tasks, promoting a more immersive learning experience. This subcategory focuses on how AI creates engaging, adaptable and participatory learning experiences.

5.3. Contextual and Repetitive Learning

Subcategory Contextual and repetitive learning refers to the use of artificial intelligence tools to present educational content in the real environment and strengthen concepts through repetition. This subcategory highlights the role of artificial intelligence in making learning more meaningful by placing it in familiar scenarios and providing students with multiple opportunities to interact with material to strengthen their understanding. Research suggests that AI tools are particularly effective in generating content linking abstract concepts to real applications, thereby making learning more accessible and easier to understand. For example, in the field of vocational education, artificial intelligence is used to create data analysis tasks that reflect workplace scenarios, helping students understand how skills they have learned are applied in real life. This contextual approach has enabled students to see the relevance of their lessons and increase their involvement and retention. In addition to contextual learning, artificial intelligence supports repetitive learning by providing students with repeated exposure to key concepts in different ways. The research shows that artificial intelligence tools (such as adaptive tests and exercises) are used to improve learning by presenting the same concepts in different formats and ensuring that students have multiple opportunities to practice. For example, if students complete AI-generated exercises, they may receive additional tasks or questions, which gradually increase complexity and allow for continuous reinforcement of the class.

5.4. Customized Task Difficulty

Subcategory Customized task difficulty refers to the use of artificial intelligence tools to adapt the complexity of learning tasks to the individual needs and skills of students. This subcategory focuses on how AI can dynamically adjust the difficulty of exercises, quizzes and learning activities based on students' performance, ensuring that each learner is appropriately challenged without feeling overwhelmed. The research demonstrates that artificial intelligence tools such as adaptive learning platforms can customize learning experiences by adjusting tasks. In addition, if students struggle with some concepts and learning materials, the AI tools provide a simpler task, reconstructing the material into more manageable steps that can help students to understand content. This flexible approach allows each student to work at their own pace and level and promotes a more personalized learning environment. Students who need more support receive basic data sets with clear instructions, while advanced students receive complex scenarios requiring independent problem solving. This personalization helps ensure that all students are engaged and challenged appropriately, regardless of their initial skills.

LEARNING SCENARIOS FOR IMPLEMENTING FRAMEWORK FOR USING AI TOOLS FOR PERSONALIZED TEACHING AND LEARNING IN EDUCATIONAL ENVIRONMENT

The following learning scenarios are designed for teachers to explore how AI can be integrated into various subjects based on the proposed framework. These scenarios provide practical examples of how AI tools can be used to improve and upgrade traditional teaching methods, offering students a more interactive, adaptive, and personalized learning experience. Each scenario is structured to guide teachers through the process of using AI tools to create and adjust learning activities and to demonstrate how AI can be used as an addition to the classroom. These learning scenarios aim to help teachers to integrate AI tools into their teaching practices, ensuring that each student receives the support they need to improve their learning skills in an educational environment. Each scenario is designed and developed with the help of ChatGPT 4.0 but it is based on the proposed framework for using AI tools for conducting personalized teaching. There are a total of 15 scenarios, 3 for each category from the framework. Each scenario is related to one or more of the subcategories from the framework so that teachers get insight and a few examples of how AI tools could be used for conducting personalized teaching and learning at their institutions.

Learning Scenarios for Category 1
AI Literacy and Training

Scenario 1: AI-Assisted Lesson Planning for Mixed-Ability Classrooms

Subcategory: *1.1 Understanding AI Fundamentals; 1.2 Generative AI Tools*

Objective of the scenario: Teachers will use AI tools like ChatGPT to create lesson plans that are for students with different levels of understanding in a mixed-ability classroom.

Process:

1. The teacher introduces students to basic AI concepts, explaining how generative AI can create personalized learning materials.
2. The teacher uses ChatGPT to create three different versions of the same lesson (beginner, intermediate, and advanced) on a topic like "The Life Cycle of Plants."
   a. Beginner Level: ChatGPT generates simplified explanations, diagrams, and vocabulary for students who need more support.
   b. Intermediate Level: ChatGPT offers moderately complex content with more detailed visuals and questions requiring critical thinking.
   c. Advanced Level: ChatGPT provides in-depth scientific explanations and challenges students to apply their knowledge in new contexts, such as creating their own experiments.
3. Each student receives a lesson tailored to their ability level. The teacher uses ChatGPT to support real-time question answering during the class.
4. The teacher uses ChatGPT to generate personalized quizzes and homework assignments for students at different levels, ensuring that each student's learning path is appropriately challenging.

Personalization Benefits:

- AI adapts lesson content to individual student levels.
- Real-time interaction with AI allows teacher to monitor students assignments.
- Students struggling with the material can ask ChatGPT for additional explanations in simpler terms.

Scenario 2: AI-Facilitated Peer Learning and Feedback

Subcategory: *1.3 Critical AI Evaluation; 1.4 Facilitation and Customization*

Objective of the scenario: Students will use AI tools like Gemini to collaborate on projects while receiving personalized AI-generated feedback to improve their work and critical thinking skills.

Process:

1. The teacher introduces the concept of peer learning and how AI tools can enhance collaboration by offering personalized feedback.
2. Students work in pairs or small groups to complete a project, such as creating an infographic on "Renewable Energy Sources." They use Gemini to research, generate content, and check the accuracy of the information.
3. Each group submits their project to Gemini, which provides feedback on the accuracy of the content, clarity, and suggestions for improvement. Students can ask Gemini to customize their project by simplifying complex terms, adding visuals, or suggesting additional sources of information.
4. As part of AI literacy, students critically evaluate the feedback provided by Gemini. They discuss what suggestions they agree with and which parts of their project they want to revise based on AI-generated insights.
5. Students submit their final project, having customized it based on AI feedback and peer discussions.

Personalization Benefits:

- AI tools provide customized feedback that targets specific areas of improvement for each group.
- Students learn to evaluate and critique AI feedback, developing critical thinking skills.
- Collaboration is enhanced by AI's ability to suggest tailored improvements for each team.

Scenario 3: Continuous Professional Development for AI-Enhanced Lesson Customization

Subcategory: *1.5 Continuous Professional Development; 1.4 Facilitation and Customization*

Objective of the scenario: Teachers will engage in continuous professional development by using AI tools like Bard or Eduaide.ai to enhance their skills in customizing lessons for personalized learning experiences.

Process:

1. The teacher participates in an online training session on how to use generative AI tools like Bard and Eduaide.ai for customizing lessons.
2. The teacher practices using these tools to create lessons for their subjects. Bard is used to generate content, including timelines and visual aids, while Eduaide.ai is used to create personalized exercises for different student learning levels. Teacher can divide learning materials for two types of learners, ones that are struggling to comprehend learning materials and ones that are more advanced and need more challenging materials.
3. The teacher reviews the AI-generated lessons and tailors them to the cultural context of their classroom. The teacher also adjusts the complexity of tasks for students based on their previous performance and feedback.
4. The teacher delivers these AI-enhanced lessons, using the platform to provide real-time, personalized support to students as they progress through the material.
5. The teacher keeps using AI tools to enhance lesson plans continuously, incorporating student feedback and AI suggestions to adjust the lesson difficulty, engagement strategies, and assessment techniques.

Personalization Benefits:

- Teachers engage in continuous learning by using AI to improve lesson customization.
- AI tools save time in generating personalized content, allowing teachers to focus more on student interaction.
- The ongoing use of AI tools can improve both teaching opportunities and student outcomes by creating dynamic and evolving learning environments.

Learning Scenarios for Category 2 Pedagogy

Scenario 1: AI-Supported Flipped Classroom for Personalized Content Creation

Subcategory: *2.1 Integration with Teaching Strategies; 2.3 Guidelines for Personalized Content Creation*

Objective of the scenario: Teachers will use AI tools like ChatGPT to create personalized pre-class learning materials for students, allowing for a flipped classroom model where class time is dedicated to problem-solving and deeper exploration of topics.

Process:

1. The teacher uses ChatGPT to generate personalized reading materials, videos, and quizzes for students to review at home. The content is tailored based on the students' current proficiency levels. For students struggling with the topic, the teacher will ask ChatGPT to generate simplified texts with basic concepts and visual aids. For advanced students teacher will ask ChatGPT to provide more complex materials, including supplementary research articles and challenging exercises.
2. In class, students work in groups to solve problems related to the topic they studied at home. The teacher acts as a facilitator, answering questions and providing additional resources generated by ChatGPT for students who need more clarification or deeper insights.
3. During group work, students can use AI tools like Gemini to clarify doubts or generate examples, which they then explain to their peers. This allows students to reinforce their learning by teaching others, with AI as a support system.
4. The teacher uses ChatGPT to create personalized quizzes based on each student's progress during class, ensuring that students are tested on content relevant to their understanding level.

Personalization Benefits:

- Pre-class materials are developed to different student abilities, ensuring every student comes prepared for classroom activities.
- AI-generated resources during class help students reinforce their learning.

- Personalized assessments allow the teacher to track student progress effectively and provide targeted feedback.

Scenario 2: AI-Enhanced Curriculum Alignment and Cross-Subject Integration

Subcategory:*2.2 Curriculum Alignment; 2.5 Cross-Subject Integration*

Objective of the scenario: Teachers will use AI tools to integrate multiple subjects into a single lesson plan, aligning learning materials with the curriculum while ensuring cross-disciplinary learning opportunities.

Process:

1. The teacher uses ChatGPT and Eduaide.ai to generate lesson plans that integrate subjects like science, mathematics, and language arts. For example, a lesson on the “Water Cycle” can include:
    a. Science: Explaining the biological and chemical processes involved.
    b. Mathematics: Students calculate precipitation rates and evaporation statistics.
    c. Language Arts: Students write essays on the importance of water conservation, guided by AI-generated prompts.
2. The teacher customizes AI-generated content to align with individual student learning goals. For instance, students who are more interested in science can receive deeper explanations of the water cycle, while others focused on writing can receive additional writing prompts.
3. During the lesson, students use Gemini to further explore the topic from different subject perspectives, creating personalized projects (e.g., a visual presentation on water's impact on the environment, or a statistical report on water usage in their town).
4. The teacher uses AI tools to generate interdisciplinary quizzes or assignments, assessing students not only on their knowledge of the water cycle but also their ability to integrate mathematical, scientific, and language skills.

Personalization Benefits:

- AI supports curriculum alignment while integrating multiple subjects into a cohesive learning experience.

- Students can explore the topic through different views, based on their individual interests and strengths.
- AI-generated cross-subject assessments ensure that students apply knowledge from various domains.

Scenario 3: AI-Driven Student Engagement and Motivation through Gamified Learning

Subcategory: *2.6 Student Engagement and Motivation; 2.7 Collaboration and Peer Learning*

Objective of the scenario: Teachers will use generative AI tools like ChatGPT to gamify lessons, creating personalized challenges that engage students in collaborative problem-solving.

Process:

1. The teacher uses ChatGPT to create a gamified learning environment by designing challenges related to the lesson topic. For example, in a history class, students are tasked with solving a mystery about ancient civilizations, with different challenges focusing on specific historical facts or events. ChatGPT can generate different levels of difficulty for each challenge, ensuring students are appropriately challenged based on their proficiency. The AI can provide immediate feedback and hints as students progress through the challenges.
2. Students are grouped into groups based on their interests and abilities. Each group uses AI tools like Gemini to collaborate and solve the challenges. For example, one student can research specific facts, while another summarizes them, and a third presents their findings.
3. As students collaborate, they can ask ChatGPT to clarify difficult concepts or generate explanations for their peers, reinforcing peer learning. Teams compete to complete the challenges, and the AI keeps track of scores and progress.
4. At the end of the class, students use AI to generate a report reflecting on what they learned, how they contributed to their team, and areas where they struggled. The teacher reviews these AI-generated reports to provide personalized feedback and suggestions for improvement.

Personalization Benefits:

- Gamified challenges created by AI boost student engagement and motivation through fun, interactive learning.
- Challenges are personalized to different ability levels, ensuring that every student is appropriately challenged.
- Collaborative activities foster peer learning, with AI acting as both a resource and a guide.

Learning Scenario for Category 3 Language and Accessibility

Scenario 1: AI-Enhanced Language Support for Non-Native Speakers

Subcategory:*3.2 Language and Cultural Inclusivity; 3.4 Supporting Special Education Needs*

Objective of the scenario: Teachers will use AI tools like ChatGPT to provide personalized language support for non-native speakers, helping them overcome language barriers in the classroom.

Process:

1. The teacher uses ChatGPT to adapt lesson materials into simpler language or into the students' native languages. For example, a history lesson on ancient civilizations is simplified for non-native speakers by using shorter sentences, simpler vocabulary, and culturally familiar examples. For students with limited proficiency, ChatGPT translates key terms and generates summaries in their native languages (e.g., Croatian or Spanish). ChatGPT can generate visual aids, such as timelines or maps, to supplement the text and make content more accessible to visual learners.
2. During class, students can use ChatGPT as an interactive language assistant. If they encounter difficult words or concepts, they can type questions into the AI, which provides real-time translations, simplified explanations, or audio pronunciations. For practice, ChatGPT can generate vocabulary quizzes or short writing tasks that allow students to use the new terms they've learned.

3. Non-native speakers pair with native speakers in small groups to collaborate on class projects. AI tools like Gemini can generate prompts and conversation starters that help bridge language gaps. Native speakers help explain more complex concepts, while the AI supports non-native speakers in real-time language translation.
4. The teacher uses ChatGPT to create assessments that evaluate language comprehension as well as subject understanding. Non-native speakers receive tests with simplified language, while still covering the same core concepts.

Personalization Benefits:

- AI-generated content adapts lessons to the language proficiency of each student, ensuring inclusivity.
- Real-time language support from AI helps non-native speakers participate fully in class discussions and activities.
- Personalized assessments ensure that students are evaluated fairly without the barrier of language complexity.

Scenario 2: AI-Supported Accessibility for Students with Special Educational Needs

Subcategory:*3.1 Accessibility; 3.4 Supporting Special Education Needs*

Objective of the scenario: Teachers will use generative AI tools like ChatGPT and Eduaide.ai to create accessible and personalized learning materials for students with cognitive, physical, or learning disabilities.

Process:

1. The teacher uses ChatGPT to adapt classroom materials for students with disabilities. For example, Students with dyslexia receive materials in a dyslexia-friendly font, and ChatGPT can reformat text into shorter paragraphs with visual cues. For visually impaired students, ChatGPT generates audio versions of lessons or creates tactile-friendly materials using simple, descriptive language. For students with cognitive disabilities, ChatGPT simplifies complex instructions, breaking tasks into smaller, manageable steps.
2. The teacher integrates multiple learning modes by using AI-generated materials that cater to different sensory needs. For example, visual learners receive AI-generated infographics and diagrams. Auditory

learners can engage with lessons narrated by AI in clear, easy-to-understand language. Kinesthetic learners receive AI-generated task instructions that involve hands-on activities, like building models or drawing.

3. During class, students can use AI tools like Gemini to ask for further simplification of tasks or to request alternate formats for materials (e.g., audio explanations, enlarged text, or video demonstrations). For students with limited mobility, Gemini can provide voice-activated assistance, enabling them to interact with lessons through speech.
4. The teacher uses ChatGPT to generate assessments that cater to the needs of each student, ensuring that all students are evaluated based on their abilities. Students can receive additional time or alternate formats (e.g., multiple-choice vs. open-ended) for assessments, based on the AI's suggestions.

Personalization Benefits:

- AI tools enable personalized learning materials and assessments that cater to diverse needs.
- Multimodal learning ensures that all students, regardless of their disabilities, can access the content in a way that suits their learning style.
- AI-generated feedback is accessible and provides individualized support to each student.

Scenario 3: Culturally Inclusive AI-Generated Content for Diverse Classrooms

Subcategory:*3.2 Language and Cultural Inclusivity; 3.3 Age-Specific Guidelines*

Objective of the scenario: Teachers will use AI tools like ChatGPT and Bard to generate culturally inclusive and age-appropriate content for diverse student populations, ensuring that learning materials resonate with students' cultural backgrounds and experiences.

Process:

1. The teacher uses ChatGPT to create culturally inclusive learning materials that reflect the backgrounds of the students. For example, in a geography class ChatGPT generates examples and case studies

from various regions of the world, ensuring that students from different cultural backgrounds see their home countries represented in the lesson. The AI can develop content to include culturally relevant examples, such as local festivals, historical events, or cultural practices, helping students connect with the material.

2. ChatGPT provides bilingual materials, allowing students to study in both their native language and the target language of instruction. Students receive translations for key concepts, and AI generates glossaries of important terms in multiple languages (e.g., Croatian, English, and Spanish). For younger students, ChatGPT simplifies content into age-appropriate language, ensuring that students of different ages can engage with the same topic at a level suitable for their understanding.
3. Students explore their cultural backgrounds using AI tools like Gemini. For example, they can ask Gemini to generate reports on specific cultural phenomena from their home countries and present them to the class. Students can also use ChatGPT to create personalized narratives or essays that draw on their cultural heritage, making the lesson more meaningful and relevant to their personal experiences.
4. The teacher uses AI tools to create assessments that are culturally sensitive, avoiding language or examples that may be unfamiliar to certain students. For example, ChatGPT generates math problems based on scenarios from various cultures, ensuring that no student feels excluded by unfamiliar contexts.

Personalization Benefits:

- AI-generated content is tailored to each student's cultural background, making lessons more inclusive and relatable.
- Bilingual support ensures that multilingual students can fully engage with the material.
- Age-appropriate and culturally relevant assessments ensure fair and inclusive evaluation for all students.

Learning Scenarios for Category 4 Evaluation

Scenario 1: AI-Supported Formative Assessment for Personalized Feedback

Subcategory:*4.1 AI Evaluation; 4.2 Students Feedback*

Objective of the scenario: Teachers will use AI tools like ChatGPT to provide personalized formative assessments and real-time feedback, helping students understand their progress and areas for improvement.

Process:

1. The teacher uses ChatGPT to generate quizzes tailored to individual students based on their performance in previous lessons. For students who excel in math ChatGPT generates more challenging questions involving problem-solving and critical thinking. For students who struggle the AI generates simpler, step-by-step questions with guided prompts.
2. After students complete the quiz, ChatGPT provides instant feedback, explaining their mistakes and suggesting areas for improvement. For example, if a student answers a question incorrectly, ChatGPT provides a detailed explanation of the correct answer and recommends additional resources for further practice. If the student excels, ChatGPT suggests more advanced topics or additional reading material to challenge them further.
3. Students are encouraged to interact with ChatGPT to reflect on their performance. The AI guides students through a series of reflective questions (e.g., "What did you find difficult?" or "How can you improve next time?"), helping them develop self-awareness of their learning process.
4. The teacher reviews ChatGPT's feedback to identify patterns in student performance, allowing them to adjust future lessons based on individual needs. They can use the AI tool to further personalize follow-up quizzes or exercises.

Personalization Benefits:

- AI-generated quizzes and feedback are personalized to each student's learning level.

- Immediate feedback helps students understand their mistakes and encourages self-directed improvement.
- Teachers gain insights into student performance, allowing for targeted instruction in future lessons.

Scenario 2: AI-Assisted Summative Assessment with Adaptive Difficulty

Subcategory:*4.1 AI Evaluation & 4.3 Transparency and Accountability*

Objective of the scenario: Teachers will use AI tools like Eduaide.ai to conduct summative assessments with adaptive difficulty, ensuring that each student is tested at their appropriate learning level.

Process:

1. The teacher uses Eduaide.ai to generate summative exams with questions that adapt to student performance in real-time. For example, if a student answers a question correctly, the next question becomes more challenging. If a student struggles, the AI generates simpler questions to ensure they remain engaged and motivated.
2. The AI tool keeps track of the difficulty level of questions and provides a transparent breakdown of the student's performance in each section. The system generates reports that show how students performed across various difficulty levels, ensuring fairness in assessment.
3. After the assessment, Eduaide.ai generates personalized reports for each student, highlighting their strengths and areas where they need improvement. The AI also suggests customized study materials for students to review based on their performance.
4. The teacher reviews the AI-generated results and reports, verifying that the difficulty levels matched each student's abilities and ensuring the assessment was fair and transparent. The teacher also uses the AI's suggestions to plan targeted revision lessons for the entire class or for individual students.

Personalization Benefits:

- Adaptive difficulty ensures that each student is tested at the appropriate level, preventing frustration or disengagement.
- AI-generated performance reports give both students and teachers a clear understanding of strengths and weaknesses.

- Teachers maintain oversight, ensuring that AI-generated assessments align with their instructional goals and are conducted fairly.

Scenario 3: AI-Guided Ethical Evaluation of AI Tools in the Classroom

Subcategory: *4.4 Ethical AI Usage; 4.3 Transparency and Accountability*

Objective of the scenario: Teachers will use AI tools like Bard or ChatGPT to evaluate the ethical implications of using AI in the classroom, ensuring that AI-generated content and assessments are fair, transparent, and free of bias.

Process:

1. The teacher introduces the concept of ethical AI usage by engaging students in a discussion about fairness, bias, and accountability. ChatGPT provides examples of both ethical and unethical uses of AI in education, allowing students to reflect on the implications of AI in their learning.
2. Students work in groups to use Bard or ChatGPT to critically evaluate AI-generated content or assignments. Each group reviews AI-generated lesson materials or assessments, analyzing whether the content is free from bias or if any group (e.g., gender, culture, or ability level) is unfairly represented. Students use AI tools to help generate a checklist of ethical standards to evaluate the content (e.g., Does the content favor one group over another? Are all learning styles and needs considered?).
3. After the group evaluations, students present their findings to the class, highlighting any potential issues of bias or lack of transparency. The teacher facilitates a discussion on how AI-generated materials can be improved to ensure fairness and inclusivity.
4. The teacher reviews the AI's output and ensures that all materials used in the classroom meet ethical standards. The teacher also uses AI tools to generate follow-up questions for students, encouraging them to think critically about how AI can be used ethically in education.

Personalization Benefits:

- Students develop critical thinking skills by evaluating the fairness and ethics of AI-generated content.

- The teacher ensures that AI-generated materials are used responsibly, promoting an inclusive and transparent learning environment.
- AI tools foster a discussion about the ethical implications of using AI in education, empowering students to engage with the topic.

Learning Scenarios for Category 5 Engagement Strategies

Scenario 1: AI-Powered Multimodal Learning for Diverse Learning Styles

Subcategory: *5.1 Multimodal Learning; 5.5 Supporting Diverse Learning Styles*

Objective of the scenario: Teachers will use generative AI tools like ChatGPT to create multimodal learning experiences that engage students with different learning styles, ensuring personalized content delivery.

Process:

1. The teacher uses ChatGPT to create different types of content for a lesson on "Photosynthesis," tailoring materials to various learning styles, visual learners receive AI-generated infographics, diagrams, and flowcharts explaining the stages of photosynthesis. *Auditory learners* are provided with AI-generated audio recordings or podcasts that explain the process in simple terms. Kinesthetic learners are given AI-generated project instructions for hands-on activities, such as growing plants to observe photosynthesis in action. Text-based learners receive AI-generated reading materials that summarize the process with key points highlighted for easy review.
2. Each student selects the type of content that aligns with their preferred learning style, engaging with the material in the format that suits them best.
3. During classroom discussions, students can ask ChatGPT to clarify concepts or provide additional resources based on their chosen mode of learning (e.g., asking for another visual example or a detailed explanation of a specific phase).
4. The teacher uses ChatGPT to generate quizzes or assignments for each learning style, assessing how well students engage with and retain information from their preferred modality.

Personalization Benefits:

- Students engage with content in a format that best supports their learning style, ensuring maximum engagement and retention.
- AI-generated content is tailored to individual preferences, making learning more accessible and enjoyable.
- The teacher can monitor how well each learning style performs and adjust future lessons accordingly.

Scenario 2: Interactive AI-Driven Storytelling for Active Learning

Subcategory:*5.2 Interactive Learning; 5.3 Contextual and Repetitive Learning*

Objective of the scenario: Teachers will use generative AI tools like Gemini to create interactive storytelling experiences that engage students in active and context-based learning.

Process:

1. The teacher uses Gemini to generate an interactive historical fiction story about Ancient Egypt. As students read the story, they are prompted to make decisions based on the historical context, such as choosing how to advise a Pharaoh or managing resources during a famine. The AI personalizes each story based on the students' previous knowledge and interests, making the experience more engaging and relevant.
2. At key points in the story, students are asked to complete tasks that reinforce the historical context. For example, they use Gemini to research real-life events from Ancient Egypt and compare them to the events in the story. ChatGPT generates historical questions that prompt students to reflect on the choices they made and how they align with historical facts.
3. After the story is completed, students can re-engage with the material by choosing different paths and outcomes. The AI generates new scenarios each time, allowing students to repeatedly explore the topic from different perspectives, enhancing retention.

4. The teacher facilitates a class discussion, where students share their different story outcomes. Gemini assists by generating follow-up questions that encourage students to think critically about the historical decisions they made.

Personalization Benefits:

- Interactive storytelling keeps students actively engaged and allows them to connect with the material in a personal, meaningful way.
- Repetitive engagement with AI-generated scenarios reinforces learning and aids memory retention.
- The story adapts to each student's interest and knowledge level, creating a more personalized and engaging experience.

Scenario 3: AI-Supported Gamified Learning with Customized Task Difficulty

Subcategory:*5.4 Customized Task Difficulty; 5.2 Interactive Learning*

Objective of the scenario: Teachers will use AI tools like ChatGPT to create a gamified learning environment, where students engage with personalized challenges and progress through levels based on their performance.

Process:

1. The teacher uses ChatGPT to design a gamified math lesson on solving algebraic equations. The AI generates different difficulty levels for each challenge, e.g. for beginner level creates basic problems with step-by-step guidance from the AI. For intermediate level creates more complex problems with hints provided by ChatGPT upon request and for advanced level creates challenging problems that require critical thinking, with minimal guidance from the AI.
    1. As students solve problems, ChatGPT tracks their progress and adjusts the difficulty of subsequent tasks. Students who solve problems quickly and correctly are moved to more advanced levels, while those who struggle receive simpler problems and additional explanations.
    2. The AI provides instant feedback for each problem, highlighting mistakes and offering suggestions for improvement. The teacher organizes a class competition where students work in teams to solve

the most problems. ChatGPT generates team-based questions that challenge each group at their collective skill level, ensuring that each team receives personalized tasks based on their combined abilities.

3. After the gamified session, the AI generates a personalized report for each student, highlighting their strengths and areas for improvement. The teacher uses these reports to tailor future lessons and provide individualized support where needed.

Personalization Benefits:

- Gamified learning keeps students engaged and motivated, with tasks that adapt to their performance level.
- AI provides real-time feedback and personalized challenges, ensuring that students are neither under- nor over-challenged.
- The personalized progress reports help the teacher monitor individual growth and make informed decisions for future instruction.

PROMPTS FOR FRAMEWORK FOR USING AI TOOLS FOR CONDUCTING PERSONALIZED TEACHING

For teachers to get better results from generative AI tools it is important to use rightly written and constructed prompts. More about prompts is available in chapter 3 Personalized Learning Through Generative AI.

This section contains a list of informative prompts that teachers can use during the preparation of personalized learning materials for their students. Table 8 contains prompts for category AI literacy and training, Table 9 contains prompts for category Pedagogy, Table 10 contains prompts for category Language and accessibility, Table 11 contains prompts for category Evaluation and Table 18 contains prompts for category Engagement strategies. These prompts have informative character, and teachers can adapt, change or upgrade them to their needs, students' needs and possibilities, curriculum, education level, school level, subject, etc.

Table 8. List of prompts for category AI literacy and training

Subcategory	Prompts
1.1. Understanding AI Fundamentals	*Create a simple lesson plan that explains the basics of artificial intelligence (AI) to middle school students. Focus on explaining AI concepts like machine learning, data input, and algorithms using simple, relatable examples. Include a short activity where students can brainstorm real-life examples of AI they encounter in their daily lives (e.g., voice assistants, online recommendations).*
1.2. Generative AI Tools	*Create an introductory lesson for 9th-grade students that teaches them how to use ChatGPT to assist with their homework. The lesson should include a step-by-step guide on how to ask effective questions, how to evaluate the AI's responses, and how to use ChatGPT ethically for research purposes.*
1.3. Critical AI Evaluation	*Design a lesson that teaches secondary school students how to evaluate the accuracy and reliability of AI-generated content. Include examples of common mistakes AI tools might make and a classroom discussion on why it is important to fact-check information provided by AI. End with an activity where students use ChatGPT to answer a question, then research the accuracy of the response.*
1.4. Facilitation and Customization	*Design a customization lesson for teachers. The lesson should focus on helping teachers quickly adapt lesson content based on student feedback. Provide examples of how teachers can ask Gemini for simpler explanations or more complex challenges on a topic like 'Photosynthesis' during class to ensure all students are engaged at their own level.*
1.5. Continuous Professional Development	*Create a lesson for teachers on how to use AI tools like Bard and ChatGPT to boost collaboration among students. Include strategies for teachers to design group activities where students use AI to research, generate ideas, or solve problems together. Provide examples of how to incorporate AI feedback into group projects and peer review sessions.*

Table 9. List of prompts for category pedagogy

Subcategory	Prompts
2.1. Integration with Teaching Strategies	*Create a differentiated lesson plan for a 7th-grade math class on solving linear equations. Provide simple step-by-step instructions for students who struggle with the topic, intermediate practice problems for students with some understanding, and more complex, real-world application problems for advanced students.*
2.2. Curriculum Alignment	*Design a history lesson on the American Revolution for 8th-grade students that aligns with the common core standards. Ensure the lesson includes key facts, important figures, and the causes and effects of the revolution. Provide suggestions for personalized tasks where advanced students can research lesser-known historical figures, while struggling students can focus on key events and dates.*
2.3. Guidelines for Personalized Content Creation	*Develop a personalized science project on renewable energy for 9th-grade students. Provide simplified project instructions for students who need more guidance, intermediate-level projects for students with some knowledge, and complex, research-based projects for advanced students. Include tips on how students can use AI tools to gather data and analyze their findings.*
2.4. Resource Recommendations	*Generate a list of AI-recommended resources for a lesson on climate change. Provide easy to read articles and videos for students who need more support, as well as advanced scientific journals and interactive simulations for students who are interested in further exploration of the topic.*
2.5. Cross-Subject Integration	*Create an integrated lesson for 8th-grade students that combines history and language arts. Focus on a key historical event, such as the Civil Rights Movement, and have students analyze primary sources (historical documents) and write essays from different perspectives. Offer simplified materials for students who struggle with reading comprehension, and advanced tasks for students who excel in writing.*
2.6. Student Engagement and Motivation	*Create a personalized lesson on environmental science that engages students by allowing them to choose their own research topics (e.g., deforestation, ocean pollution, wildlife conservation). Include guidelines for students who need more structure in their research process, and suggest in-depth, independent projects for students who are more advanced.*
2.7. Collaboration and Peer Learning	*Develop a collaborative project for a secondary school history class where students use AI tools like ChatGPT to research and present on key battles of World War II. Provide instructions for group work, where each student takes on a different role (researcher, writer, presenter), and suggest how they can use AI to gather and organize their information. Include tips on how to facilitate peer feedback and reflection.*

Table 10. List of prompts for category language and accessibility

Subcategory	Prompts
3.1. Accessibility	*Create a vocabulary list for a secondary school biology lesson on genetics for students who speak both English and Spanish. Include definitions and explanations in both languages and provide simplified sentences that students can use to understand the terms in context. Add pronunciation guides for key scientific terms in both languages.*
3.2. Language and Cultural Inclusivity	*Design a culturally inclusive literature lesson on the theme of family in different cultures. Provide short stories from diverse cultures (e.g., African, Asian, Latin American) that reflect different perspectives on family values. Ensure that the reading level and vocabulary are appropriate for students at different proficiency levels, and suggest reflection questions that promote cross-cultural understanding.*
3.3. Age-Specific Guidelines	*Generate an age-appropriate lesson on climate change for 3rd-grade students. Use simple language to explain the causes and effects of climate change, and include a short video or cartoon that visually demonstrates the concept. Provide an activity where students can draw what they think the world will look like if we take care of the environment.*

Table 11. List of prompts for category evaluation

Subcategory	Prompts
4.1. AI Evaluation	*Generate a set of reflection questions for teachers to evaluate the educational value of using AI tools in a science unit on ecosystems. The questions should guide teachers in reflecting on whether the AI-generated content facilitated deeper understanding of ecological relationships, how well it supported personalized learning, and whether it encouraged critical thinking. Include suggestions for how teachers can adjust the use of AI tools to improve educational outcomes.*
4.2. Student feedback and critical thinking	*Create a student feedback survey that teachers can use to measure student engagement and satisfaction with AI-generated content in a 9th-grade literature class. The survey should ask questions about the clarity of AI-generated explanations, how well the AI helped students understand complex texts, and how engaging students found the AI-generated activities. Include options for students to suggest improvements or share concerns about the AI-generated content.*
4.3. Transparency and accountability	*Design a lesson plan for explaining to secondary school students how AI-generated feedback on their essays works. The lesson should break down how AI analyzes grammar, structure, and content, and what criteria it uses to provide suggestions. Include transparency guidelines that help students understand the limitations of AI feedback and how the teacher reviews and adjusts the AI's suggestions to ensure fairness.*

Table 12. List of prompts for category engagement strategies

Subcategories	Prompts
5.1. Multimodal Learning	*Generate a hands-on learning activity for a 6th-grade science lesson on energy transformation. Include instructions for a simple experiment where students can create their own circuits or models to demonstrate energy transformation, such as turning chemical energy into electrical energy. Provide step by step guides with real-world examples that explain each type of energy transformation.*
5.2. Interactive Learning	*Create an interactive dialogue-based lesson for students learning Spanish. Use AI to generate role-playing scenarios where students practice conversational Spanish in real-world situations, such as ordering food at a restaurant or asking for directions. The AI should provide feedback on their grammar, vocabulary, and pronunciation.*
5.3. Contextual and Repetitive Learning	*Design a contextual biology lesson for high school students on the topic of genetics. Include real-world examples where students explore how genetics plays a role in disease inheritance, agricultural practices, and biodiversity. Use AI to generate follow-up activities where students apply genetic concepts to real-life scenarios, such as predicting genetic traits in offspring or analyzing genetic modification in plants.*
5.4. Customized Task Difficulty	*Create a personalized reading lesson on Shakespeare's Romeo and Juliet for secondary school students. For students who struggle with the text, provide simplified summaries of each scene and vocabulary support. For intermediate students, generate discussion questions that encourage them to analyze character motivations. For advanced students, suggest activities like comparing different film adaptations or writing a modern retelling of a scene.*
5.5. Supporting diverse learning styles	*Design a lesson on ecosystems for 7th-grade students that incorporates multiple learning styles. For visual learners, include AI-generated diagrams showing different types of ecosystems and food chains. For auditory learners, provide a podcast or audio lecture on ecological balance. For kinesthetic learners, include a project where students build their own ecosystem models or conduct outdoor observations.*

When writing prompts, it is important to remember a few tips on how to get the most out of the generative AI tools. For better results the prompts need to be specific and targeted, the use key words such as "Write", "Classify", "Summarize", "Translate", "Order", etc. (Prompt Engineering Guide, n.d.) is encouraged. The prompting is the focal point when working with generative AI models. These examples are informative and can be altered, upgraded and changed in any way. It is important for teachers to be educated about writing quality prompts so that they could get constructive feedback and quality materials from the AI models that can be included in the learning materials and classroom.

REFERENCES

A framework for AI literacy. (n.d.). EDUCAUSE Review. https://er.educause.edu/articles/2024/6/a-framework-for-ai-literacy

AI Guidance for Schools Toolkit. (n.d.). https://www.teachai.org/toolkit

Azukas, M. E. (2019). Cultivating a Blended Community of Practice to Promote Personal Learning. *Journal of Online Learning Research*, 5(3), 275–310.

CAST. (n.d.). *Universal Design for Learning (UDL) guidelines*. Retrieved from: https://www.cast.org

Chan, C. K. Y. (2023). A comprehensive AI policy education framework for university teaching and learning. *International Journal of Educational Technology in Higher Education*, 20(1), 38. DOI: 10.1186/s41239-023-00408-3

Europaea, S. (2020). *Digital Competence Framework for the European Schools*. Schola Europaea, Office of the Secretary-General Pedagogical Development Unit.

European Commission. (2023). European Education and Culture Executive Agency, *AI report – By the European Digital Education Hub's Squad on artificial intelligence in education*, Publications Office of the European Union. https://data.europa.eu/doi/10.2797/828281

FOI. (2024). *The framework of using artificial intelligence tools in teaching, student work, and research at the Univeristy of Zagreb Faculty of Organization and Informatics.*

Guo, P. J., Kim, J., & Rubin, R. (2014). How video production affects student engagement: An empirical study of MOOC videos. *Proceedings of the first ACM conference on Learning@ scale conference*. Retrieved from: https://dl.acm.org/doi/10.1145/2556325.2566239

Keengwe, J. (Ed.). (2023). *Creative AI Tools and Ethical Implications in Teaching and Learning*. IGI Global. DOI: 10.4018/979-8-3693-0205-7

Luckin, R., Holmes, W., Griffiths, M., & Forcier, L. B. (2016). *Intelligence Unleashed: An argument for AI in Education*. Pearson Education. Retrieved from: https://www.pearson.com

Miao, F., & Cukurova, M. (2024). *AI competency framework for teachers* [Report]. UNESCO. DOI: 10.54675/ZJTE2084

Miao, F., & Shiohira, K. (2024). *AI competency framework for students*. UNESCO. DOI: 10.54675/JKJB9835

Moreno, R., & Mayer, R. E. (2007). Interactive multimodal learning environments: Special issue on interactive learning environments: Contemporary issues and trends. *Educational Psychology Review*, 19(3), 309–326. DOI: 10.1007/s10648-007-9047-2

NCAI. (2021). *AI and Multimodal Learning: Enhancing Education Through Artificial Intelligence*. Retrieved from: https://www.ncai.org

Ng, D. T. K., Leung, J., Su, J., Ng, C. W., & Chu, S. (2023). Teachers' AI digital competencies and twenty-first century skills in the post-pandemic world. *Educational Technology Research and Development*, 71(1), 137–161. DOI: 10.1007/s11423-023-10203-6 PMID: 36844361

OCDE. (2023). Opportunities, guidelines and guardrails for effective and equitable use of AI in education. In *OECD Digital Education Outlook 2023: Towards an Effective Digital Education Ecosystem*. Éditions OCDE. DOI: 10.1787/2b39e98b-

Open, A. I. (2024). *ChatGPT* [Large language model]. https://chat.openai.com/chat

Prompt Engineering Guide. (n.d.). Retrieved from https://www.promptingguide.ai/

Punie, Y. (Ed.). (2017). European Framework for the Digital Competence of Educators: DigCompEdu, EUR 28775 EN. Publications Office of the European Union. DOI: 10.2760/178382

Team, M. E. (2024b, July 18). *Explore insights from the AI in Education Report | Microsoft Education Blog*. Microsoft Education Blog. https://www.microsoft.com/en-us/education/blog/2024/04/explore-insights-from-the-ai-in-education-report/

The National Center on Education and the Economy. (2024). *Framework for AI-Powered Environments*. National Center on Education and the Economy.

Thongprasit, J., & Wannapiroon, P. (2022). Framework of Artificial Intelligence Learning Platform for Education. *International Education Studies*, 15(1), 76–86. DOI: 10.5539/ies.v15n1p76

Tzafilkou, K., Perifanou, M., & Economides, A. A. (2022). Development and validation of students' digital competence scale (SDiCoS). *International Journal of Educational Technology in Higher Education*, 19(1), 30. DOI: 10.1186/s41239-022-00330-0 PMID: 35602658

UNESCO. (2019). Beijing consensus on artificial intelligence and education. *International Conference on Artificial Intelligence and Education, Planning Education in the AI Era: Lead the Leap*.

UNESCO. (2021). *AI and Education: Guidance for Policy-makers*. Retrieved from: https://unesdoc.unesco.org

Varsik, S., & Vosberg, L. (2024). The potential impact of Artificial Intelligence on equity and inclusion in education.

Vuorikari, R., Kluzer, S., & Punie, Y. (2022). *DigComp 2.2: The Digital Competence Framework for Citizens - With new examples of knowledge, skills and attitudes*. EUR 31006 EN, Publications Office of the European Union. DOI: 10.2760/490274

World Economic Forum. (2021). *The inclusive revolution: Artificial intelligence for accessibility*. Retrieved from: https://www.weforum.org

Chapter 9
Conclusion

ABSTRACT

The chapter examines the evolving role of teachers in AI-enhanced learning environments, positioning them as facilitators of learning rather than being replaced by AI. Teachers are now tasked with integrating AI tools responsibly to align with pedagogical and ethical standards. In addition to exploring the benefits of AI, the chapter also addresses challenges, such as the need for continued human oversight in AI-driven education and the limitations of AI-generated responses. Recommendations for future research include focusing on AI's impact in under-resourced educational environments and developing comprehensive ethical frameworks for its use in education.

CONCLUSION

The book explores the transformational role of artificial intelligence (AI) in education and focuses on how AI technologies can improve learning experiences and support teachers and students in different educational environments. The study examined various AI tools and their applications and provided an overview of the current and future potential of AI in education. The main conclusion derived from this research is that AI can improve education by creating a more personalized, inclusive and effective learning environment by applying thoughtful and ethical approaches. The main contributions of artificial intelligence include the automatization of routine tasks such as classification and planning, enabling teachers to focus on student interaction and personalized support. The ability of artificial intelligence to provide real-time feedback, identify learning gaps, and adapt educational strategies to the

DOI: 10.4018/979-8-3693-3474-4.ch009

needs of students makes personal learning accessible and conducive in large or diverse classrooms. Furthermore, AI can offer learning experiences that adapt to the pace and style of each student, thus improving learning outcomes across different subjects and educational levels. In addition, it is necessary to consider that the use of AI in the educational context involves risks and limitations, such as problems of privacy, misinformation, plagiarism, biases and cultural differences, as well as the lack of human connection (Bayly-Castaneda et al., 2024, p. 3).

The research also points to the evolving role of educators in AI-enhanced learning environments. Rather than replacing teachers, AI is repositioning them as facilitators of learning, where their expertise in critical thinking, emotional intelligence, and ethical decision-making is essential. AI in education does not aim to replace teachers but rather to collaborate with them where educators play a critical role in integrating AI effectively and maintaining a human-centered approach to teaching and this requires teachers to remain active facilitators of learning while leveraging AI to optimize instructional strategies (Keengwe, 2023). Educators are now responsible for managing the complexities of AI tools while supporting students in personalized learning and ensuring that AI is implemented in alignment with both pedagogical objectives and ethical principles.

The future of AI in education will bring further advancements, including more sophisticated AI systems capable of real-time data analysis, immersive learning experiences through AI-powered simulations, and improved accessibility for students with disabilities. Realizing the full potential of AI in education requires a commitment to ethical principles, transparency, and a focus on equity. As this research has shown, AI can be a powerful tool in education, but only if it is developed and deployed responsibly. The continuous evolution of AI in education will certainly continue to shape the future of education, and it is the responsibility of teachers, stakeholders, developers, etc. to ensure that this future benefits all students, teachers, and society as a whole. The findings of this book highlight the potential of AI to transform educational practices across all levels of education, from primary education to higher education. Through the research, several concrete conclusions have been drawn regarding AI's role in improving teaching and learning. One of the conclusions is that AI can improve personalized learning by analyzing student data to identify strengths, weaknesses, and learning gaps, and by adjusting instructional content to fit the needs of individual students. Moreover, the research concludes that AI can alleviate administrative burdens on teachers, automating repetitive tasks such as grading, attendance tracking, and lesson planning. This allows teachers to focus more on interactive teaching and personalized student engagement. By freeing up teachers' time, AI also opens opportunities for educators to innovate and incorporate more creative, critical-thinking-focused activities into their lessons. However, the integration of AI in education is not without its challenges.

RESEARCH QUESTIONS

The research examines several research questions about how AI tools influence education, specifically focusing on their role in improving learning outcomes, student engagement, and instructional methods. These questions aim to explore both the benefits and limitations of AI in various educational contexts.

RQ1. How Do AI Tools Improve the Understanding of New Concepts Compared to Traditional Learning Methods?

A central research question investigates whether AI tools can enhance students' understanding of new concepts more effectively than traditional, teacher-led approaches. The research found that while AI provides advantages in task-solving and information retrieval, it often falls short in promoting deep understanding. Many students still prefer traditional teacher-led instruction for mastering complex theoretical concepts. This finding supports the work of Susskind & Susskind (2015), who argue that while technology can transform how information is delivered, human experts remain crucial for fostering deep learning. Similarly, Chen et al. (2020) found that although AI tools can efficiently assist students in solving problems, they lack the nuance required for mastering complex theoretical concepts. These insights suggest that AI tools might complement traditional learning but are not a sufficient replacement for teacher-led instruction in fostering comprehensive understanding.

RQ 2. What Are the Benefits, Challenges, and Limitations Students Experience When Using AI Tools Independently?

Another important question focuses on the advantages and difficulties students encounter when using AI tools independently. Students reported that AI tools allow them to learn at their own pace and complete tasks more efficiently, supporting findings from Luckin (2017), who emphasizes the value of personalized learning. However, challenges such as the shallow depth of AI-generated responses and the need for additional teacher support, particularly for abstract or new concepts, were frequently commented by students. Holmes et al. (2019) similarly highlight the limitations of AI tools in delivering in-depth learning experiences. These findings suggest that while AI can help in task efficiency, its limited ability to conduct deeper understanding can slow down students' learning without teacher intervention. However, challenges included the lack of depth in AI-generated responses and the need for additional teacher support, particularly when learning new or abstract concepts. The research also highlighted concerns about over-reliance on AI tools, which could reduce personal engagement and critical thinking.

RQ 3. How Do AI Tools Impact Students' Confidence and Self-Efficacy in Learning?

The research also explores the impact of AI tools on students' confidence and self-efficacy in learning. While some students expressed increased confidence in their ability to complete tasks with AI support, the overall effect on long-term confidence in mastering new materials was unclear. Some students expressed that AI tools improved their confidence, but a significant portion remained neutral or skeptical about the tool's ability to boost their self-efficacy. This reflects Bandura's (1997) theory of self-efficacy, which stresses the importance of sustained confidence for long-term success. Similarly, Kim & Baylor (2016) found that while AI companions could improve task completion, their impact on student self-efficacy was less consistent. These studies suggest that while AI can support learning processes, its influence on building long-term self-efficacy remains uncertain and may require additional pedagogical support.

RQ 4. Can AI Tools Effectively Supplement Traditional Learning Models?

This research question addresses whether AI tools can effectively supplement traditional learning models. The findings suggest that AI tools are particularly useful in technical subjects such as computer science, where task-oriented activities and practical examples are essential. However, they are best seen as complementary to, rather than a replacement for, traditional methods. Woolf (2009) supports this view, arguing that while AI-based intelligent tutors are valuable for specific task-based learning, they cannot fully replicate the adaptive and empathetic nature of human teachers. Means & Neisler (2021) also highlight the importance of balancing AI integration with teacher-led instruction, especially for fostering conceptual understanding. This balanced approach strengthens the concept that AI tools are a valuable supplement but not a replacement for traditional pedagogical methods. The integration of AI into traditional models requires a balanced approach where AI supports but does not replace teacher-led instruction.

RQ 5. How Can AI Tools Support the Personalization of Learning Materials for Students With Learning Difficulties?

This research question examines how AI tools can help in personalizing learning experiences, particularly for students with learning difficulties. The results indicate that while AI can generate customized content for diverse learning needs, effective personalization still depends on teacher oversight. Pane et al. (2017) found that while technology-driven personalization improved engagement and learning outcomes, it was most effective when combined with active teacher involvement. Rose (2016) also stresses the importance of moving beyond a one-size-fits-all approach to education, a goal that AI tools can help achieve, but only when thoughtfully integrated with teacher guidance. These findings highlight the importance of human involvement in adapting AI-generated content to meet the specific needs of individual learners.

The potential of artificial intelligence in education is great, providing students with opportunities to participate in a more inclusive, personalized, and effective learning environment, and also helping teachers to customize learning materials. To fully exploit these potential educators, policymakers and developers need to work together collaboratively to overcome the existing ethical concerns and technological gaps. As AI develops, the future of education will depend on how well these tools are integrated, improving learning while preserving the human touch in the center of equity, privacy and education.

LIMITATIONS OF THE RESEARCH

The research provides a comprehensive exploration of AI's role in education, but several limitations must be acknowledged. First, much of the research focuses on case studies in developed educational systems, where access to advanced technology is available. This limits the generalizability of the findings to regions or institutions where technological infrastructure is less developed. Future research should examine AI's impact in a wider range of contexts, including low-resource settings, to gain a more understanding of its global applicability. Another limitation of this research is the lack of longitudinal studies. Most of the data reviewed are based on short-term implementations of AI tools, making it difficult to assess the long-term impact of AI on student outcomes and teaching practices. Longitudinal studies are needed to track the sustained effects of AI integration in education over time, particularly in terms of learning retention and changes in teaching methodologies. Additionally, while the research explores various AI tools and platforms, it is limited in its scope regarding the technical understanding of AI systems. This book primarily focuses on the educational implications of AI, rather than the algorithms and technical advancements that make these systems possible. Future research could research the technological side of AI development in education to provide more technical guidance for AI developers working in the educational space.

FUTURE RESEARCH

To build on the findings of this research, future studies should address several areas. One of the areas is exploring the impact of AI in under-resourced educational environments. Research should investigate how AI can be adapted to work in settings with limited access to technology, infrastructure, and training, and how it can be scaled to benefit students globally, not just in high-tech regions. Another important direction for future research is examining long-term outcomes of AI-supported education. Studies that track the impact of AI tools over several years would provide valuable insights into whether personalized learning and AI-driven instruction result in sustained improvements in academic achievement, critical thinking, and problem-solving skills. There is also a need for more research into AI literacy for educators. As AI becomes more integrated into classrooms, teachers must develop a deeper understanding of how to effectively use AI tools. Future studies could explore the best practices for AI training and professional development, ensuring that teachers are not only comfortable using AI but are equipped to critically assess its outputs and guide students in responsible AI use. In addition, research into the ethical frameworks for AI in education should continue to evolve. Further exploration is needed to create robust guidelines that address emerging challenges, such as AI's role in influencing student behaviour, safeguarding data privacy, and ensuring fairness and transparency in AI-powered decision-making systems.

REFERENCES

Bandura, A. (1997). *Self-efficacy: The exercise of control.* W.H. Freeman and Company.

Bayly-Castaneda, K., Ramirez-Montoya, M. S., & Morita-Alexander, A. (2024). Crafting personalized learning paths with AI for lifelong learning: A systematic literature review. *Frontiers in Education*, 9, 1424386. DOI: 10.3389/feduc.2024.1424386

Chen, L. (2020). How AI-based tools impact cognitive development in classrooms: A comparative study. *Journal of Educational Technology Research*, 47(3), 251–269.

Holmes, W. (2019). *Artificial intelligence in education: Promises and implications for teaching and learning*. UNESCO.

Keengwe, J. (Ed.). (2023). *Creative AI Tools and Ethical Implications in Teaching and Learning*. IGI Global. DOI: 10.4018/979-8-3693-0205-7

Kim, Y., & Baylor, A. L. (2016). Pedagogical agents as learning companions: The role of agent competency and type of interaction. *Educational Technology Research and Development*, 64(6), 753–776.

Luckin, R. (2017). *Enhancing learning and teaching with technology: What the research says*. UCL Institute of Education Press.

Means, B., & Neisler, J. (2021). *Technology use in education: Emerging trends and issues*. American Educational Research Association.

Pane, J. F. (2017). *Does personalized learning work? Evidence from U.S. schools*. RAND Corporation.

Rose, L. T. (2016). *The end of average: How we succeed in a world that values sameness*. HarperOne.

Susskind, R. E., & Susskind, D. (2015). *The future of the professions: How technology will transform the work of human experts*. Oxford University Press. DOI: 10.1093/oso/9780198713395.001.0001

Woolf, B. P. (2009). *Building intelligent interactive tutors: Student-centered strategies for revolutionizing e-learning*. Morgan Kaufmann.

ADDITIONAL READING

Delello, J. A., Watters, J. B., & Garcia-Lopez, A. (2024). Artificial intelligence in education: Transforming learning and teaching. In Delello, J., & McWhorter, R. (Eds.), *Disruptive Technologies in Education and Workforce Development* (pp. 1–26). IGI Global. DOI: 10.4018/979-8-3693-3003-6.ch001

Fernández-Llamas, C., Conde, M., Rodríguez-Sedano, F. J., Rodríguez-Lera, F. J., & Matellán-Olivera, V. (2020). Analyzing the computational competences acquired by K-12 students when lectured by robotic and human teachers: Can a robot teach computational principles to pre-university students? *International Journal of Social Robotics*, 12(5), 1009–1019. DOI: 10.1007/s12369-017-0440-9

Frąckiewicz, M. (2023). OpenAI and the risks of AI bias: Addressing stereotypes and discrimination. *TS2 Space*. https://ts2.space/en/openai-and-the-risks-of-ai-bias-addressing-stereotypes-and-discrimination

Jauhiainen, J. S., & Guerra, A. G. (2023). Generative AI and ChatGPT in school children's education: Evidence from a school lesson. *Sustainability (Basel)*, 15(18), 14025. DOI: 10.3390/su151814025

Kayyali, M. (2024). Future possibilities and challenges of AI in education. In Sharma, R., & Bozkurt, A. (Eds.), *Transforming Education With Generative AI: Prompt Engineering and Synthetic Content Creation* (pp. 118–137). IGI Global. DOI: 10.4018/979-8-3693-1351-0.ch006

Keengwe, J. (Ed.). (2023). *Creative AI Tools and Ethical Implications in Teaching and Learning*. IGI Global. DOI: 10.4018/979-8-3693-0205-7

Marrone, R., Cropley, D., & Medeiros, K. (2024). How does narrow AI impact human creativity? *Creativity Research Journal*, 36(1), 1–18. DOI: 10.1080/10400419.2024.2378264

Seldon, A., & Abidoye, O. (2023). AI and the future of learning: Will artificial intelligence redefine educational practices? *International Journal of AI in Education*, 5(2), 88–105. DOI: 10.1007/s41539-023-00152-w

Xiao, X., & Wang, L. (2021). AI in education: Examining the role of intelligent tutoring systems in modern classrooms. *Journal of Educational Technology & Society*, 24(4), 58–72. DOI: 10.1109/ETS.2021.9808329

KEY TERMS AND DEFINITIONS

AI Literacy: AI literacy is the theoretical and practical knowledge required to effectively use AI tools in educational settings. Some examples of AI knowledge could include basic concepts of AI, how AI can support teaching and learning, and ethical considerations for the implementation of AI.

Content Customization: Content customization is the process of adapting educational materials to the specific needs of students which is leading and upgrading personalized learning and teaching. Generative AI tools can help teachers to design and adjust educational content based on student's abilities, learning styles and interests.

Curriculum Alignment: Curriculum alignment is a process of ensuring that AI tools and outputs comply with established educational programs, objectives and standards. This process can help teachers to develop personalized and curriculum-based content for students.

Ethical AI: Ethical AI is a practice that ensures the development and use of AI tools transparently and fairly. In education, ethical AI focuses on issues such as data privacy, equal learning opportunities and accountability for decisions based on AI.

Generative AI: Generative AI technologies have the possibility to generate new content based on user prompts such as text, images, videos, audio, etc. In education, generative AI tools such as ChatGPT can be used to generate learning materials, simplify concepts and create personalized content for students.

Interactive Learning: Interactive learning is a process where generative AI tools can help teachers create additional educational materials and exercises, e.g. simulations, quizzes, and games to actively involve students in their learning processes.

Language and Cultural Inclusivity: Language and cultural inclusivity refers to the generative AI tools ability to personalize educational materials for students from diverse linguistic and cultural backgrounds, ensuring accessibility and relevance for all learners.

Multimodal Learning: Multimodal learning refers to the use of different methods of teaching, e.g. visual, auditory and kinesthetic approaches, to address students' different learning styles. Generative artificial intelligence tools can provide various ways of presenting information such as images, texts, and interactive activities with a goal to improve multi-modal learning.

Personalized Learning: This is a method of education that adapts the pace and method of instruction to the needs, goals and abilities of each student. Personalization education is often supported by technology to create unique experiences that adapt to different learning environments.

Appendix

APPENDIX A

Appendix A shows a survey which was given to students from higher education institution in Croatia who participated in this research and who were using generative AI tools for learning new concepts and resolving exercises. Results of Appendix A are shown and interpreted in chapter 5.

Working With AI Tools

The questionnaire aims to assess your experience working with AI tools during the Informatics course. All fields are mandatory, and the questionnaire is anonymous. Thank you all for participating.

1. Gender

a. Male

b. Female

c. Other

2. Age

a. 18-22

b. 23-27

c. 28-32

d. 33-37

e. more than 37

3. Study program

a. Rehabilitation

b. Speech Therapy

c. Social Pedagogy

4. Year of study

a. First

b. Second

c. Third

5. Have you used AI tools before?

a. Yes

b. No

6. If yes, for what purpose?

a. Learning

b. Information retrieval

c. Reviewing learning material

d. Creating additional exercises for repetition of learning materials
e. Personal purposes
7. How often do you use AI tools?
a. I never use AI tools.
b. I use AI tools once or twice a month.
c. I use AI tools once or twice a week.
d. I use AI tools several times a week.
e. I use AI tools every day.
f. Never.
8. Which AI tools have you used so far?
9. Were you able to successfully master new material using AI tools?
a. I fully mastered the material.
b. I partially mastered the material.
c. Some parts remained unclear to me.
d. I did not master the material at all.
10. Do you think you needed additional assistance from the teacher?
a. Yes
b. No
11. Were the instructions you received from the AI tool clear?
a. Completely unclear
b. Unclear
c. Neither clear nor unclear
d. Clear
e. Completely clear
12. Would you use AI tools again to assist with learning?
a. Yes
b. No
13. Would you use AI tools again to assist with solving tasks?
a. Yes
b. No
14. Level of satisfaction working with the AI tool.

Table 1.

	Completely dissatisfied	Dissatisfied	Neutral	Satisfied	Completely satisfied
How satisfied are you with the AI tool for solving tasks?					
How satisfied are you with the AI tool for mastering new material?					
How satisfied are you with the explanations you received from the AI tool?					

15. Experience working with the AI tool.

Table 2.

	I completely disagree	I disagree	Neutral	I agree	I completely agree
The AI tool helped me solve tasks more easily.					
The AI tool helped me better understand new material.					
The AI tool saved me time and effort.					
The AI tool was easy to use.					
I would recommend the AI tool to others.					
The AI tool helped me feel confident in my knowledge.					

continued on following page

Table 2. Continued

	I completely disagree	I disagree	Neutral	I agree	I completely agree
The AI tool helped me understand the concept of the tasks.					
I will use the AI tool for solving tasks in the future.					
The AI tool helped me develop problem-solving skills.					
The AI tool allowed me to tailor my learning approach to my needs.					
The AI tool provided me with incorrect examples.					
The AI tool gave me unclear information.					
Additional interpretation of the information was needed for a clearer understanding of the AI content.					
The AI tool gave me incorrect information.					

16. How easy was the AI tool to use?

a. Very easy

b. Easy

c. Neutral

d. Difficult

e. Very difficult

17. Did you need to use other sources to interpret the responses and guidance from the AI tool?

a. Yes

b. No

18. If yes, what was the reason for using other sources?

19. Would you use the AI tool in the future?

a. Yes

b. No

20. How often did you use the AI tool while solving tasks?

a. Never

b. Rarely

c. Sometimes

d. Often

e. Always

21. Accuracy of information while using the AI tool.

Table 3.

	Always accurate	**Mostly accurate**	**Often accurate**	**Sometimes accurate**	**Rarely accurate**
The AI tool was accurate in solving tasks.					
The AI tool was reliable in providing accurate information for learning new material.					

22. Please write any comment related to the use of AI tools in teaching.

APPENDIX B

Appendix B contains list of all questions which were included in the interviews with teachers from primary and secondary schools in Croatia. Results of Appendix A are shown and interpreted in Chapter 6 and 7.

First Interview on the Structure of the Teaching and Knowledge of Working with AI Tools

How long have you been working as a primary school teacher?

What subject do you teach?

How many students do you have in your class?

What is the age of the student?

Are you getting a kick out of using AI tools? (for lesson preparation, for personal purposes or something else)

Before this research, how often was the AI tool used and for what purposes?

What type of material is the most difficult for students to learn?

What type of material do students learn the easiest/quickest?

How would you define personalized learning in the context of primary school education?

Have you ever implemented personalized learning for your students? If yes, please explain the procedure.

What is the age?

Do you use digital tools for lesson preparation?

If yes, how often do you use digital tools for lesson preparation?

Do you use digital tools in direct teaching with students?

If yes, how often and for what type of material/teaching do you use digital tools in direct teaching with students?

If yes, which digital tools have you used or are you using?

How would you define artificial intelligence?

Are you getting a kick out of using AI tools? (for lesson preparation, for personal purposes or something else). If so, for what purpose did you use them?

If so, which AI tools are we talking about?

What material will you prepare using AI tools? Explain why you think a particular material would be suitable for preparation using AI tools?

What professional development opportunities are available for teachers to effectively use artificial intelligence tools in teaching international students?

What is the structure of students in your class?

What is the grade point average of the students in your class?

Do you need to adapt the teaching content for individual students in the class?

Second Interview with the Teacher About the Process of Lesson Preparation Using AI Tools

How would you describe your experience using AI tools to create personalized materials?

Describe the process of preparation and production of materials.

Does AI save you time for lesson preparation or has the preparation time increased? Explain the answer.

To what extent has AI helped you?

What are the challenges you faced when preparing your lessons using AI tools?

What are the positive sides of using AI tools for lesson preparation?

Which AI tool or tools have you used to adapt your teaching?

How did personalized teaching materials differ from other materials?

Explain the reason why you have chosen a particular AI tool for lesson preparation.

To what extent did the AI tool help you prepare the teaching unit?

Did the AI tool help you prepare personalized lessons for foreign students?

What were the advantages and what were the disadvantages of using AI tools for lesson preparation?

Was the AI tool applicable to teaching your subject?

Was it more time-consuming for you to use an AI tool for preparing personalized lessons compared to traditional preparation? Or did the preparation time get longer? Do you think that the AI tool saved you time preparing your lessons? Explain the answer.

Have you been able to personalize materials using AI tools for students?

In your experience, what were the advantages and disadvantages of using AI tools for lesson preparation?

Did you need to customize the examples and content that the AI tool generated?

Have you come across any wrong examples or information while working with the AI tool?

Were the examples of exercises generated by the AI more useful and interesting for the students?

Will you use the AI tool again to prepare personalized lessons for foreign students?

Have the introduction of AI tools changed your approach to planning and preparing teaching content? In what way?

What functionalities of AI tools do you find most useful in preparing your teaching materials?

What are the advantages, in your opinion, of using AI tools in teaching? Are there any drawbacks or challenges you have faced?

How would you rate the effectiveness of AI tools compared to your traditional teaching methods?

Has using AI tools fueled your professional development or changed your perceptions about teaching and technology?

Will you use AI tools for teaching in the future? If so, in what ways do you plan to expand your use of AI technology in the classroom?

How have you used an AI tool to adapt teaching materials to the individual needs and understanding levels of students?

What are the best practices for integrating AI tools into the curriculum to ensure it supports students' diverse learning styles?

How would you evaluate the effectiveness of using AI tools in improving students' achievement and understanding of the material?

Do you think that AI tools can be used to encourage creativity and self-confidence in students in the learning process?

What are the possibilities for customizing and adapting the AI tool's responses to better suit the specific needs of the learner?

What are the opportunities for professional development for teachers to train them to effectively use AI tools in teaching?

What guidelines or resources do you recommend for educators who want to better understand and use AI tools more effectively in their practice?

How can AI tools be integrated into existing curricula and educational programs to ensure personalization of learning?

How can AI tools support the differentiation of instruction to meet the different needs and learning styles of students?

In your experience, what were the advantages and disadvantages of using AI tools to prepare lessons?

The Third Interview with the Teacher on the Experience of Using AI Tools in Direct Teaching With Students and the Results of Students' Independent Use of AI Tools for Solve Exercises and Tasks

Explain the reason why you chose certain AI tools for use in direct teaching.

How did the students react to the integration of AI tools in direct teaching?

How would you describe your own experience in applying AI tools in direct teaching with students?

Were there any obstacles during classes and mastering the material?

How successfully did the students learn the material?

For which age group do you think AI tools would be suitable for use in teaching with students? Was it appropriate for the age group of your class?

Have you used an AI tool to overcome language barriers? If yes, did it help the students to overcome the language barrier?

Do you think that students can overcome language barriers faster by using AI tools?

How does an AI tool affect your interaction with students during class?

Did students show interest or reaction to using AI tools in class? What was their feedback?

How do you deal with potential technical difficulties or limitations of AI tools when using them in class?

What was the most interesting for the students during the lesson?

What were the advantages and disadvantages of using AI tools in direct teaching with students?

Has an AI tool helped you prepare personalized lessons for your students?

During class, did you manage to implement personalized learning for individual students who learn the material better?

During class, did you manage to implement personalized learning for individual students who are less able to learn the material?

Have you been able to adapt the materials using AI tools for individual students who have difficulty learning the material?

Have you been able to adapt the materials using AI tools for individual students who learn the material better and faster?

Which material did you use the AI tool to prepare?

What was the students' interest in assisted teaching using AI tools?

Was the students' motivation better?

Were the results of the exercises more successful?

Were the assignments more successful?

Did the students copy the answers from the AI tool or did they use it as an additional tool to complement and successfully solve the tasks?

How did students react to the possibility of using AI tools to create assignments?

Did the students know how to use the AI tool or did you have to take the time to teach them how to use the AI tool?

If you had to teach them how to use the tool, how much time did you spend on training?

Do you think the time invested is worthwhile considering the results?

In your experience, what were the advantages and disadvantages of using AI tools to solve tasks?

Given your research experience, will you use the AI tool again to prepare lessons, exercises, homework or directly in class?

Did the students have problems using the AI tools to solve the tasks? If yes, describe the problems they encountered?

Do you think that students responded better to the application of AI tools in direct teaching or to solve tasks at home?

Is AI applicable to teaching your subject?

Do you think that incorporating AI tools into working directly with students would be an approach you would use in your teaching?

What are the challenges faced by students using AI tools during class?

What are the positive sides of using AI tools in direct teaching with students?

Do you find that AI tools have made it easier for you to prepare personalized lessons for the students in your class?

APPENDIX C

Appendix C shows teacher's A materials which were prepared during this research for students in vocational school in Croatian for data analysis and interpretation using Excel. An explanation of exercises and materials in Appendix C is shown and interpreted in chapter 6.

Task 1

Table for interpretation

Question:

- Which student has the highest number of unexcused absences?
- What is the average grade of Ivan Hemingway?
- How many students have an average above 3.00?
- Which student has the least number of excused absences?
- How many students are travelers?

Task 2

Graph for interpretation

Questions:

- Which student has the highest average grade?
- What is the average grade of the student with the lowest average?
- Are there more students with an average grade above 3.5 or below 3.0?

APPENDIX D

Appendix D shows teacher's B teaching units (materials) which were prepared during this research for students in primary school in Croatia for biology class. An explanation of exercises and materials in Appendix C is shown and interpreted in chapter 6.

Written Preparation for Conducting a Lesson

Textbook Unit: Life Cycle of Flowering Plants

Domain/Concept: B. CHANGES AND RELATIONSHIPS

Outcome: The student analyzes and connects living conditions and the diversity of living beings in different habitats and describes cycles in nature.

Outcome Elaboration: Describes the life cycle using the example of a flowering plant.

Interdisciplinary Theme: The student shows interest in different areas, takes responsibility for their learning, and perseveres in learning.

Interdisciplinary Connections:

• Language expression.

• Interprets different content through artistic and visual expression (the life cycle of the plant is illustrated with a drawing).

Assessment for learning: Completion of worksheets/exit cards.

Assessment as learning: Self-assessment of understanding the content.

Teaching and Learning Methods: discussion method, demonstration method, oral presentation method, writing method

Teaching Resources and Aids: Textbook "Exploring Our World 4," additional digital content, teaching worksheets.

Literature: Curriculum for the Subject of Nature and Society. 2019. MZO. Textbook "Exploring Our World 4," additional digital content, teaching worksheets.

The course of the lesson

1. Introduction:

• I announce to the students that we will watch the video "Life Cycle of a Plant" at the link https://hr.izzi.digital/DOS/56495/72387.html.

• Students briefly summarize the video content.

• I pose a motivational question from the textbook:

• What is a cycle? By solving sequences given in the textbook, the student concludes that a cycle is a circular sequence of events that repeat.

• I announce the learning of new content.

• Duration: 10 min

2. Main Part of the Lesson:

• Familiarization with new content

• I conduct familiarization with new content by having students read the text in the textbook on page 196. I explain unfamiliar words from the text. Students describe images from the textbook, solve the task - Explain the life cycle of the dandelion on page 197, and ask questions.

• Summarizing/Generalizing

• Students copy the board plan. They illustrate the life cycle of flowering plants.

• Duration: 25 min

3. Conclusion of the Lesson:

• Verification of new content

• Completion of worksheets/exit cards.

• Self-assessment of the acquisition of new knowledge - I can describe the life cycle using the example of a flowering plant.

• Duration: 10 min

Teaching Activities

1. Teacher's Activities:

• directs to the video and the motivational question in the textbook

• announces new content

2. Students' Activities:

• develop interest in learning new material

3. Teacher's Activities:

• directs to reading the text in the textbook, describing images, and solving tasks

• checks accuracy and provides feedback

4. Students' Activities:

• describe life cycles in nature – flowering plants

• read the text in the textbook

• connect prior knowledge with new insights

5. Teacher's Activities:

• directs to complete the worksheet and provides feedback

6. Students' Activities:

• applies acquired knowledge in solving various tasks

7. Teacher's Activities:

• checks if students have copied the board plan

• confirms new insights using various knowledge sources

8. Students' Activities:

• checks whether they have acquired the expected outcomes

• assesses the effectiveness of their learning in the specific learning situation

Additional Tasks (problem-solving research, etc.)

• Textbook p. 197 – Investigate

• Choose one plant from the forest or meadow community.

• Draw the stages of its life cycle and explain them.

Adjustments for Students with Difficulties:

• depending on the type of difficulty, provide an individualized approach to the student

• adapt teaching methods and procedures to the student based on their needs and capabilities

• adjust teaching materials to the needs and capabilities of the student

Activities for Gifted Students: /

Multimedia and Interactive Content:

https://hr.izzi.digital/DOS/56495/72387.html

Project Tasks: Create a herbarium by May 27, 2024.

Board Plan:

• Life Cycle of Flowering Plants

• LIFE CYCLE OF THE CHESTNUT TREE

• SEED

• GERMINATION

• GROWTH AND DEVELOPMENT OF THE CHESTNUT TREE

• FLOWERING AND POLLINATION

• FRUIT DEVELOPMENT

• DISPERSAL

• Worksheet/Exit Card

• LIFE CYCLE OF FLOWERING PLANTS

Explain the life cycle of flowering plants by arranging the given terms: growth, germination, pollination, dispersal, flowering, seed.

Name two plants that develop from seeds: ______________________________ ________.

What conditions are necessary for a seed to begin germinating and for a young plant to develop?

APPENDIX E

Appendix C shows exercises used with students in higher education for learning Excel functions during the Computer Science collegium. An explanation of exercises is shown and interpreted in chapter 5.

Task 1

Use the generative AI tool of your choice to search for the following functions in Excel:

- SUM
- SUMIF
- COUNT
- COUNIF
- COUNT
- MIN
- MAX
- AVERAGE
- IF
- MODE.

Write a description for each of the functions and write two practical examples for each function. If you used an additional AI tool, please put a note at the end of the document. Save the file with the *name functions_name_surname.docx.*

Task 2

The file *functions_tables.xlsx* contains data on which you will apply the knowledge gained from the previous task. You can use the help of AI tools to help solve the tasks.

Compilation of References

A framework for AI literacy. (n.d.). EDUCAUSE Review. https://er.educause.edu/articles/2024/6/a-framework-for-ai-literacy

Abbes, F., Bennani, S., & Maalel, A. (2024). Generative AI and Gamification for Personalized Learning: Literature Review and Future Challenges. *SN Computer Science*, 5(8), 1154. DOI: 10.1007/s42979-024-03491-z

Adams, C., Pente, P., Lemermeyer, G., & Rockwell, G. (2023). Ethical principles for artificial intelligence in K-12 education. *Computers and Education: Artificial Intelligence*, 4, 100131. DOI: 10.1016/j.caeai.2023.100131

Adobe Firefly. (n.d.). Retrieved May 18, 2024, from https://firefly.adobe.com

AI Guidance for Schools Toolkit. (n.d.). https://www.teachai.org/toolkit

Akgun, S., & Greenhow, C. (2022). Artificial intelligence in education: Addressing ethical challenges in K-12 settings. *AI and Ethics*, 2(3), 431–440. DOI: 10.1007/s43681-021-00096-7 PMID: 34790956

Almasri, F. (2024). Exploring the Impact of Artificial Intelligence in Teaching and Learning of Science: A Systematic Review of Empirical Research. *Research in Science Education*, 54(5), 977–997. DOI: 10.1007/s11165-024-10176-3

Ayeni, O. O., Al Hamad, N. M., Chisom, O. N., Osawaru, B., & Adewusi, O. E. (2024). AI in education: A review of personalized learning and educational technology. *GSC Advanced Research and Reviews*, 18(2), 261–271. DOI: 10.30574/gscarr.2024.18.2.0062

Azukas, M. E. (2019). Cultivating a Blended Community of Practice to Promote Personal Learning. *Journal of Online Learning Research*, 5(3), 275–310.

Bandura, A. (1997). *Self-efficacy: The exercise of control*. W.H. Freeman and Company.

Bayly-Castaneda, K., Ramirez-Montoya, M. S., & Morita-Alexander, A. (2024, August). Crafting personalized learning paths with AI for lifelong learning: a systematic literature review. In *Frontiers in Education* (Vol. 9, p. 1424386). Frontiers Media SA. *ChatGPT*. https://chatgpt.com/?oai-dm=1&model=auto

Bayly-Castaneda, K., Ramirez-Montoya, M. S., & Morita-Alexander, A. (2024). Crafting personalized learning paths with AI for lifelong learning: A systematic literature review. *Frontiers in Education*, 9, 1424386. DOI: 10.3389/feduc.2024.1424386

Bernacki, M. L., Greene, M. J., & Lobczowski, N. G. (2021). A systematic review of research on personalized learning: Personalized by whom, to what, how, and for what purpose (s)? *Educational Psychology Review*, 33(4), 1675–1715. DOI: 10.1007/s10648-021-09615-8

Brass, J., & Lynch, T. L. (2020). Personalized learning: A history of the present. *Journal of curriculum theorizing, 35*(2).

Briskteaching. (n.d.). Retrieved March 6, 2024, from https://briskteaching.com

CAST. (n.d.). *Universal Design for Learning (UDL) guidelines*. Retrieved from: https://www.cast.org

Chan, C. K. Y. (2023). A comprehensive AI policy education framework for university teaching and learning. *International Journal of Educational Technology in Higher Education*, 20(1), 38. DOI: 10.1186/s41239-023-00408-3

ChatGPT. (n.d.). Retrieved May 25, 2024, from https://chatgpt.com/

Chen, L. (2020). How AI-based tools impact cognitive development in classrooms: A comparative study. *Journal of Educational Technology Research*, 47(3), 251–269.

Chen, S. Y., & Wang, J. H. (2021). Individual differences and personalized learning: A review and appraisal. *Universal Access in the Information Society*, 20(4), 833–849. DOI: 10.1007/s10209-020-00753-4

Cheung, S. K. S., Fu, L. W., Kwok, L. F., & Poulova, P. (2021). In search of the good practices of personalized learning. *Interactive Learning Environments*, 29(2), 179–181. DOI: 10.1080/10494820.2021.1894830

Copilot. (n.d.). Retrieved May 10, 2024, from https://copilot.microsoft.com/

Cukurova, M. (2024). The interplay of learning, analytics and artificial intelligence in education: A vision for hybrid intelligence. *British Journal of Educational Technology. Gemini*. Retrieved August 15, 2024, from https://gemini.google.com/

Data, I. B. M., & Team, A. I. (2023, October 16). *Understanding the different types of artificial intelligence*. IBM Blog. https://www.ibm.com/blog/understanding-the-different-types-of-artificial-intelligence/

DIFFIT. (n.d.). https://web.diffit.me/

du Boulay, B. (2023). Artificial Intelligence in Education and Ethics. In Zawacki-Richter, O., & Jung, I. (Eds.), *Handbook of Open, Distance and Digital Education*. Springer. DOI: 10.1007/978-981-19-2080-6_6

Europaea, S. (2020). *Digital Competence Framework for the European Schools*. Schola Europaea, Office of the Secretary-General Pedagogical Development Unit.

European Commission. (2022). Directorate-General for Education, Youth, Sport and Culture, Ethical guidelines on the use of artificial intelligence (AI) and data in teaching and learning for educators, Publications Office of the European Union. https://data.europa.eu/doi/10.2766/153756

European Commission. (2023). European Education and Culture Executive Agency, *AI report – By the European Digital Education Hub's Squad on artificial intelligence in education*, Publications Office of the European Union. https://data.europa.eu/doi/10.2797/828281

Filipsson, F., & Filipsson, F. (2024). Top 10 use cases for Microsoft Copilot in Education. *Redress Compliance - Just another WordPress site*. https://redresscompliance.com/top-10-use-cases-for-microsoft-copilot-in-education/

Fitria, T. N. (2021, December). Artificial intelligence (AI) in education: Using AI tools for teaching and learning process. In *Prosiding Seminar Nasional & Call for Paper STIE AAS* (pp. 134-147).

FOI. (2024). *The framework of using artificial intelligence tools in teaching, student work, and research at the Univeristy of Zagreb Faculty of Organization and Informatics.*

Foltynek, T., Bjelobaba, S., Glendinning, I., Khan, Z. R., Santos, R., Pavletic, P., & Kravjar, J. (2023). ENAI Recommendations on the ethical use of Artificial Intelligence in Education. *International Journal for Educational Integrity*, 19(1), 12. DOI: 10.1007/s40979-023-00133-4

Formative, A. I. (n.d.). Retrieved June 13, 2024, from https://www.formative.com/

Frąckiewicz, M. (2023). OpenAI and the Risks of AI Bias: Addressing Stereotypes and Discrimination. TS2 SPACE. https://ts2.space/en/openai-and-the-risks-of-ai-bias-addressing-stereotypes-and-discrimination

Gašević, D., Siemens, G., & Sadiq, S. (2023). Empowering learners for the age of artificial intelligence. Computers & Education. *Artificial Intelligence*, 4, 100130. DOI: 10.1016/j.caeai.2023.100130

Gašević, D., Siemens, G., & Sadiq, S. (2023). Empowering learners for the age of artificial intelligence. *Computers & Education: Artificial Intelligence*, 4, 100130.

Gemini. (n.d.). https://gemini.google.com/

GEMINI. (n.d.). Retrieved June 13, 2024, from https://gemini.google.com

Ghimire, A., Prather, J., & Edwards, J. (2024). Generative AI in Education: A Study of Educators' Awareness, Sentiments, and Influencing Factors. *arXiv* preprint *arXiv*:2403.15586.

Google. (2024). *Tips to write prompts for Gemini*. Available at: https://support.google.com/a/users/answer/14200040?hl=en

Gunawardena, M., Bishop, P., & Aviruppola, K. (2024). Personalized learning: The simple, the complicated, the complex and the chaotic. *Teaching and Teacher Education*, 139, 104429. DOI: 10.1016/j.tate.2023.104429

Guo, P. J., Kim, J., & Rubin, R. (2014). How video production affects student engagement: An empirical study of MOOC videos. *Proceedings of the first ACM conference on Learning@ scale conference*. Retrieved from: https://dl.acm.org/doi/10.1145/2556325.2566239

Holmes, W. (2019). *Artificial intelligence in education: Promises and implications for teaching and learning*. UNESCO.

Holmes, W., & Bialik, M. (2020). *Artificial intelligence in education: Learning systems and intelligent learning environments for personalized education*. Springer.

Hwang, G. J., & Tu, Y. F. (2021). Roles and research trends of artificial intelligence in education. *Computers & Education: Artificial Intelligence*, 2, 100011.

Ifenthaler, D., Majumdar, R., Gorissen, P., Judge, M., Mishra, S., Raffaghelli, J., & Shimada, A. (2024). Artificial Intelligence in Education: Implications for Policymakers, Researchers, and Practitioners. *Tech Know Learn*, 29(4), 1693–1710. DOI: 10.1007/s10758-024-09747-0

Introduction to large language models. (n.d.). Google for Developers. https://developers.google.com/machine-learning/resources/intro-llms

Jackley, M. (2024, February 16). *What is a Large Language model (LLM)?*https://www.oracle.com/artificial-intelligence/large-language-model/

Jauhiainen, J. S., & Guerra, A. G. (2023). Generative AI and ChatGPT in school Children's education: Evidence from a school lesson. *Sustainability (Basel)*, 15(18), 14025. DOI: 10.3390/su151814025

Katsamakas, E., Pavlov, O. V., & Saklad, R. (2024). Artificial Intelligence and the Transformation of Higher Education Institutions: A Systems Approach. *Sustainability (Basel)*, 16(14), 6118. DOI: 10.3390/su16146118

Keengwe, J. (Ed.). (2023). *Creative AI Tools and Ethical Implications in Teaching and Learning*. IGI Global. DOI: 10.4018/979-8-3693-0205-7

Kim, Y., & Baylor, A. L. (2016). Pedagogical agents as learning companions: The role of agent competency and type of interaction. *Educational Technology Research and Development*, 64(6), 753–776.

Laak, K. J., & Aru, J. (2024). AI and personalized learning: bridging the gap with modern educational goals. *arXiv* preprint *arXiv*:2404.02798.

Large language models (LLM). (2024, May 13). European Data Protection Supervisor. https://www.edps.europa.eu/data-protection/technology-monitoring/techsonar/large-language-models-llm_en

Lee, D., Huh, Y., Lin, C. Y., & Reigeluth, C. M. (2018). Technology functions for personalized learning in learner-centered schools. *Educational Technology Research and Development*, 66(5), 1269–1302. DOI: 10.1007/s11423-018-9615-9

Luckin, R., Holmes, W., Griffiths, M., & Forcier, L. B. (2016). *Intelligence Unleashed: An argument for AI in Education*. Pearson Education. Retrieved from: https://www.pearson.com

Luckin, R. (2017). *Enhancing learning and teaching with technology: What the research says*. UCL Institute of Education Press.

MagicSchool. (n.d.). Retrieved May 30, 2024, from https://app.magicschool.ai

Makhambetova, A., Zhiyenbayeva, N., & Ergesheva, E. (2021). Personalized learning strategy as a tool to improve academic performance and motivation of students. *International Journal of Web-Based Learning and Teaching Technologies*, 16(6), 1–17. DOI: 10.4018/IJWLTT.286743

Marrone, R., Cropley, D., & Medeiros, K. (2024). How Does Narrow AI Impact Human Creativity? *Creativity Research Journal*, 1–11. DOI: 10.1080/10400419.2024.2378264

Martinez, M. (2002). Designing learning objects to personalize learning. *The instructional use of learning objects*, 151-171.

Means, B., & Neisler, J. (2021). *Technology use in education: Emerging trends and issues*. American Educational Research Association.

Miao, F., & Cukurova, M. (2024). *AI competency framework for teachers* [Report]. UNESCO. DOI: 10.54675/ZJTE2084

Miao, F., Holmes, W., Huang, R., & Zhang, H. (2021). *AI and education: Guidance for policy-makers*. UNESCO., DOI: 10.54675/PCSP7350

Miao, F., & Shiohira, K. (2024). *AI competency framework for students*. UNESCO. DOI: 10.54675/JKJB9835

Moreno, R., & Mayer, R. E. (2007). Interactive multimodal learning environments: Special issue on interactive learning environments: Contemporary issues and trends. *Educational Psychology Review*, 19(3), 309–326. DOI: 10.1007/s10648-007-9047-2

NCAI. (2021). *AI and Multimodal Learning: Enhancing Education Through Artificial Intelligence*. Retrieved from: https://www.ncai.org

Ng, D. T. K., Leung, J., Su, J., Ng, C. W., & Chu, S. (2023). Teachers' AI digital competencies and twenty-first century skills in the post-pandemic world. *Educational Technology Research and Development*, 71(1), 137–161. DOI: 10.1007/s11423-023-10203-6 PMID: 36844361

OCDE. (2023). Opportunities, guidelines and guardrails for effective and equitable use of AI in education. In *OECD Digital Education Outlook 2023: Towards an Effective Digital Education Ecosystem*. Éditions OCDE. DOI: 10.1787/2b39e98b-

OECD. (2022). *OECD Framework for the Classification of AI systems. OECD Digital Economy Papers, No. 323*. OECD Publishing. DOI: 10.1787/cb6d9eca-

Open, A. I. (2024). *ChatGPT* [Large language model]. https://chat.openai .com/chat

Padlet. (n.d.). Retrieved June 12, 2024, from https://padlet.com/

Pane, J. F. (2017). *Does personalized learning work? Evidence from U.S. schools*. RAND Corporation.

Peng, H., Ma, S., & Spector, J. M. (2019). Personalized adaptive learning: An emerging pedagogical approach enabled by a smart learning environment. *Smart Learning Environments*, 6(1), 1–14. DOI: 10.1186/s40561-019-0089-y

Perplexity. (n.d.). Retrieved June 2, 2024, from https://perplexity.ai

Porayska-Pomsta, K. (2024). A manifesto for a pro-actively responsible AI in education. *International Journal of Artificial Intelligence in Education*, 34(1), 73–83. DOI: 10.1007/s40593-023-00346-1

Prompt Engineering Guide. (n.d.). Retrieved August 15, 2024, from https://www.promptingguide.ai/

Prompt Engineering Guide. (n.d.). Retrieved from https://www.promptingguide.ai/

Prompt Lab working with Minecraft Education and Microsoft Copilot: Vol. 1.3. (2024). Microsoft Corporation. https://aka.ms/promptlab1

Punie, Y. (Ed.). (2017). European Framework for the Digital Competence of Educators: DigCompEdu, EUR 28775 EN. Publications Office of the European Union. DOI: 10.2760/178382

QUIZZIZ. (n.d.). Retrieved May 10, 2024, from https://quizizz.com/?lng=en

Ramirez, E. A. B., & Fuentes Esparrell, J. A. (2024). Artificial Intelligence (AI) in Education: Unlocking the Perfect Synergy for Learning. *Educational Process: International Journal*, 13(1), 35–51. DOI: 10.22521/edupij.2024.131.3

Redding, S. (2013). *A perspective on personalized learning and practice guide for teachers*. Center on Innovations in Learning.

Reiß, M. (2021). The use of AI in education: Practicalities and ethical considerations. *London Review of Education*, 19(1). Advance online publication. DOI: 10.14324/LRE.19.1.05

Rillig, M. C., Ågerstrand, M., Bi, M., Gould, K. A., & Sauerland, U. (2023). Risks and benefits of large language models for the environment. *Environmental Science & Technology*, 57(9), 3464–3466. DOI: 10.1021/acs.est.3c01106 PMID: 36821477

Rose, L. T. (2016). *The end of average: How we succeed in a world that values sameness*. HarperOne.

Saylam, S., Duman, N., Yildirim, Y., & Satsevich, K. (2023). Empowering education with AI: Addressing ethical concerns. *London Journal of Social Sciences*, 6(6), 39–48. DOI: 10.31039/ljss.2023.6.103

Schmidt, P., & Niekler, A. (2020). Challenges and opportunities: Artificial intelligence in education. *Proceedings of the 13th International Conference on Educational Data Mining*, 1-9.

School, A. I. (n.d.). Retrieved May 10, 2024, from https://schoolai.com/tools

Shemshack, A., Kinshuk, , & Spector, J. M. (2021). A comprehensive analysis of personalized learning components. *Journal of Computers in Education*, 8(4), 485–503. DOI: 10.1007/s40692-021-00188-7

Susskind, R. E., & Susskind, D. (2015). *The future of the professions: How technology will transform the work of human experts*. Oxford University Press. DOI: 10.1093/oso/9780198713395.001.0001

Team, M. E. (2024b, July 18). *Explore insights from the AI in Education Report | Microsoft Education Blog*. Microsoft Education Blog. https://www.microsoft.com/en-us/education/blog/2024/04/explore-insights-from-the-ai-in-education-report/

The National Center on Education and the Economy. (2024). *Framework for AI-Powered Environments*. National Center on Education and the Economy.

The School District of Clayton. (n.d.). Available at: https://www.claytonschools.net/Page/13457

Thongprasit, J., & Wannapiroon, P. (2022). Framework of Artificial Intelligence Learning Platform for Education. *International Education Studies*, 15(1), 76–86. DOI: 10.5539/ies.v15n1p76

Tzafilkou, K., Perifanou, M., & Economides, A. A. (2022). Development and validation of students' digital competence scale (SDiCoS). *International Journal of Educational Technology in Higher Education*, 19(1), 30. DOI: 10.1186/s41239-022-00330-0 PMID: 35602658

UNESCO International Bureau of Education. (2017). Personalized learning. Available at: https://unesdoc.unesco.org/ark:/48223/pf0000250057

UNESCO. (2019). Beijing consensus on artificial intelligence and education. *International Conference on Artificial Intelligence and Education, Planning Education in the AI Era: Lead the Leap*.

UNESCO. (2021). *AI and Education: Guidance for Policy-makers*. Retrieved from: https://unesdoc.unesco.org

Varsik, S., & Vosberg, L. (2024). The potential impact of Artificial Intelligence on equity and inclusion in education.

Vuorikari, R., Kluzer, S., & Punie, Y. (2022). *DigComp 2.2: The Digital Competence Framework for Citizens - With new examples of knowledge, skills and attitudes*. EUR 31006 EN, Publications Office of the European Union. DOI: 10.2760/490274

W3schools. (n.d.). Retrieved August 15, 2024, from https://www.w3schools.com/gen_ai/gen_ai_prompt_intro.php

What are Large Language Models (LLMs)? (n.d.). https://www.ibm.com/topics/large-language-models

What is Artificial Intelligence (AI)? (2024, January 31). https://www.iso.org/artificial-intelligence/what-is-ai

Wolf, M. A. (2010). *Innovate to educate: System [re] design for personalized learning, a report from the 2010 symposium*. Software and Information Industry Association.

Woolf, B. P. (2009). *Building intelligent interactive tutors: Student-centered strategies for revolutionizing e-learning*. Morgan Kaufmann.

World Economic Forum. (2021). *The inclusive revolution: Artificial intelligence for accessibility*. Retrieved from: https://www.weforum.org

Wu, S., Cao, Y., Cui, J., Li, R., Qian, H., Jiang, B., & Zhang, W. (2024). A Comprehensive Exploration of Personalized Learning in Smart Education: From Student Modeling to Personalized Recommendations. *arXiv* preprint *arXiv*:2402.01666.

Yim, I.H.Y., & Su, J. (2024). Artificial intelligence (AI) learning tools in K-12 education: A scoping review. *J. Comput. Educ.* DOI: 10.1007/s40692-023-00304-9

Zawacki-Richter, O., Marín, V. I., Bond, M., & Gouverneur, F. (2019). Systematic review of research on artificial intelligence applications in higher education – Where are the educators? *International Journal of Educational Technology in Higher Education*, 16(39), 1–27. DOI: 10.1186/s41239-019-0171-0

About the Author

Kristina Posavec is a research associate and educator with a strong focus on integrating Information and Communication Technologies (ICT) into education and advancing open science practices. She holds a PhD in Information and Communication Science from the University of Zagreb and has a diverse academic background, including master's degrees in Museology and Journalism. Currently, she works as a research associate at the Institute for Migration Research and as a lecturer at the Faculty of Education and Rehabilitation Sciences, University of Zagreb. She is the Editor-in-Chief of the International Journal of Adult Education and Technology (IJAET), where she oversees the publication of cutting-edge research in adult education and technological advancements. Kristina's research interests span across ICT and AI in education, assistive technologies, digital competencies, gamification, open science, and mixed reality applications in teaching. Her career includes contributions to numerous international projects under the Horizon2020 and Horizon Europe frameworks. She is an active member of editorial boards, a published author, and a speaker at international conferences. Her work bridges the gap between technology and education, fostering innovation and accessibility in learning environments.

Index

A

C

D

E

F

G

R

S

T

U

V

www.ingramcontent.com/pod-product-compliance
Ingram Content Group UK Ltd.
Pitfield, Milton Keynes, MK11 3LW, UK
UKHW050946290926
15470UKWH00005B/1673